RECOLLECTIONS FROM MY LIFE

AN AUTOBIOGRAPHY BY ADOLPH BERNHARD MARX

D1521748

Recollections From My Life

An Autobiography by Adolph Bernhard Marx

Translation by Stephen Thomson Moore

Introduction and notes by R. J. Arnold

LIVES IN MUSIC SERIES No. 14

PENDRAGON PRESS
HILLSDALE, NY

OTHER TITLES IN THE LIVES IN MUSIC SERIES

Library of Congress Cataloging-in-Publication Data

Names: Marx, Adolf Bernhard, 1795-1866, author. | Moore, Tom, 1956-
  translator.

Title: Recollections from my life / by Adolf Bernhard Marx ; translated by
  Stephen Thomson Moore ; introduction and notes by R.J. Arnold.

Other titles: Erinnerungen aus meinem Leben. English

Description: Hillsdale, NY : Pendragon Press, [2016] | Series: Lives in music
  series ; No. 14

Identifiers: LCCN 2016054571 | ISBN 9781576472491

Subjects: LCSH: Marx, Adolf Bernhard, 1795-1866. |

  Composers--Germany--Biography. | Music--Germany--19th century--History
    and criticism. | LCGFT: Autobiographies.

Classification: LCC ML410.M3828 A3 2016 | DDC 780.92 [B] --dc23 LC record
  available at https://lccn.loc.gov/2016054571

TABLE OF CONTENTS

CONTENTS OF VOLUME ONE

CONTENTS OF VOLUME TWO

INTRODUCTION

When reading autobiographies written in the nineteenth century, it is important to remember that this was a form that was both relatively new, and still experimental. The self-reflexive habits and attitudes of the present, which have helped create an accepted set of autobiographical literary strategies, verging in the worst hands on the formulaic, were simply not yet present. Of course, there were isolated autobiographies before 1800, most notably Jean-Jacques Rousseau's *Confessions* of 1782, which cast its shadow over almost all subsequent attempts at forthright self-exposure. But the trickle became a flood only after the turn of the century: according to one persuasive line of thinking, the generation that grew up around the period of the French Revolution and Napoleonic Wars had not just lived through stirring events, but had as a result a new consciousness of the forward march of history, and consequently of their lives as narratives of change.[1]

The novelty of the autobiography was especially marked in the field of music. While practitioners of the other arts had found ways of exploring and displaying their individuality – in, for example, the painter's self-portrait, a feature of visual culture since at least the sixteenth century – the musician remained a reticent figure until surprisingly late. It is perhaps again the year 1800 that provides a convenient, if approximate, locus of a major perceptual shift, from the notion of the musician as a sort of superior servant, noteworthy only as an adjunct to his master, to a self-aware, self-reliant creative force in his own right. While Franz-Joseph Haydn, who died in 1809, wore the livery of his aristocratic employer, Ludwig van Beethoven, thirty-eight years his junior, is seen as the vanguard of a new romantic ideal of the composer as assertive genius.[2] Composers had resorted rarely to prose, and when they did, it was usually to explain their technique, not themselves; the first example of an autobiographical work by a composer was arguably the *Mémoires* of André-Ernest-Modest Grétry,

---

[1] There is a substantial literature on modernity and memory. See, for example, Philip Dwyer, 'Public Remembering, Private Reminiscing: French Military Memoirs and the Revolutionary and Napoleonic Wars', *French Historical Studies* 33/2 (Spring 2010), pp.231-58; Peter Fritzsche, 'Specters of History: On Nostalgia, Exile, and Modernity', *American Historical Review* 106 (2001), pp.1587-1618; idem, *Stranded in the Present: Modern Time and the Melancholy of History* (Cambridge, MA, 2004); Richard Terdiman, *Present Past: Modernity and the Memory Crisis* (Ithaca, NY, 1993); Damien Zanone, *Écrire son Temps: Les Mémoires en France de 1815 à 1848* (Lyon, 2006).
[2] The case for this rapid shift in status has been most persuasively made in T.C.W. Blanning, *The Culture of Power and the Power of Culture: Old Regime Europe 1660-1789* (Oxford, 2002), pp.266ff; and in his *The Triumph of Music: Composers, Musicians and Their Audiences, 1700 to the Present* (London, 2008), pp.7-72.

published in 1789-1797, and even here, the personal reminiscence was packed within layers of musicological exegesis. With a few colorful exceptions, the life of a musician is not dramatic, but bounded by solitary desk-work and the routines of professional duty.

Yet what particularly characterizes the new autobiographical approaches of the nineteenth century is a belief that one's inner life ought to be at least as important as the events that take place externally. It is given to very few people to have a life so rich in public incident and significance – or such an unusual degree of self-importance – to render a simple recitation of their deeds worth writing, let alone reading. Instead, the task of the autobiographer is to weave together the historiographical and the personal, laying out how the individual is shaped by his times, and perhaps how he in turn helps to shape those times. In the absence of a literary tradition of conveying the meaning of one's individuality to a public audience, it is not surprising that these early attempts tended to struggle with questions of register, tone, balance and subjectivity, and might often appear gauche, or even risible, to our eyes.

These considerations, I would argue, help us approach the memoirs of Adolf Bernhard Marx with a degree more understanding. This understanding is required because these reminiscences can appear to the impatient modern reader as in various ways a flawed work, offering insufficient clarity and depth of information both on Marx himself, and on the exceptionally interesting epoch and place in which he lived. Yet these very flaws have not only a charm of their own, but an importance, revealing to us a tone of voice and patterns of thought intensely expressive of the fluid, combative and energetic cultural milieu of post-Napoleonic Germany.

II.

At the very least, Marx's memoirs are invaluable in rounding out our conception of him as primarily a musicological theorist, the sphere of his activity for which he has the most prominent claim on posterity. His reputation in this regard rests principally on his monumental compositional method, *Die Lehre von der Musikalischen Komposition*, published in four volumes between 1837 and 1847, and widely read both inside and outside Germany for the rest of the century. This work contained, most famously, his theory of musical form, notably the adumbration of sonata form – an achievement that in some quarters has tended to bracket Marx as a promoter of normative formal analysis, a dreary and scholastic imposition of rigid categories onto the free-flowing material of musical inspiration.

But as Scott Burnham, the leading modern scholar of Marx's theory, has argued, this would be a misrepresentation. Marx's formal analysis, far from being a narrow academic exercise, emerges from an engagement with the living tissue of the music, and in particular its dynamic opposition of rest and motion. All Marx's musicological thinking intends to tie apparently small details into more significant wholes, not only the structures of the larger musical unit that contains them, but also in relation to the thinking of the composer and the aesthetic impact on audiences. In Burnham's argument, Marx's work is further grounded in reality in that it never loses touch with its pedagogical role, and therefore, as Marx himself makes clear towards the end of his memoirs, with the fortunes of the nation itself.[3] In Marx's extensive other writings, this worldly quality is expressed even more plainly. Marx wrote book-length texts on, among other practical subjects, the art of song, musical pictorialism, Prussian musical administration and education, musical history, and the significance of Mozart and Haydn. Among these, two stand out for the impact they have arguably had as far as our times. His life-and-works study of Christoph Willibald Gluck, published in 1863, helped resurrect the reputation of a composer who, while dominant in the latter decades of the eighteenth century, was regarded as too austere to find much favor after 1800, even in the German lands. And his work on Ludwig van Beethoven, notably in his biography of 1859, played a role in the development of the composer's canonical status that has only recently been fully comprehended. For Marx, Beethoven was not only the supreme exponent of the dynamic forms that gave life to music, but was also – in the shape of his *Eroica* symphony – the harbinger of the culminating phase in the historical development of music, an embodiment of the special vitality and decisive destiny of German musical culture.[4]

Marx's theoretical work was inseparable from his practical activities, which touched upon almost every aspect of Prussian musical life. He was a prominent journalist and critic, contributing to a number of publications, and for seven years editing the *Berliner Allgemeine Musikalische Zeitung*, a journal that aimed towards a more profound, even spiritual understanding of musical creation, one

[3] Scott Burnham, 'Introduction: Music and Spirit' in A.B. Marx, *Musical Form in the Age of Beethoven: Selected Writings on Theory and Method* (tr. and ed. Scott Burnham, Cambridge, 1997), pp.1-14. This valuable work presents a selection of Marx's theoretical writings in English, with commentary, and including numerous otherwise obscure texts.

[4] On Marx's role as an evangelist of Beethoven, see Elisabeth Bauer, *Wie Beethoven auf den Sockel Kam: Die Entstehung eines Musikalischen Mythos* (Berlin, 1992); Scott Burnham, 'Criticism, Faith, and the *Idee*: A.B. Marx's Early Reception of Beethoven', *19th-Century Music*, 13/3 (1990), pp.183-92; id., 'The Four Ages of Beethoven: Critical Reception and the Canonic Composer' in G. Stanley (ed.), *The Cambridge Companion to Beethoven* (Cambridge, 2000), pp.272-91.

rooted in the intentions of the creative artists themselves.[5] He was an educator, rising rapidly from what he admitted were highly amateurish beginnings as a music teacher to a chair at Berlin University by 1830.[6] He was from his childhood a composer, and produced a number of works that achieved at least a toehold in the repertoire; his inability invariably to translate his inner urgings into functioning music, or to carve out enough time and solitude in his schedule for composition, represents a persistent theme of frustration and disappointment in his memoirs.[7] And not least, he was a leading musical personality of Berlin, constantly sociably engaged in what seems to have been an unusually intense exchange of opinions, advice and ideas, especially in the influential circles that radiated out from the Mendelssohn household; Marx's intimate but often strained relationship with Felix Mendelssohn, which encompassed teamwork on the words and music of both men's compositions, and a general sense of collaborative give and take, is another recurrent thread.[8]

Even leaving aside such specific enterprises, Marx's was a lifetime replete in, if not precisely dramatic incident, the headiest of atmospheres. Born at the end of the eighteenth century, he was old enough to appreciate the sight of the Napoleonic armies sweeping eastward through his Prussian hometown, affording him a heart-stopping glimpse of the emperor himself, and then trudging back westward seven years later. As soon as his legal career would permit it (certainly by 1822), he moved to Berlin, at the time perhaps the most exciting city on the planet. The fabric of the Prussian capital was ceaselessly in flux: its population more than doubled during Marx's time there, and many of the young architects, sculptors and artists who were remaking its built environment were among his acquaintances. Culturally, it was transforming from the dour backwater it had been as recently as the period of the French occupation, into a city that was rivaling Paris for European hegemony. This was the city of Alexander Humboldt, of E.T.A. Hoffmann, of August Schlegel and Georg Hegel, of Bettina von Arnim and Heinrich Heine; Marx did not

---

[5] Arno Forchert, 'Adolf Bernhard Marx und Seine *Berliner Allgemeine Musikalische Zeitung*' in Carl Dahlhaus (ed.), *Studien zur Musikgeschichte Berlins im Frühen 19. Jahrhundert*, pp.381-404.
[6] There is a touching appreciation of Marx's gifts as a teacher in Gustav Selle (ed.), *Aus Adolf Bernhard Marx' Litterarischen Nachlass: Ein Gedenkblatt zum Hundertjährigen Geburtstag* (Berlin, 1898), pp.53-59.
[7] There is an invaluable listing and exploration of Marx's compositions, many of which are no longer extant, in Leopold Hirschberg, 'Der Tondichter Adolph Bernhard Marx', *Sammelbände der Internationalen Musikalischen Gesellschaft*, 10/1 (1908), pp.1-72.
[8] On Marx and Mendelssohn, see *Adolf Bernhard Marx' Verhältnis zu Felix Mendelssohn-Bartholdy* (Leipzig, 1869), a work published by Theresa, his widow; and George Marek, *Gentle Genius: The Story of Felix Mendelssohn* (New York, NY, 1972); Judith Silber Ballon, 'Marxian Programmatic Music: A Stage in Mendelssohn's Musical Development' in R. Larry Todd (ed.), *Mendelssohn Studies* (Cambridge, 1992), pp.149-61.

restrict himself to musical circles, and his accounts of Berlin sociability paint a picture of an unbuttoned interdisciplinary mingling altogether more fertile than the more compartmentalized etiquette of the Parisian salon. Very broadly speaking, the spirit of Berlin expressed itself in two divergent trajectories: first, in a strenuous military-industrial-intellectual effort, fired by nationalistic ardour and a sense of Germanic manifest destiny; and second, a dreamy romanticism, an easygoing quality that fostered a fondness for fantasy and satire, and which made pre-unification Berlin unusually tolerant and socially fluid.

III.

Given these rich materials, Marx's memoirs might strike the reader as unsatisfactory, or at least frustrating. As a source of information, the work can prove highly elusive. Its very first sentence contains a factual confusion, over whether his birth had been in 1795 or 1799; Marx inclined toward the latter, while most subsequent authorities have tended to fix on the earlier date. Later in the first chapter we encounter Marx's father, a most imprecisely drawn figure. Although "benevolent and righteous", he also comes across as dogmatic and unyielding, a hard-line post-Voltairean atheist; in a later chapter, he punishes Adolf quite unjustly for a childish misunderstanding over a pocket-knife. Apparently on his death-bed in the first chapter, he goes on to live, according to Marx, "for many years more", but he essentially vanishes from the memoirs as an active presence after the first few pages. We never even learn his name.[9] Throughout the work, this sort of vagueness recurs, particularly in regard to dating and chronology. The reader is, for example, able to date Marx's arrival in Berlin, a milestone of great importance in his life, only by the fact that he had a chance to meet Hoffmann, who died in June 1822. Marx was, it might seem, taking the notion of *Erinnerungen*, or memoirs, quite literally: in place of the somewhat rigorous, linear, testamentary quality of an autobiography proper, this book gives the impression of a man rummaging about in his memory, with results as eclectic and fallible as one might expect. Some objects emerge brightly colored and distinct (notably some of his earliest memories), while others remain veiled by the mists of history. It appears that Marx wrote these memoirs *ad libitum*, without recourse to notes or other corroborative research: his quotations are often misquotations, and he frequently misspells or otherwise jumbles the names of the

[9] It was, it has since emerged, Moses. The omission of the name might be taken as significant by those interested in seeking psychological explanations: Moses was one of Adolf Bernhard Marx's birth names (although not used by him), and was the name of that other patriarch in his life, Moses Mendelssohn, who died before Marx's birth but among whose descendants Marx spent so much of his time. It might also be noted that Marx's principal compositional project, on which he worked for most of his adulthood, was *Mose*. On this work, and the significance of the theme to Marx, see Michael Zywietz, *Adolf Bernhard Marx und das Oratorium in Berlin* (Eisenach, 1996).

people and works that he cites. The point is quickly reached at which it becomes difficult fully to credit his most straightforward assertions.

In particular, there are three large areas in which the reader would like more definition. The first is Marx's work. We hear a great deal about his early legal training and employment: the exams he sat, the appointments he secured and failed to secure, the qualities of his teachers and colleagues, even extensive details of some of his cases. Yet his musical activities, and in particular his prose writings and compositions, are only thinly detailed. His life's work, the compositional method, is alluded to on a number of occasions tangentially, but the issue of its creation and reception – surely of central importance in Marx's life – are simply not addressed. Marx gives a certain amount of space to the genesis and performances of *Mose*, but his many other compositions are only glancingly cited, if at all. It might be concluded that Marx considered his musical activities would be sufficiently well-known to require little introduction to his likely readership, who might conversely cherish an insight into the more obscure corners of his career; the priorities of the modern reader, however, are likely to be rather different.

A second area of dissatisfaction is the topic of religion. Marx begins his memoirs with a vivid evocation of the synagogue, and goes on to describe, in extremely brisk terms, his seemingly rapid process of apostasy. How this loss of faith brought him eventually to Christianity is not detailed. Had religion been a matter of little account to Marx, such casual handling might be excused, but his memoirs are in fact suffused by references to the divine; while Marx was a Lutheran, his religious notions come across in these memoirs as more broadly deist, but at no point does he address precisely what his doctrines were, and how he arrived at them. Conversion to Christianity was a path taken by many prominent Jewish families in Marx's Prussia, notably most of Moses Mendelssohn's children, but was also rejected by many. It must, therefore, have been a perennial point of discussion in the circles in which Marx moved, which included many Jews of varying degrees of secularity; if it was, we do not learn so from Marx. This is particularly frustrating since the extent of the assimilation and success of nineteenth-century Prussian Jewry has become a major element in attempts to get at the roots of the horrors that would strike the community in the twentieth century. Again, however, taking Marx on his own terms, what comes across is a picture of an unusually liberal social world in which the precise orientation of one's religious beliefs – Jewish, Protestant or Catholic, and all the degrees inbetween – was not a factor in one's public interactions, however important it might be in the privacy of one's soul.[10]

---

[10] This type of positive interpretation of the status of nineteenth-century German Jewry, as both high-achieving and comfortably integrated, emerges from Amos Elon, *The Pity of it All: A Portrait of Jews in Germany, 1743-1933* (London, 2004). Some notion of the difficulties inherent in such an argument, with particular reference to the circles in which Marx moved,

The third area concerns Marx's judgment about what should be considered interesting, and therefore what space should be allotted to each topic. Marx rubbed shoulders with a great selection of extraordinary people during his career, and one of the charms of the book is the pen-portraits he provides of many of them. It is hardly surprising that the modern reader is likely to want more on some topics and less on others than Marx is willing to provide; tastes, priorities and perspectives change over time. It is notable that Robert Schumann, for example, although now a revered name, appears only briefly in Marx's memoirs, and in the capacity of a fellow journalist. Yet while Marx's greatest veneration and interest was reserved for Beethoven, very little is written about him or his works in the memoirs. And at the same time, fully two chapters are devoted to Gaspare Spontini, an Italian operatic composer whose standing was severely contested even during his own lifetime.

IV.

Yet the Spontini chapters ought to be considered as the heart of Marx's memoirs, both spatially – straddling the end of his first volume and the beginning of his second – and in terms of their theme. They anatomize the evolution of Marx's conception of the composer during the 1820s, from his initial enthusiastic appreciation and championing of the Italian's music in the face of powerful domestic cliques, towards a more skeptical apprehension of Spontini as a representative of a sort of theatricality that was dangerously at odds with the emergent German spirit. In the process, Marx was learning to set aside his admiration for Spontini's warm personal qualities, his musicianship and intellect – an admiration that remained undimmed during the Italian's long residence in Berlin – in favor of an allegiance to what he took to be an ultimately decisive underlying ideal, one rooted in the cultural integrity of the nation. As such, these two chapters are not so much about Spontini *per se*, and far more about Marx's sense of coming of age as a critic, and as a German.[11]

Again and again in his memoirs, Marx describes his groping towards, grasping of, and eventually subservience to, big underlying ideals and inner convictions. The urgings of expediency, short-term advantage, or personal

can be found in Deborah Sadie Hertz, *How Jews Became Germans: The History of Conversion and Assimilation in Berlin* (New Haven, CT, 2007); Jeffrey Sposato, *The Price of Assimilation: Felix Mendelssohn and the Nineteenth-Century Anti-Semitic Tradition* (Oxford, 2006).

[11] The importance of national considerations in Marx's musical criticism, including his evolving views on Spontini, are explored in Sanna Pederson, 'A.B. Marx, Berlin Concert Life, and German National Identity', *19th-Century Music*, 18/2 (1994), pp.87-107. See also Celia Applegate, 'How German is It? Nationalism and the Idea of Serious Music in the Early Nineteenth Century', *19th-Century Music*, 21/3 (1998), pp.274-96.

likings and dislikings, needed to be overcome if they did not accord with this most profound ideological underpinning. He ascribed, for example, his relative failure as a composer to the fact that, in spite of the advice of his peers and the models presented by the marketplace, he was unable to write music that did not emerge "from my own deepest inner feelings". As a coda to his interesting remarks on the virtuosic performances of Niccolò Paganini, he averred that great creative men fell into two classes. Those of one class applied the force of their personality to their circumstances, shaping them to give their inclinations the structure of an idea. These men – and he named Paganini, Napoleon and Lord Byron as examples – he labeled demonic. Although he was at pains to insist that he imputed no malign intention by his use of the term, he regarded such men as less admirable than a second class, those who put their personality and their talents at the service of some great idea, "brightly illuminated by the eternal or absolute, and holding to it, and exalting it". Beethoven and Goethe were of this second type, and while Marx did not presume to range his own achievements alongside theirs, he was eager to stress that the practice of abnegation of the ego was something that might unite people of every station.

This notion was, of course, a practical outgrowth from the idealism that – most famously and influentially articulated by Hegel – was overwhelmingly the dominant philosophical strand in nineteenth-century German thought. There are persuasive reasons for classifying Marx as a thoroughgoing Hegelian: his commitment to pedagogy; his faith in the centrality of the "world spirit" – and his assurance that this was displayed to best effect in Germany; his sense of historical progress.[12] Yet this Hegelian inheritance, essentially rational, purposeful and forward-looking, sat alongside a very different aspect of his outlook that might be characterized as more romantic, more mystical, perhaps even Schopenhauerian – although if Marx did know anything of Schopenhauer's writings, far less influential in their time than Hegel's, he did not mention them in his memoirs. This tendency manifests itself in the memoirs in a variety of ways: in the rhapsodic language he often uses to convey musical experiences; in his attraction to the exotic, for example his fascination for Indian painting; in his belief in the uncanny and the supernatural; and in his frequent moments of foreboding and pessimism.

In thus bestriding two countervailing tendencies, Marx was an apt representative of a time and place that was, as I have noted above, itself

---

[12] For a nuanced discussion of the effect of Hegelian thought on Marx's ideas about musical form, see the chapter devoted to Marx in Holly Watkins, *Metaphors of Depth in German Musical Thought: From E.T.A. Hoffmann to Arnold Schoenberg* (Cambridge, 2011), pp.51-85.

somewhat conflicted in character. (One might be reminded also of Schumann's self-presentation in the guise of the introvert Eusebius and the extrovert Florestan.[13]) The more closely one reads the memoirs, the more frequently one is struck by the ways that Marx was able to live with – indeed, frequently thrived upon – apparently jagged dualities: between his roles as musical creator, and as musical analyst and critic, for example; or variously in his imperfectly-sketched religious views – between Jew and Gentile, Lutheran and Catholic, believer and non-believer. One example in particular deserves to be highlighted, since it features strongly in these memoirs: his long-running attempt to juggle the two careers of jurist and musician. Unlike most artists who begin life in some more respectable profession, Marx was not evidently eager to quit the law, and seems to have spent some years considering his position. Quite apart from the financial implications, this was an interesting time to be a lawyer: the unimaginable complexities of the legal system of the Holy Roman Empire – dissolved by Napoleon in 1806 – were being unwound, and the eyes of many were on the possibility of German unification, with all the reform and rationalization that would necessitate. It is clear that Marx brought something of a lawyer's sensibility to his approach to music. He recounts, for example, his early teacher Daniel Gottlob Türk's cringing obeisance to the rules of composition; Marx, by contrast, had a lawyerly appreciation that rules were there to be made use of, to be respected but not feared, to be constantly probed, questioned and their limits tested. It might be speculated that his later work on musical form was strongly informed by a legal mind: in its feeling for rhetoric and argumentation; in its concern for justice and resolution; in its tendency to classify and establish persuasive precedents, to neaten what is untidily various.

At first glance, Marx's legal and musical careers are at variance; he himself makes it clear that his judicial work crowded out his music. But while the two appeared to pull in different directions, the conflict was in a sense creative: Marx the musician – or at least the particular type of musician he turned out to be – would have been unimaginable without Marx the lawyer. This sort of dynamic was evidently fundamental to Marx's character and method: one might be reminded here that Marx's notion of musical form was itself based in the energetic confrontation of rest and motion. If Marx's memoirs, therefore, come across as at times inconsistent, incoherent or inconclusive, that is an expression of the various competing forces that are at work in his personality. His attempts

---

[13] This facet of Schumann's art, although long seen as little more significant than a sign of his mental disturbance, now tends to be regarded as something rooted more firmly in the particularities of German romantic culture: see in this regard Judith Chernaik, 'Schumann's Doppelgängers: Florestan and Eusebius Revisited', *The Musical Times*, 152/1917 (2011), pp.45-55; Eric Sams, 'Why Florestan and Eusebius?', *The Musical Times*, 108/1488 (1967), pp.31-34.

to express some of the contingency of the human experience result in a prose that can be seen as clumsy or garbled, but this is deeply eloquent of an era that was itself garbled, that was making itself anew with extraordinary vigor, and that was conscious of the complexity and conflict inherent in that process.

V.

The great strength and weakness of Marx's memoirs is this time-capsule quality, the fact that they are so defiantly representative of their time. As a literary experience, they give us access to a highly characteristic tone of voice. The wordy exuberance – amounting sometimes to verbosity – that is a feature of almost all prose of the first half of the nineteenth century is to some extent even more present in German, with its complex nests of subordinate clauses, its heavy reliance on separable and auxiliary verb constructions, and its fondness for abstract expressions; to this structural mix Marx adds his particular ingredient, which is a conversational quality infused by a boyish enthusiasm that verges on breathlessness. Marx appears to write as he speaks, and his prose is littered with exclamations, self-interruptions and admonishments, and tangential veerings-off. For some readers, the result is a text that is idiosyncratic to the point of unreadability. Birgitte Plesner Vinding Moyer, author of a study of Marx's formal theory, wrote that his "unregulated profusion of rhetorical questions, pseudo-historical asides, bombast, and condescension" means that he "will not be remembered as a purveyor of elegantly honed prose."[14] Not elegant, perhaps, but a more recent assessment by Ian Bent was altogether more charmed by the sense of being in the presence of an articulate and recognizable individual voice. "The bubbling energy, the drive, the vitality radiates off the page at you!" he wrote.[15] Both Bent and Moyer were judging Marx's writing in his composition method, his most formal and academic piece of work, but the same sort of remarks, positive and negative, might be made in respect of the memoirs; clearly, this was simply the way that Marx naturally wrote, irrespective of target audience, and rejecting all bookish artifice.

It is an open question as to how this most German of writers will function in English. In his time, Marx had a substantial currency outside his homeland: his didactic works, notably the *Lehre von der Musikalischen Komposition*, and the more accessible *Allgemeine Musiklehre* of 1839, were translated on multiple occasions, often immediately after their initial German publication; these gained

---

[14] Birgitte Plesner Vinding Moyer, *Concepts of Musical Form in the Nineteenth Century with Special Reference to A.B. Marx and Sonata Form* (PhD diss., Stanford, CA, 1969), p.55.

[15] Ian Bent, 'Foreword' in Scott Burnham's *Musical Form in the Age of Beethoven*, p.xii.

a wide circulation in the third quarter of the century, especially in America, without apparently encountering any revulsion at their Teutonic prose – indeed, readers seem to have welcomed Marx's conversational manner as an antidote to the pedantic, technical style of many textbooks. The memoirs are a somewhat different proposition, since they deserve to be judged as relatively early examples of an autobiography, a form with at least some pretensions to literary merit. Rendering Marx's words into acceptable modern English poses some challenges. There are particular technical difficulties, such as Marx's extensive deployment of the long dash as an all-purpose mark of punctuation, serving for example to associate grammatically distinct utterances, or to provide a rhetorical caesura within one utterance, or to separate items in a list, or speakers in a dialogue, all often mingled indiscriminately together with full-stops, colons and commas. It would perhaps not be possible to translate Marx's memoirs into wholly idiomatic English prose without doing violence to the peculiar color and rhythms of his writing that are, as I have argued, a major part of the reward for reading it.

Beyond this essentially touristic pleasure, finally, why read Marx's memoirs today? The cliché that biography humanizes its subject is perhaps not entirely banal in this connection. In all their fallibility and eccentricity, Marx's memoirs are a powerfully human work – nowhere more so than in the concluding chapters, where the increasing prestige of Marx's official position, buttressed by professorial dignity and royal favor, is strikingly counterpointed against his regretful acceptance of the failure of his compositional ambitions; and in the poignant final lines, wherein Marx – only months from death – feebly hopes for a renewal of his energies for the many tasks left unfinished. This intimate perspective is an invaluable aid to our historical understanding of the stern figures of nineteenth-century intellectual life, all too easily occluded behind their formal portraits, academic titles and lists of publications. And Marx's own constant intertwining of the personal and the professional, of the scholarly and the subjective, is a reminder that musical theory – and by extension, all intellectual appreciation of culture – needs to remain inseparable from emotion, physicality and the human spirit.

James Arnold; Birkbeck, University of London

SELECT BIBLIOGRAPHY

(Excluding works by Marx himself; for a listing of these, see Scheidler below)

Celia Applegate, *Bach in Berlin: Nation and Culture in Mendelssohn's Revival of the* St. Matthew Passion (Ithaca, NY, 2014)

Elisabeth Bauer, *Wie Beethoven auf den Sockel Kam: Die Entstehung eines Musikalischen Mythos* (Berlin, 1992)

Ian Bent (ed.), *Music Theory in the Age of Romanticism* (Cambridge, 2005)

Scott Burnham, 'The Role of Sonata Form in A.B. Marx's Theory of Form', *Journal of Music Theory*, 33/2 (1989), pp.247-71

'Criticism, Faith, and the *Idee*: A.B. Marx's Early Reception of Beethoven', *19th-Century Music*, 13/3 (1990), pp.183-92

[as tr. and ed.] A.B. Marx, *Musical Form in the Age of Beethoven: Selected Writings on Theory and Method* (Cambridge, 1997)

'The Four Ages of Beethoven: Critical Reception and the Canonic Composer' in G. Stanley (ed.), *The Cambridge Companion to Beethoven* (Cambridge, 2000), pp.272-91

Carl Dahlhaus, 'Formenlehre und Gattungstheorie bei A.B. Marx' in Richard Jakoby and Günter Katzenberger (eds.), *Heinrich Sievers zum 70. Geburtstag* (Tutzing, 1978), pp.29-35

Aesthetische Prämissen des "Sonatenform" bei Adolf Bernhard Marx', *Archiv für Musikwissenschaft*, 41 (1984), pp.73-85

Arnfried Edler, 'Zur Musikanschauung von Adolf Bernhard Marx' in Walter Salmen, *Beiträge zur Geschichte des Musikanschauung im 19. Jahrhundert* (Regensburg, 1965), pp.103-12

Kurt-Erich Eicke, *Der Streit zwischen Adolph Bernhard Marx und Gottfried Wilhelm Fink um die Kompositionslehre* (Regensburg, 1966)

Amos Elon, *The Pity of it All: A Portrait of Jews in Germany, 1743-1933* (London, 2004)

Arno Forchert, 'Adolf Bernhard Marx und Seine *Berliner Allgemeine Musikalische Zeitung*' in Carl Dahlhaus (ed.), *Studien zur Musikgeschichte Berlins im Frühen 19. Jahrhundert*, pp.381-404

Deborah Sadie Hertz, *How Jews Became Germans: The History of Conversion and Assimilation in Berlin* (New Haven, CT, 2007)

Francien Markx, *E.T.A. Hoffmann, Cosmopolitanism, and the Struggle for German Opera* (Leiden, 2016)

Birgitte Plesner Vinding Moyer, *Concepts of Musical Form in the Nineteenth Century with Special Reference to A.B. Marx and Sonata Form* (PhD diss., Stanford, CA, 1969)

Sanna Pederson, 'A.B. Marx, Berlin Concert Life, and German National Identity', *19ᵗʰ-Century Music*, 18/2 (1994), pp.87-107

Alexander Ringer (ed.), *Music and Society: The Early Romantic Era. Between Revolutions: 1789 and 1848* (Basingstoke, 1990), chapters by Christoph-Hellmut Mahling on Berlin, pp.109-40; and Sieghart Döhring on Dresden and Leipzig, pp.141-59.

Ulrich Scheidler, 'Marx, Adolf Bernhard' in *Musik in Geschichte und Gegenwart* (1994-2008), Personenteil, pp.1234-38

Gustav Selle (ed.), *Aus Adolf Bernhard Marx' Litterarischen Nachlass: Ein Gedenkblatt zum Hundertjährigen Geburtstag* (Berlin, 1898)

Arnold Schering, *Geschichte des Oratoriums* (Hildesheim, 1988)

Howard Smither, *A History of the Oratorio. Volume IV: The Oratorio in the Nineteenth and Twentieth Centuries* (Chapel Hill, NC, 2000), pp.3-248

Jeffrey Sposato, *The Price of Assimilation: Felix Mendelssohn and the Nineteenth-Century Anti-Semitic Tradition* (Oxford, 2006)

R. Larry Todd (ed.), *Mendelssohn Studies* (Cambridge, 1992)

Mendelssohn and his World (Princeton, NJ, 2012)

Holly Watkins, *Metaphors of Depth in German Musical Thought: From E.T.A. Hoffmann to Arnold Schoenberg* (Cambridge, 2011), pp.51-85

Michael Zywietz, *Adolf Bernhard Marx und das Oratorium in Berlin* (Eisenach, 1996)

CHAPTER 1

MY FATHER'S HOUSE

I was born on May 15, 1799 in Halle on the Saale, the son of a doctor, and certainly in the bosom of the Jewish community. Oddly enough the latter led to uncertainty regarding the date. The notations of the synagogue official contradict those of my father in a family bible. It might well be that my birthday is not May 15, but rather November 28, and the year of my birth 1795. Family information speaks in favor of the former date[1]. But it makes no difference. My father remained connected to the Jewish community until the end of his life, firm and unshakable, without having the least inclination to the old church. Basically he was neither Jew nor Christian, but a genuine follower of Voltaire. Naturally, from his point of view he had nothing to conceal from me – and he could not have, for he often invited me to accompany him to the synagogue, strangely enough for his point of view. My relation to the old church was so easy hereafter, and religiosity was kept so far from the child, but one would be in error, if one were to assume that, the latter was entirely lacking; oriental fantasy was too hard at work for that in me and my dark-haired playfellows. Even the unintelligible language in which God himself, as we were taught, had put together the Holy Scriptures, inspired our imaginations with the power of a continuing miracle. For to doubt the fact, taken for granted, was something that occurred to none of us; rather, we were ready to regard the extremely ancient rolls of the Torah, which were carried in procession about the synagogue in their gold-brocade decorated cover, as being the true and original writing by God's hand. On days of repentance and fasting the main section of the temple was filled with the men of the community, each in their burial shroud, as they named them for us – these were usual, but very whitely washed shirts, which they only wore over their clothes at this time, and which probably offered the ancient and original form of garment before our eyes; and we boys were very serious and awfully impressed, especially by the oriental and violent exclamations, with each of the loudly praying worshipers beating indefatigably against their breasts, every time he named one of the many sins indicated in the formula of prayer, or raised one of the many prayers to heaven. That the community fasted from all food on this day had a great effect on our minds; perhaps we were so much the more receptive, because we, being less than thirteen years of age, were not yet called upon to do the same fasting. Thus the community, with the women's section separated

---

[1] Most subsequent reference works prefer the earlier date, however.

by a veiled grating in a side-nave, was gathered from early morning on until the first star appeared. We remained as well, naturally with many escapes included. We did not weary in telling each other the story of a pious Rabbi, who had once been seduced after many years of practice in piety, to depart for a short time from the temple in the long night. Soon however, his guilty conscience had filled him with the power of desperation, and he did not stop begging and crying until someone would cut off both feet, which had led him to sin. Bleeding, he had dragged himself back into the temple and laid himself down in front of the ark with the Torah scrolls. Here he died in fervent prayer with the hope of divine clemency. This legend never failed to draw our eyes to a 97-year-old man whom we always viewed as the first and last in the synagogue. The friendly old man was named Herz; a peddler, not well-off, he enjoyed the reverent attention of all, even the richest. For us boys he incontestably was a saint; we only argued about the extent of the miraculous power of his prayer, whether he could make the sun disappear, or the rain to come streaming down, or who knows what all else! Please do not laugh at the miraculous faith, always relating to the earth, which heated up our young brains. Where did such a lively imagination come from? We had not even heard of the "Bosom of Abraham" then! And it certainly would not have been very appealing.

Alas! This same long night that opened in the far distance the realm of the beyond-earthly to us, also held the seeds of doubt and unbelief.

It could not long remain hidden from curious young eyes, that not a few practiced open deception on that same holy night, that one had more concern for the eyes of the neighbors than for the Godhead and one's own conscience.

What did we see! — One after another of these well-dressed women, who gave the appearance of strictly fasting, complained of exhaustion and left the temple, in order to slip into a room of the temple caretaker, which had already been prepared. From outside, however, as soon as one of these was visible, a servant, doubtless attracted through magnetism, crept in with a well-prepared basket – and soon the fugitive returned, wondrously restored, to fasting and praying in the temple. I too, as grand-student of Voltaire, moved, in my sleeve, one plum after another from my pocket, so that it could stroll to my mouth. My comrades stared at the disappearing fruit, not without some longing, but also with the grim expectation that now flame, or some kind of dread punishment, would break forth. I, an impatient free-thinker, had at that point not yet realized that any statute of any church had to lead unavoidably to deception and self-deception of the individual, since it is impossible that laws should entirely agree with the disposition and way of thinking of that individual.

And my father? And my mother?

My dear mother, whose life's occupation was only worries and care, left all matters of conscience to the higher insight of my father. And he may well have taken a secret pleasure in my little heresy, because for him the entire synagogue service was, like every positive religion, whether Christianity or Judaism, without meaning. Later he took pleasure in giving me the treatise, then widely read, *De tribus impostoribus*[2]. The three charlatans were well-known - Moses, Christ and Mohammed. The breeze from the west had blown together so much aversion to churches, priests and their harmful influences, that people preferred to throw all religion over board, and no longer recognized that nothing great and salutary in the world could have arisen and come to light that did not have its roots in the field that those men had prepared, who they boldly called the three betrayers.

But even now, after such a long time for reflection, has the intimate relationship between worldly affairs and the leading religions - the frequent differences between faith and church, revelation and priesthood - really become clear?

So this entirely benevolent and righteous man found a standpoint like thousands before and alongside him, and had no belief whatever to pass down to his son. Insisting on the principles of Voltaire and the Enlightenment, at that time rather frivolous and superficial, he pointed thoughtlessly to every positive religion, Judaism or Christianity, as superstition and balderdash, overflowed with insults against the old religion, and did not hesitate to point out to me how much fraud and self-deception was in fashion. At the same time he held it to be a point of honor not to fall away from it, then even more than now oppressed and limited in rights in society. When I later in my own individual way – namely through an acquaintance with Mozart's *Requiem* and then Handel's *Messiah*, was led first to the study of the Bible, and to a lively inclination to Christianity and particularly to Lutheranism, and decided to convert to the Christian faith, I found in him the most obstinate resistance – which was that much less comprehensible for me, since I had long realized inwardly that for him very religion was a matter of complete indifference, and thus the choice for one or the other must have appeared meaningless as well.

For both of us it was a serious matter. Since no arguments were effective, the already very elderly man lay down on his bed and explained to me: this was his dying place, should I convert to Christianity. For my part I had already completed catechism in the Christian faith, and the day had been set for my baptism. With inner certainly I felt that that threat was only the expression of

<hr>

[2] This was an essentially apocryphal work of atheism, whose existence was much rumored during the Middle Ages, but which never existed in any settled form. Marx probably saw an edition in French from the later eighteenth century.

a momentary mood, without serious meaning, and I went to the altar of the Church. My father continued healthy, and lived on for many years more.

Certainly the instruction in the tenets of Christian belief that I received from the preacher Marks[3] was valuable. I cannot deny however, that what led me to Christianity, and has always attracted me more, was not so much the theological instruction, which, avoiding explanation, simply pointed to unrestricted faith, but rather – after the first impulse, given by that sacred music – aroused by Handel's *Messiah*, which stimulated pleasant and eager study of the Bible, which I have not been able to turn away from my whole life long, so much did the poetic sublimity and deep wisdom of the Book of Books grasp me. It was particularly the greater part of the Old Testaments, and from the New Testament, the Gospels of Matthew and Luke, that moved me. In them I believed that I received the true information regarding Judaism, and furthermore, regarding Christianity, purer and truer than in all the theological writings that I knew, and among which, probably more through boyish impertinence than with justification, I also included the epistles. In the Sermon on the Mount and the philippic against the Pharisees, I believed that I saw the fullest expression of the character and the mission of Christ.

It was only later, and at that time yet entirely unanticipated, that the great influence appeared, which would express the intimate relationship with the Bible that I had as composer and writer.

With respect to my paternal house, which gradually sank from earlier prosperity into deep penury, and my upbringing there, I will remain silent. My father's guiding rule, which he reproached me with incessantly: I had to learn everything; this continued, as it seem, to exert its influence on me. Its danger and impracticability could understandably not be clear for a boy. But from its effects there was at least the inclination, to look in all directions that might open up, and to strive for insight. First I searched through my father's medical library. For a long time I looked with spine-chilling fascination at the instruments of torture and bloody operations from the book on surgery by old Heister[4], including the hot irons in order to cauterize bleeding. I recall fondly Unger's weekly, *The Doctor*[5]; here for the first time I saw the possibility and advantages of a popular treatment of scientific matters.

---

[3] This was presumably Benjamin Adolph Marks, 1775-1847, a theologian who had a benefice at the Ulrichskirche, and was university preacher and instructor at the University of Halle.

[4] A *Compendium Anatomicum*…by Laurentius Heister was published in Amsterdam around 1732. The book in question here is more likely to be *Laurentii Heisters der Medicin, Chirurgie und kräuterwissenschaft Professoris zu Helmstädt, practisches medicinisches Handbuch, oder kurzer, doch hinlänglicher Unterricht, wie man die innerlichen Krankheiten am bestern curiren soll*, Leipzig, J.C. Gollner, 1763, of which a copy is held at the University Library in Halle.

[5] *Der Arzt*, a weekly medical journal, published from 1760 by Johann August Unger.

After this first deviation, which would not be the last, the Gymnasium followed, the Latin School of the Waisenhaus with its modest polyhistory. Along with everything there burbled an unending stream of the brightest collection of books, novels of knights and outlaws, stories from Homer, love stories, the most attractive pictures by Wieland and his French predecessors, along with *Faust*, Corneille – in short, everything and much more swam past the young soul in innocent and peaceful concord. What it found appealing remained. Others produced stimuli, that perhaps had later effect, and many sank without a trace. From this confused wandering I have at least retained the conviction that a person reads nothing in books that not already present in his own nature. All these lubricious things from Wieland's *Idris und Zenide*, from his *New Amadis*, from Crebillon[6], slid into my ear without the least comprehension, and indeed even unperceived, while those things that appealed to me remained, partly until this moment. Only one of the lubricious books, Voltaire's *Pucelle*[7], was and will be hated by me until my death. For I had already gotten to know Schiller's *Maid of Orleans*, was mad about it with all the inner fervor of a young heart, and could not understand how a Frenchman could have so shamelessly treated the heroine of his people.

In addition to all this, I drew much, partly invented, and partly copied, especially after the pictures of Raphael, unfortunately only in black ink. I had had drawing lessons in the community drawing hours of Professor Prange, a fine and benevolent man, if perhaps not so committed to art and art teaching. As soon as I was past the teaching of the rudiments, his troubles with me began. He was kind enough to leave the choice of models to us students; and soon I was happy with none of them. So it happened that he once offered me page after page in vain, until I finally cried out for one of them: I will do that one! As soon as the word was heard, I could hear the general laughter of my fellow students, and of the good Prange himself. What I had chosen was a copy of Raphael's *"Healing of the paralytic."* The people were surrounding a poor house, and thus blocked the entrance. Inside were the Apostles and Christ. Since there was no more space left, the man had broken through the roof and lowered the unfortunate down on his bed by ropes into the inner sanctum before Christ. This produced a very rich and crowded group. If I am not mistaken, the page

[6] Claude Prosper Jolyot de Crébillon, 1707-1777, novelist, who wrote works of a light-hearted and occasionally scurrilous nature. Christoph Martin Wieland's works, although now regarded with more appreciation than Marx's dismissive assessment might indicate, were generally witty, mock-heroic and occasionally libertine tales and verses in the manner of Voltaire.
[7] Voltaire's *La Pucelle d'Orléans*, begun in 1730 and frequently revised, was banned for its licentious and irreligious treatment of the life of Joan of Arc.

held about twenty figures.[8] Precisely that, the difficulty of the task, had aroused people's scorn against me. I bore it, certainly not without some anger, but held my tongue, and asked him to send the picture home with me. So I sat down without any bystanders and completed my copy. How – that I really can't say!

A copy of the *Transfiguration*, after the well-known engraving, but with the correction of some of the heads according to larger depictions, which were available to me, was dedicated to a benevolent society.

I have never stopped drawing and painting, but never felt the real vocation that would have made it my life's work.

Daniel Gottlob Türk, 1750-1813. His piano method was an early influence.

[8] This miracle, although frequently depicted by Medieval and Renaissance artists, does not seem to have been the subject of a work by Raphael. The artist did depict Saint Paul's healing of a lame man, but the details in the scene were not precisely as Marx described.

CHAPTER 2

Musical beginnings

It is evident that amongst this tumult of activities music could not be lacking. An understanding and pleasure in music awoke in me very early on. Already between my fifth and seventh years I recall bombarding my father, who at the time was visiting nearby Leipzig for his diversion, with requests for him to bring me a keyboard from the fair, and for it to be just so, perhaps a half-ell long[1]. How the instrument builder and the acoustics might accomplish this was naturally of no concern to the boy. Soon thereafter, perhaps at age seven, I had keyboard lessons. But our finances were already very restricted; I had to be satisfied with an old clavichord, then with a *Kielenflügel* by Oesterlein[2] (at the price of 13 thalers) , which, with its sprinkling tones, which were produced by the impact of quill tangents on the strings, had neither duration of sound, nor gave the possibility of distinguishing between forte and piano. And there was also no longer any good teacher available. I certainly carried it far enough, given my age and circumstances, that I even attracted attention in private circles. All that I was lacking was sufficient variety and increasingly challenging tasks. So my studies ended and became an entirely willful phantom; my lessons had to be given up.

Two, if not three years went by in this dreamy activity; the only more solid connection, which still bound me to music, was Türk's piano method[3] and its readings. Thus I often read: there was a composer, Wolf[4], who had in six (!) sonatas depicted the quarreling of a married couple. The absurdity escaped me, but I grasped the basic notion that music could also reproduce more substantial ideas as well. Just then the first musical lending library had opened in Halle. I hurried to the proprietor and asked for those six sonatas. "Those we don't have", was the dreary response. What now? To leave empty-handed seemed shameful. "So give me another sonata!" — I received a sonata (in A-flat, probably op. 26, which begins with the variations) by Beethoven, whom at the time I did not even know by name.

Thus I turned around to go home, with my first Beethoven in my hands. Not without some grim foreboding did I put it on the music rack and lift my

---

[1] An ell, originally a cubit, or forearm length, was in this period used for various somewhat longer measurements; in any case, however, the keyboard described by Marx would be unfeasibly small.

[2] Johann Oesterlein, 1717-1792, active Berlin, with one surviving harpsichord.

[3] Daniel Gottlob Türk, 1750-1813, composer and director of music at the university of Halle. His *Clavierschule* was published Leipzig/Halle, 1789, with a second enlarged edition in 1802. His *Clavierschule* was published Leipzig/Halle, 1789, with a second enlarged edition in 1802.

[4] Ernst Wilhelm Wolf, 1735-1792, a composer principally active at the Weimar court.

hands to play. Ach! — They did not descend to the keys. Notes, markings, everything disappeared or became uncertain. I was deeply ashamed, indeed, disgusted by this event. I shared it with no one, and the only helpers in my need were Türk's book and Beethoven's sonata. With these guides, gripped by grim and boyish determination, I learned to play piano for the second time. Means were lacking – and also my desire – to seek instruction once more. Never again did I take piano lessons. Naturally we cannot talk about regular formation of technique. All had to be replaced by tireless determination and newly awoken pleasure. It was not entirely misguided. Having arrived at the upper grades in the gymnasium, I formed a concert society.

We boys managed, from our means and with the assistance of others, to put together an orchestra, and to attract members of the excellent city chorus, so that with the favor of the Rector, we performed Haydn symphonies (the easier ones), choruses from Winter's *Macht der Töne*[5] and Mozart concertos. For the latter the solo parts were performed by the brilliant ballade and song composer Löwe[6] (at the time a soprano with a wonderful voice), by myself, and others. I do not know, how meager my playing may have been. But at least the performance was possible, and was not without applause, although Löwe's playing was at a level far above my own. The direction, as well, was shared in turn among us and other "high heads".

One should however not have too high an impression of our undertakings, more bold than solid. We were lacking in both inner and outer resources. Thus I recall the first performance of the Mozart E-flat concerto[7], which before the opening of the concert had only been rehearsed in my room. I sat at the grand piano; the two violin parts were lightly manned – naturally one on a part; the viola was done by a third violin, who happily rested for all the notes that were too low; we managed to find a violoncello, and we – all sopranos and altos – could not manage to arrange a contrabass. It was very easy to find the two flutes; out of necessity the oboes were replaced by two other flutes; and the two B-flat clarinets had also to be performed by two flutes – we had nothing else. Everything else went lacking. O, you poor Mozart, never have you experience more zeal and more lack of talent united together!

Now the playing began. A frightful missed note! We repeated and repeated the beginning; all the parts seemed to be playing the right notes, and yet the missed note remained; for how were we unfortunates to know that the B-flat

---

[5] eter von Winter's *Timotheus oder die Macht der Töne* was a choral work of 1809, also produced in an Italian version, setting words from John Dryden's *Alexander's Feast*..

[6] Carl Löwe, 1796-1869, a composer best known for his large number of songs and ballads.

[7] Evidently K.482, number 22, which was the first to include clarinets in its scoring.

clarinets were supposed to play their part a whole tone lower than written, so that the note C sounded a B-flat? So the B-flat clarinets had to be left out; and thus everything went very well, at least in our judgment at the time.

O blessed school years! And thrice blessed the boys, who spend their youth in smaller, and especially old cities! How quickly is every woe, and every embarrassment forgotten! We were also merry, all the best of friends, and content with ourselves and with the world!

Each of us had no doubt about his own excellence and that of all his comrades. Each of us believed that he was the best, and all the rest were his equals! And what a future was waiting for us! Novels of knight-errantry had opened the lands of fantasy, Schiller (and to a lesser extent, Goethe) rang the alarm bells of boyish hearts with audacity and freedom, their "give them freedom of thought" gave enthusiasm to the calls of the classics from Rome and Greece, as if with "freedom of thought" everything might be done, even if word and deed were left out.   And then there was the old city with its cliffs nearby, with the ruined castle, to which, from our Lutheran Gymnasium (a former cloister of discalced monks, to which I at first belonged), an underground passageway led, unfortunately walled-up in the middle. And if that were not enough, we lived in an old house from the time of the cloister, which belonged at the time to a Professor Tieftrunk[8]. It had a deep cellar, and under it a second and deeper level, both from hewn stone. And from the lower level an underground passage led sideways to the Ulrichskirche, not far away. The passage was sealed up to the cellar vault with bricks, and there were some gaps, probably of recent origin. What a frightening pleasure it was for us boys to clamber down into the cellar. Especially in the twilight! How curiously we peered through the holes into the passageway, and imagined that we spied ever more frightening things, the less that we could actually make out!

But the most lasting were, in spite of all incidents and fistfights, our feelings of camaraderie and friendship. Never have I seen any of my comrades once more, without experiencing that complete sensation of belongingness. Even if we had been distant in school, I considered myself happy if I was able to do something nice for someone later in Berlin. Certainly, my comrades, and everyone who had a happy and lighthearted time at school, have had the same experience.

At the school, however, we were all one for the other. I recall an event in which the leading role happened to be mine, but certainly anyone else from our merry band would have behaved in the same way. Our highly regarded and

---

[8] Johann Heinrich Tieftrunk, 1759-1837, a prolific philosopher of religion and Freemason.

beloved Rector Rath asked to begin with the Primus[9] a question; after his answer resounded "the next! The next!" until one of those sitting far away repeated the answer of the Primus. Now it was: "Correct!" — "I said that already", the Primus was heard to say. Rath looked angrily at him, and directed the next question to me, the Second, and continued to ask in this way through the whole class until the end of the hour, always overlooking the First. Before the beginning of the next class I let the others understand: the honor of the class required that we should not let our Primus be hurt without there being a cost. When the Rector directed his first question to me, once again overlooking the Primus, I looked him right in the eye and kept my mouth shut. "The next! The next!" Everyone kept silent. "Didn't you prepare?" exclaimed the Rector harshly. "We prepared", I answered, modestly, but firmly, "and could have answered the question; but we believed, that the turn to answer should not come to us, before it comes to our Primus." The worthy man, certain of our honor and love, gazed at me for a long time with his spirit-bright eyes, asked no more questions in this hour, but in the following class began with the Primus. We however, especially myself, who would soon thereafter become Primus, were always full of enthusiasm for him from then on.

---

[9] The leading student in the school.

CHAPTER 3

WARTIME

As if all these intrigues and dreams were not enough, the war arrived for us boys (we must now travel back a few years from the most recent school experiences); all of Europe was filled with its bluster, and resounded with the name of Napoleon and the martial fame of his troops.

My first clear reminiscence goes back to the year 1805. At that time Prussia had set masses of troops in motion, in order to support the demand that Haugwitz[1] was supposed to issue to Emperor Napoleon in Vienna[2]. Various divisions even marched through Halle. I still recall with complete clarity the grenadiers and their unusual headgear. A very low cloth-hat, flat on top, covered the head. The front half, however, enclosed a sort of shield, rounded on the top, and bent backwards on both sides, connecting to the cap. This shield was made of black and shiny leather, and surrounded with a sort of woolen beehive; it increased the man's height by at least a half-foot.

When a regiment had marched by, it was followed by long rows of pack horses, carrying bundles hanging on both sides with equal weights; these were the tents, for the event that they were unable to find or use accommodation in houses. The bundles were covered with a white cover, and on the highest points a plume swayed as an ornament. In addition, there were many reserve horses for the officers, the baggage-wagons for the officers as well, the latter even with armchairs attached for the commanders. Now and then a field-bakery, with numerous wagons, would crash by. Our young eyes were drunk with the bright drama stretching for such a long distance. There was none among us who did not dream of being an officer, and if possible, general, in order to play with these soldiers in their shining uniforms. In the meantime the small change wheedled from our parents all went to the tinsmith for tin grenadiers and pack animals. We certainly had reason to be impressed with what we had seen. For a year later the French came, and seven years later the *Volksheer* of Prussia – how different that all looked!

1806 brought the real war to us.

---

[1] Christian August Heinrich Kurt Graf von Haugwitz, 1752-1832, foreign minister for Prussia.
[2] The literature on the Napoleonic Wars is too immense to be cited here in detail. Helpful handbooks for this chapter are, however, David Gates' *The Napoleonic Wars 1803-1815*, London, Pimlico, 2011; and the more geographically and chronologically specific Francis Petre, *Napoleon's Conquest of Prussia*, London, John Lane, 1907.

The Battle of Jena[3] was fought; in Halle we heard the thunder of the cannons. First of all, the news arrived: the French were beaten, shattered, obliterated, "Bonaparte" was captured and put in chains. Then sinister rumors crept near, which said entirely otherwise. The reserve army gathering by Halle encamped east of the city, but began to move and to occupy a position on the Saale, west of Halle, and to send cavalry out to nearby Passendorf[4].

This position west of the city is extremely strong. Before the bridge there is a wide space of meadow, not protected by any heights, or any buildings besides the not very useful Gymritzer mill, and uninterrupted by any forest. Three branches of the Saale form the foremost section of terrain on the west, which can only be forded in places, and also permit no vehicles except for a few very small and low fishing boats. Over all of this in one span goes the "long bridge", entirely built of stone, with low stone railings, only provided on one arm with beams and boards, which can very easily be thrown down or set one fire. Only to the east on the side of the exit from the bridge does interrupted and light shrubbery appear, called the "Powdermeadow", before the "Powderwall", an insignificant but certainly usable elevation, probably built there in earlier days for defensive purposes. And then there is fourth, impassable branch of the Saale before the city, crossed by the "Klausbrücke", which, at least at that time, had a roofed bridge-house, as one still can find in Switzerland, rather well-protected against shot, covering the access from the high bridge. Here one first really enters the city, fortified with a stone wall on this side. It rises, if only slightly; but inside it are several high points, the Freimaurerberg, the Botanical Garden, the Moritzburg, provided with stone buildings, and a view and line of fire to the bridges and the western terrain. This not being enough, the rocky heights at a farther remove were occupied, called the Stonebreak, high enough in order notably strengthen the defense with heavy artillery. Thus the situation with respect to defense to the west is so advantageous, that a small corps can hold off a much larger one, until it is surrounded in a wide arc, or is made defenseless by superior artillery. But what happened for the defile of the bridge, which was intrinsically so strong? — On a meadow, to the side of the bridge, which lay before the last branch, the most easterly one, of the stream, and which consequently, once the bridge was taken, had no line of retreat[5] Hinrich's fusilier-battalion, with a detachment of *Jägers* [a type of German infantry, originally hunters] was emplaced. Naturally they were captured after the decision about the bridge; of those, who tried to save themselves by wading and swimming across the branch of the stream into the city, few or none made it across, but

---

[3] October 14, 1806; the battle was some 67 km from Halle
[4] About 3.3 km from the Klausbrücke.
[5] [Note by Marx] Naturally the boy had no real view of all this. But the locality was known to him in every detail, and the utterances of educated person generally agreed with each other precisely, and came, like everything, often to his ears.

drowned instead. For the defense of the bridge, from the numerous artillery of the reserve, which were estimated to be 60 to 90 pieces, only two field pieces were sent to the bridge; one stood in the middle of the bridge, and the other on its exit into the city.

The French advanced from Passendorf. The second Prussian artillery mentioned mowed down a whole troop of the advancing French, and invited them to a second try.

Then the first company of French threw down their rucksacks, and under the direction of their lieutenant it stormed the artillery, running full out, with the tall lieutenant with saber swinging leading the way. He arrived at the artillery at the moment where the gunner was putting the flame to the ignition hole. To give him a slice in the hand, throw himself over the cannon barrel, and put out the fire with his body took the officer only a moment. He clutched the cannon barrel, received countless slash and stab wounds, and the burning gunpowder ripped him a large wound in his clothing; but the shot, that possibly might have turned back the storming troops, was thwarted; the powder in the barrel did not ignite. And so the bridge, that is, the entire powerful position fell into the hands of the French. The other artillery unit galloped back to the city. One or two days later Napoleon entered the city. As soon as he had received word of the deed, he named the lieutenant, who was still hovering between life and death, as colonel of his regiment, and awarded him the Commander's Cross of the Legion of Honor. When later the report of the renewed outbreak of hostilities beyond the Vistula arrived in Halle, the new colonel, whose recovery was still far from being complete, let nothing stand in the way of hurrying after the Army. "I must go to my Emperor", he called repeatedly, "he needs his people".

It is understandable, that here I am only tracing the reports that circulated in the city, but which agreed with and confirmed the French reports[6].

On the Prussian side as well, however severely the conduct of the war was judged from here, examples of true heroism were not lacking. When the retreat into the city was already cut off by the rapidly advancing French troops, two Prussian flag-bearers, aged 16 to 18, without any cover, hurried into a side ally, that had no way out but the river. As soon as they realized this, they wound their flags around their bodies, and jumped into the water; they preferred to die rather than turn over the banner that had been entrusted to them to the enemy. — I myself saw a blue Hussar from the Usedom regiment covered with wounds, and

---

[6] This was Pierre Barrois, 1774-1860. Contrary to Marx's account, he was already a colonel at the beginning of the action and received his Legion d'Honneur in 1807, but he was promoted as a result of his personal heroism in the battle, rising to the rank of general. He was wounded at Waterloo.

exhausted, ride back, who had defended himself against 13 French hunters on his horse, and luckily fought his way through.

We in the city were at the highest level of excitement when the messenger of bad news arrived, and soon thereafter the information that the French had been seen on our side of the Saale. Suddenly a French Hussar and immediately thereafter two riding hunters were brought as prisoners past our house to the Commandant. I remember precisely, that the Hussar was under guard by three men, of whom one held him by the collar. Now the French were here! The city fell into ferment, even though they assured us that it was only a solitary corps, cut off from the rest of the army, which we had to deal with, and that soon would be captured.

My father had dared to go to the market and gradually down the Klausstrasse to the bridge, leading me by the hand, and often carrying me. We were not the only ones. At the same time the two artillery pieces which were assigned to the bridge went by at a gallop, led by cavalry. We heard shots; a bookdealer, known in the city as the crazy Dreissig, came in a whizzing gallop over the bridge heading toward the city, and cried at the top of his voice: "Everything is fine!" Immediately thereafter the two artillery pieces came rushing back – and almost in the same moment we heard shots, the high-pitched French drums – the Prussian ones, much larger, had a deeper sound – and soon one could hear in a high tenor the unending battle cry of the French: "en avant! en avant! plus vite! plus vite!"

So these were the French? These little men in yellow or blue overcoats or uniform tunics managed to turn back our tree-high grenadiers? And where were the small weapons with the three-foot-long bayonets that we had heard about, and which they had recommended imitating on our side? We were soon ready to declare that these troops – they were the Dupont Division – were a miserable group of freebooters and call them a "Löffelbande", because many had tin spoons stuck in their hats, and other had a pair of live hens or ducks tied to their packs.

The bridge was taken, and in a moment the city was overrun, and the reserve army on that side overthrown; I soon thereafter saw many hundreds of prisoners under the guard of a few watchmen gathered at the market. Many escaped into the Marktkirche or the Marienkirche, or escaped elsewhere with the help of the burgers. These soldiers, the majority of them foreigners, brought together through the not always honest practices of the recruiter to hard service – how could they be equal to the Prussians? And yet they had battled well, ransomed themselves, often in danger for their lives, crept and begged from place to place back to the Prussian Army! Yes, the Germans have always shown themselves to be unshakable warriors, and have triumphed if they were supported by good leadership. Napoleon was expected.

My father led me through the overcrowded streets to the market square. Through the Klausthor, through the city and onwards to the east the "Grosse Armee" poured from early morning until evening, brigade after brigade, infantry and cavalry interspersed by artillery pieces, an unending powerful stream. Once, before our eyes, the wheel of a wagon (cannon) broke. In a moment, faster than I can describe it, it was removed, replaced by a new one, and the stream rolled further without interruption.

Both large halves of the market, over which the procession flowed onwards, offered an even more notable drama. One side was filled by the foot guard, the grenadier guard, the Jägers on foot, the Voltigeurs and Artillery, which formed an honor guard (*Gewehr bei Fuß*) opposite the Armee. The other half, the so-called Fleischmarkt was filled with the Gardekorps of the riding Grenadiers, in dark blue officer's uniforms, the trumpeters in light blue; the privates had infantry rifles hung crosswise over their shoulders. Probably the Corps was to serve on foot and on horse. On high steeds sat the very tall riders, appearing even taller with their high bear-hats (the first such, that I saw) the hair of which hung down a long way and gave their faces a warlike appearance. These were, as people said, mostly Alsatians and Walloons. For Napoleon had learned from the Romans to use the smaller and more oppressed peoples for infantry, since such folk can carry more easily and nimbly, and to use the large people for cavalry, where their longer arms and their strength can make an effect.

As if this all were not enough, new trumpets blared, and the *Kürassiergarde* marched into the marketplace, once again, giant men and giant horses. We already seen Prussian and Saxon cuirassiers; they wore iron breastplates, but with black and dull wax, and thus inconspicuous. The French cuirassiers gleamed in the sunlight, which sparkled on the clean steel armor. Along with this they wore steel helms with metal combs and waving manes; we recognized the shape from Roman depictions. How much they outshone the broad three-cornered hats of the Prussians and Saxons. Truly, it is not a small thing, to arouse fantasy! These cavalry men felt elevated, not only through their deeds and fame, but also through the vision of their truly warlike armor, shining like the blare of trumpets. And how their appearance shone in the drunken eyes of the boys! These were, so it seemed to us, the knights from our romances. Finally, there even burst forth in wild disorder a crowd of Turks – they were the Emperor's Mamelukes.

The call: der Kaiser! l'empereur! ran through the foot-guard, crowding in, and the burgers, anxious to see. We had a good spot behind the Grenadiers who had arrived out of order; my father had taken me by my arm, and I allowed myself to hope that I would see something. Suddenly a troop of the French grabbed my father, showed him a quartering order, and demanded, unsatisfied by his verbal agreement, that he lead them to the distant billet. Little hope remained, and no thought of resistance was possible; sadly we moved away. Soon, however, the way led past a group of chatting officers. My father took advantage of the shining opportunity, and complained loudly, in French, about the offense that had happened to us. An officer turned to us and asked, what the matter was. My father reported that he and his little boy had wanted to have a glimpse of the great Emperor that they would remember for their whole life long, and were now headed way back into the city. The officer immediately showed the soldiers the way, and led us through the Garde, who made way, so that we could stand in the front row. And immediately the shouts of the military crowds resounded, for just then the Emperor with his grand following rode in.

I do not know if I will be able to find anyone to believe the following, but I speak it nonetheless , since I know it to be the truth. The little boy had no eyes for the marshals, gleaming in gold, he saw only Napoleon, who, in the midst of the shining entourage, rode in wearing a light grey uniform jacket, and the world-famous hat. If my hand were still in practice, I could still today give a true portrait of the man, who, with his antique Roman, yellow-pale countenance, and the sharply cut features motionless as bronze, with the bright gray and yet abysmally deep eyes looking straight ahead, and gazing at nothing in particular, then rode by. Thus he rode into our city in the middle of his crowd of heroes, the victor over all his foes!

And yet he would be reminded in the middle of this city, that he was in the enemy's land.

He moved silently to the point of his following, as was his wont, to go down the Märkerstraße in the direction of the "grand Berlinplatze" to the residence prepared for him at Metel's, or perhaps Niemeyer's house. Suddenly he saw, on the front steps of a stately house, the high and nervous figure of a man with a powerful, brownish-red countenance, curly hair, and sparkling and lively blue eyes. This was the Justice Commissioner [*Justizkommissarius*] Dr. Scheuffelhut; he described this to me much later himself. The man stood, his eyes firmly and boldly directed at the Emperor, his right hand stuck in the buttoned-up uniform jacket, as was his custom, and far from any dangerous intentions. The Emperor turned his head, and his sharp glance met the tall figure. The pace of the horse becomes slower, and his eyes remain fixed on the bold German, who perhaps is planning something dangerous. And thus one, standing like a living marble portrait gazes at the other, carrying unshakable tranquility in his breast, as he moves down the street. Did he know, and would he still say to himself today, that the bullet for him had not yet been cast?

I learnt then, and later twice more, what a gift we receive when we, in seeing great personalities and events are lifted far beyond the narrow confines of the ego, and of daily life and activity. The historical sense awakes, and enthusiastic participation in the circumstances of humanity, of the people, of the ideal life take the place of the small and transitory, of material interests.

Naturally we boys had no inkling of this influence of the exciting events. But more tangible effects would become noticeable, which, amidst the general joy taken by the boys in martial events had their impact.

The first effect affected me personally.

Soon after those days I was attacked by strange spasms; I had lost my pleasure in and assiduousness for work, and if I tried to force myself to study for any length of time, I fell into convulsions, which pulled my eyes, lips and my whole head to the left side. My ability to speak was affected, though I remained fully conscious and master of my members. The doctors who were called in, whose questions during the attack I could only answer in writing and with an uncertain hand, seemed doubtful regarding the diagnosis; the frequently recurring seizures, which we did not how to control, debilitated me to the uttermost. Reil[7], at the time still an ornament of the University of Halle, was called in. As I was lying there, he inclined his noble countenance over me, looked deep in my eyes with his bright and yet so mild blue eyes, and said quietly, but perceptibly to himself: "Now, there probably is not much more to be done". Strangely, these words aroused in me, though I certainly loved live, and should have feared death, a curious contentment. I felt with unshakable certainly that I would continue living. It was the first time, that I became aware of that inner certainty, which is strong than all evidence and external expressions, and which lives in every human breast, but which for no one is more indispensable than for the artist, who precisely in the deepest creative moments has simply no other direction and certainty beyond this inner voice. But may no one drown in it and suffocate.

The seizures did not stop. —Then it happened, that one fine morning two regiments of French and Asenburgers were expected, and were supposed to pass by our house. How much I wanted to see them! But I could not leave my bed. Then from afar we heard the drums, moving every closer. I began to have a seizure, and my father tried to calm me. "But I want to see them!" I screamed violently. The seizure ended, my father brought me to the window, and I saw the regiments pass by, with their bright music leading the way. The seizures never returned.

The human will is stronger than most realize. It is the true doer of miracles. At the time I could not understand this properly, but I never forgot this event. Perhaps it was the first impetus to my tendency to pursue with perseverance what I wanted, as much as possible.

---

[7] Johann Christian Reil, 1759-1813, early specialist in psychiatry, active in Halle, 1788-1810.

Everyone loved playing with toy soldiers. There was not a single child, who had not had tin soldiers and cannons made. Together with a friend I had put together several hundred. We played, like everyone did, with the same war, and bravely fired volleys; for we were soon tired of simply playing at parades. Then we managed to get our hands on a copy of the *History of the Seven-year's War* by Archenholz[8]. It was avidly read and read over and over again, naturally with impassioned partisanship for old Fritz and his Prussians. We soon thought to re-enact the battles. With sticks, pieces of cardboard and sand we sought to represent the terrain for the battles, brought our soldiers into the historically documented order of battles and then – well, then the most furious cannonades had to decide. The one who had the last man standing was the victor. Our playing was taken so seriously, and we had our Archenholz so well by heart, that I am sure that even today I would be able to drawn the favorite battles according to his presentation.

More striking was the effect on the crowd. We children of the notables had already transformed ourselves into knights with cardboard armor and wooden swords. After the battle bayonets were found here and there, and occasionally cartridges as well. The great crowd of city children seized these, stuck the bayonets on long sticks, and so formed a second party, which called itself "Grannediere" (Grenadiers). Grannediers and knights met each other outside the city, and the thing became even more serious when some farm boys on horses from Giebichenstein got mixed up in it. Some old Prussian invalids – the only available reinforcements at the time – had to turn out, who happily stifled the civil war.

[8] Johann Wilhelm von Archenholz, published 1793.

CHAPTER 4

STARTING WITH COMPOSITION AND THEORY

I had improvised since I had possessed a keyboard; at least, I cannot remember a time in which that did not take place. How? Only God, who knows everything, knows! The time of the war, and certainly the years 1806 or 1807 were decisive in giving the first impulse to written composition.

My father, probably with no other goal than for play, had given me a little book with lined pages. I can see it before me in my mind's eye, with its blue and red marbled cover, and each page of the rough yellow paper covered with two systems.

Probably nothing was more amusing to me than the little post horn of the French *voltigeur* [combat soldier], which sounded so high and perky, when the handsome and brightly be-braided and be-laced troops more danced than marched by. I improvised myself such a voltigeur-march, and wrote it down with feverishly trembling hands in my notebook.

My friends, whom I allowed to hear it, seemed pleased; I, however, as is obvious, was satisfied. Why these reminiscences? I did not think about it at all, and I still can't believe it – it sounded much too *"tudesque"* [Germanic]. Why did I choose F-sharp major? Well, who can know everything? Now it is there in notes! But the longer I looked at it, the more my young heart became uneasy. Something was missing, but I did not know what; my page of music did not look like the rest. Finally, it became clear to me! It was missing the barlines! That could be remedied – the quill flew tirelessly from top to bottom, in one measure there were 4 or 5 eighth-notes, in another 1 quarter-note, according to the wanderings of the quill; for, I poor child, had never learned, what bar lines really meant; probably the loud counting of my teacher, and my inborn feeling, had reasonably straightened out the meter.

Many things followed for me as a student in the next few years. I only recall, from a somewhat later time, a more daring undertaking: my setting of Schiller's *Semele*[1]. Of course, it only went as far as the first monologue. That this poem was not really suitable for musical treatment was something that I could not know at the time; here, as in all my musical undertakings, I followed a shadowy impulse, my pleasure in the subject.

---

[1] This early work, from 1782, was described by Schiller as "a lyrical operetta", but was not set to music. It has been identified as an influence on Wagner's *Lohengrin*.

But precisely this compositional adventure would not remain without influence on the following years. At that time a young woman singer had come to Halle from Berlin, a Miss Andresse[2], who, with her well-trained voice (something entirely novel for the provincial city), and with the deep glance of her dark eyes, made quite an impression on me, as she did on everyone around me. I handed over my *Semele* to her. She was gracious to the half-boy/half young-man, and sang me my mad mixture of recitative and aria for me. Ah! It stumbled here, and stumbled there – and I could not avoid realizing that the problem lay not in her, but rather in the composition. When she spoke consolingly and very indulgently "it will yet find itself", I grabbed the innocent pages, smiling outwardly and inwardly grim, and ripped them from top to bottom, before she could stop me. The incident could not hold me back from new enterprises; for I felt constantly driven to repeated attempts. However, it did create in me an aversion to appear publicly with compositions again, which lasted for years, and obviously inhibited me. Now and then I tried to find a way around it, like our steel makers who put their products on the market as made in England, and had my attempts heard under pseudonyms, with varying degrees of success. And so I recall having an aria performed under the name of Palestrina. Ah! It was not presumption that suggested to me the name of the "Prince of Sacred Music", but rather the most innocent ignorance. A second consequence was more serious. From time to time I looked through my compositional attempts, felt unsatisfied with them, and then carried out a murderous *Auto-da-fe*. The world may not have lost much with the disappearance of these items, but I did myself. Only later did I understand that with this sort of behavior one robs oneself of insight into one's own development. The ballade and song composer Löwe, later to become so beloved, was cleverer and luckier in this regard than I was. He was at the time a soprano in the excellent *Singchor* in Halle, and had compositional instruction, paid for by the King of Westphalia, with Professor Türk. His first composition was published by subscription. This was the poem *"Lothar* "by A. W. Schlegel. We all were enchanted that the hero turned down the golden chain of honor presented, and, if I am not mistaken, the cup of honor with the golden wine, and thereby went on to say "the singer's drink is Wiesenquell[3]!" for we knew that better than the golden wine.

Only Löwe's example and my own dissatisfaction were able to teach me: one must learn something, before one can produce something.

---

[2] Probably the sister of Johann Heinrich Michael Andresse, 1756-1824, also from Berlin, and the son of Johann Michael Andresse, 1724-1801, a music teacher.
[3] Made in Blankenburg, about 77 km north-west of Halle. In fact, the ballad, set as part of Löwe's opus one, was "Klotar", and was written by Johann Friedrich Kind, not Schlegel.

Thus I found myself with the only teacher to be found in Halle, Professor Türk. From him I had instruction in figured bass, and had even wheedled permission to attend his academic lectures, although I was still in the middle classes at the Gymnasium.

The worthy man, always very dear to me, did in this instruction, what could only take place there. Along with the necessary teaching and explanations, handsome sheets with figured, and then unfigured basses, were submitted and worked on. Yes, the conscientiousness of the teacher tracked down every weakness of the student in this area of knowledge. I recall, once after the end of the lesson, when I had already stood up to depart, in exchanging the last few words, having, half-thoughtlessly to have played a couple of chords (perhaps a seventh and a six-four chord) on f and g, and then walked to the door. I was ready to open it, and I heard Türk's call: "Marx! Marx!" after me. I turned back around from the door, and looked inquiringly at Türk. "You didn't resolve them!" I had to go back to the piano, and play the final chords. Don't mock the little pedantry. The worthy old man could not imagine, could not bear for music to conclude without a formal resolution. How happy those who can hold fast to unbreakable laws, and never enter the region of eternal question and doubt!

For me, however, it was written in the stars, that I always and everywhere would be thrown back on my own attempts and strivings. I worked bravely through figured bass, as we know it from Türk or other method books; the figured basses, first with basic root-position chords, etc., were set out and played through, and – the further I worked my way in, the farther I came from any attempt at my own compositions; the source of feeling and the pleasure therein, seemed to be entirely dried up.

The valiant Türk was in no way responsible for this; I was convinced of this. Yes, I was attached to him with the full respect and youthful enthusiasm of a true disciple. Where the old man appeared, I felt only respect toward him, and was angry with many whose insulting mien I noted. This was the case at the concerts, of which he gave twenty-four annually, probably after the example of the concerts at the Leipzig Gewandhaus. When, as he was directing, and in the increasing vehemence of the affect, or during an extended crescendo, he moved ever farther upward, and finally his head, with gray, streaming hair and his flailing arms, like a musical King Saul, appeared a full head above chorus and orchestra, one thought to see the model for many conductors of our days, although their day did not have to wait long to arrive.

And when, at his lectures at the University, which he held in his private residence after having made arrangements, he laid out whole stacks of books on the table, in order to refer to these, and to provide us with insight into the depth of knowledge: thus he awoke in us a reverence which was both for the highly literate man, as for the fact that after we got to know him through art, this showed us his scholarly side. Even at this time the unusual shyness of this worthy man was a mystery to me. He presented with assurance and terseness anything that he could support from authority; in questionable cases he would decide bravely and firmly for one authority or another. Here he also trusted his own judgment. However, if any support from an outside judgment was lacking, he certainly did not dare to expound his own. Thus, he had already correctly recognized the normal minor scale at that time, long before it was publicly discussed by Gottfried Weber[4]. But only in the presence of his most trusted students, and only in the form of a daring, and perhaps foolish hypothesis, would he venture this. And in the same way he knuckled under, only secretly disagreeing with those who forbade musicians the then unplayable fifths and octaves. But neither his compositions nor his writings contain a trace of this.

Since I now found myself hindered rather than helped by figured bass, I began to tirelessly study through all the musical instruction books that I could have at hand, either from Türk's library, or anywhere else. I scarcely believe that anything whatsoever from the literature of the time remained unknown to me. In particular it was Marpurg's *"Art of Fugue*[5]*"* that occupied me on a continuing basis. In this area I had been joined by the subsequent Naue[6] (later music director), quite a few years older than myself, who also had done certain studies with Zelter[7] in Berlin, but whose volatile and weak temperament avoided any serious effort. We read the book out loud to each other, and sought to provide examples for its rules. Now the excellent Marpurg is certainly fruitful for all the individual traits which can be identified in the fugue, but the coherence of the whole —

Encheiresin naturae! (nennt's die Philosophie)

Spottet ihrer selbst und weiß nicht nie[8] —

was something he entirely left by the wayside. We learned how to make a theme, good or bad, to create the countersubjects – in short, all the details – but a fugue, an entire fugue was something never produced in this way. Only several years later would bring me there. Good old Naue! He stands before me;

---

[4] Gottfried Weber, 1779-1839, and unrelated to the composer, was an influential theorist, known for his advances in thinking on diatonic function.

[5] Probably his *Abhandlungen von der Fuge*, 1753.

[6] Johann Friedrich Naue, 1787-1858, a prolific composer who had studied with Beethoven in Vienna.

[7] Carl Friedrich Zelter, 1758-1832, composer and prolific teacher of music, who numbered Felix and Fanny Mendelssohn and Giacomo Meyerbeer among his pupils.

[8] A couplet quoted from Goethe's *Faust*, lines 417-418.
   Encheiresin naturae nennt's die Chimie,
   Spottet ihrer selbst, und weiß nicht wie.

one of those characters, who, versatile, encourage, benevolently and helpfully, where they can, but never bring the kernel of their life to maturity, because the first rudiment remained undeveloped and the power to develop has been lost. How often did his restless being, ever directed toward the external goal, and his related conceit, give an occasion for insult! And how soon we remained silent in the face of his inexhaustible good nature! And my dealings with him were a never-ending exchange of childish hostilities, and an always resurfacing positive inclination. He was the son of a rich needle manufacturer, and destined by his father, without a firm goal, for study, without however succeeding in going to the University. His next ambition when I got to know him was to go around with students and do more or less what they did, that is, where this could happen without danger. More than once I could observe him with Schelling (not the mystical philosopher, but a baker). He had some sort of confection in front of him; on the other side a student was asking for a piece of plum tort, and "give me two pieces as well!" called Naue. Another one would ask, perhaps for a glass of punch, "give me a glass of punch as well!", and so it continued until he had the entire table loaded in front of him, and then he departed, paying for everything, only touching a little, but satisfied; he had attained, what all the others had asked for. What seemed even more amazing to me was this inability to allow anyone else to take a step forward. He may have heard through the grapevine that I was thinking about a history of music, or a figured bass method (which ought rather to be called a composition method). For a long time he had nothing to say about this, but finally he led me to his library and showed me an impressive row of quarto volumes. And on the red labels, what I could I see printed? Compositional method (Figured Bass) by Fr. Naue, Vol. 1-2...; History of Music by Fr. Naue, Vol. 1-2. ...I was extremely surprised, and before he could hinder it, I pulled one of the volumes out and opened it up. What did I find? The most beautiful white paper, without a single syllable thereon. It was not boastfulness on his part, perhaps, but his soul enjoyed the vivid view of his future works. Let us not laugh too loud about this, since many devote their lives, year-in, year-out to such fantasy activities.

At first, however, this pure future-work had a fatal effect on him, and a healthy one on me. He convinced himself that he had to have a large library of musical works. So he created what would have only been achievable through his father's gold. I remember a beautiful collection of Netherlandish compositions by Orlando di Lasso and others, which later went to the collection of the library in Berlin. It also happened, that for the purchase of Handel's *Alexander's Feast*, in order to be certain, he had sent orders at the same time to three different book dealers. And so he very properly received three copies of the work, of course at double the normal price that could already be paid in the book trade. He never made serious use of these works.

I, however, for the longest time had the urge to look around everywhere, and his unlimited kindness provided me with the use of his treasures, as far as I understood them at the time. That, at that time, I could have seriously profited from their use, is quite unthinkable; it was simply incentive and preparation for riper studies in the future; it was assistance that, already at the time, even if not clearly why, seemed to be impossible to do without, and which for me in Halle, without my own means, could have come to me in no other way than this one, one not blazed by me nor for me. In so far as I have become aware of my destiny, I have always found, that everything that I needed always arrived precisely in the moment of need, not before, and not after, and certainly, where my means were insufficient, in a way that was independent of me, and impossible to foresee. No one who knows me in some degree will ascribe the foolish delusion to me that I see a [divine] favor therein. Rather I am convinced that everyone who looks attentively at his life must be drawn to the same conclusions. And does not the history of the nations, in so far as we can look through it clearly, give us this same recognition - Christianity, the Roman Empire, the fall of that Empire, Napoleon's fall, has not everything that we have realized come forward in this same way? And would anywhere a history of men or nations have more meaning and worth than the most absurd children's story, if it were not for the fact that from these stories a beam of eternal reason shines forth?

And even Naue's efforts were not without fruit. He became organist at the Marienkirche and the University music director, as well as the director of the city chorus, so excellently led before him by Türk. Yes, he tried to deliver lectures at the University, following Türk's example, which however, seemed to have but little success. Some church music by him appeared in print, and a church calendar, a collection of tonal formulas, which various churches have made use of at various times for the liturgy

Thus I had labored on the manifold ways to an education in composition – and in vain. Everything that I had read, did not lead me to where I truly wanted to go: to skill and strength in composition. Quite the opposite, if I were to judge from my own experience, it led away from this; for the more I studied, the more the source of my own invention dried up.

Thus arose for a long time a dangerous delusion for me: composition was nothing that could be taught, was nothing but an impulse or gift based on inborn talent. That this facility still needed the aid of instruction, so that not everyone would have to begin the art once again from the start, and have to doubtfully gain through the sacrifice of tiresome years, that which thousands, one after another, had achieved over many centuries, and had collected as a common inheritance for those who would come after: that was something

I could not, poor boy, either realize from within myself, or conclude from having read the music literature of the time. I certainly had an inkling that yet other teachings and ways of teaching were yet to be found somewhere. But where? In Halle there was only Türk; what he had done as a teacher for Löwe was unrecognizable for me, and indeed not very successful. This was later proved by Löwe's compositions. His lieder and ballades show a great talent; all his larger compositions were untenable, since for them the basis of a sound musical education and the general spiritual development of the composer were not present. Beside, in addition to seeking instruction, I was lacking in means. Thus, that error was still for me a way out of despair; I was thrown back on my own resources, whatever might be the result. But my drive to create and my tireless struggle to learn remained unweakened.

During this whole time many compositions were initiated; the smaller part of these were completed. Among these was my first opera. Its matter was taken from the French Revolution, no less, and the hero was none other than - Lafayette. At the same time I had enough sense or insight, to set the scene amidst the medieval battles in Italy, and to call my hero *Fayado*. The actual sources for me were Girtanner's *Erinnerungen oder Denkwürdigkeiten aus der Revolution*[9], notable for its personal and descriptive manner of presentation. I was especially excited for the second act, whose stormy prelude led to an intense recitative for bass and upper instruments. Soon the curtain rose, and we were facing the gathering in which the wild partisan struggle of parties continued the recitative. Then suddenly a single figure appears, who silently enters through the struggling parties. All fall silent. It was, as one could see, the moment when, at the city hall, the suspects, Flesselles, and his son-in-law, are threatened by their judges with immediate death and the wide plaza is full of those demanding the bloody verdict. Lafayette must skillfully bring his troops in, and is able to gradually empty the entire space, and then enters the hall, where he easily silences those demanding death, who are now abandoned by their following.

Who was the poet for this opera? None other than – myself, for I had no one, and knew no one, who could have helped me. But in my awkwardness at the time it was really out of the question for me to do a libretto. I imagined every moment in the liveliest way that I could, and then struggled to create text and musical setting at the same time. The fact that, in this way, no work of art could take shape in clarity and harmony, was unknown to me at the time, but I had to learn that from the powerful and dark struggle only individual scenes and pieces of scenes could be achieved, which would wait in vain to

[9] No book by this title by Christoph Girtanner exists. Possibly this is the *Denkwürdigkeiten* by Dumouriez, with annotations by Girtanner, published in 1794 in Berlin by Lagarde und Unger.

be joined together. Before and after me it is well known that various have made this effort to combine poet and composer in one. But these attempts separated the two activities – first created the poem, more or less completely, and then began, as a second task, to set the poem. So the practical completion was at least possible in theory, and the question simply remained: whether the musician in his poetic work would find poetic inspiration as well, or whether he might not create his text abstractly from the circumstances and the poetical recollections of others, and then, from this task, proceed to his own creative sphere, already grown cold? A question which cannot be resolved here.

My last undertaking from this period will be mentioned, since it reappeared decades later, and would then be completed in a completely altered form. Already in Halle, when I was fifteen to eighteen years old, the imposing figure of Moses appeared to my imagination, and would not let me be, until I had tried to do him justice, to the extent of my powers and direction. At that time the material appeared to me in purely dramatic form, and in fact, in a pair of two connected operas. I only recollect the first scene, which I had placed, in a highly inappropriate setting, in the forecourt of an Egyptian temple. After a short introduction by the orchestra, the procession of priests enters, two by two, and passes by the holy images in solemn procession, until it disappears into the temple. The song of the first pair is imitated in canon by the following pair, and I imagined the effect of this canonic singing, always the same, and this same always being altered, to be very solemn and mystical. Following the final pair is the youth Moses, the disciple of the Priest, joining the procession, but then remains behind at the portal of the temple, and speaks in scorn of how unbearable the temple services is for his free soul, thirsty for deeds. I had only composed this scene; to which words, I no longer recall. I had begun without having a plan for the entire thing, and had to give up on doing the rest, probably because I could sense the incompatibility of the material with the form that I had chosen. I no longer have a single note of this first effort; it was only the material that claimed and showed its power over me.

As if there were not enough marvels, I, half-boy, was at the same time tempted to do my first theoretical work. I had, as it happened, a friend at school and university, who also was my constant companion at the piano. He played more fluently and more cleanly than I did; but he was not successful in improvising, and yet he was stimulated to imitate me every time I sat down at the keyboard. I was disturbed by this pointless activity, the basis of which I did not understand, and I never stopped wondering what one really is doing when one improvises. I probably may have imagined all sorts of repetition, replacement and alternation of a theme; well, then, I sat down to my sheet of paper, and wrote thereon: "Introduction to Improvisation." The little volume was dedicated to my friend, who enjoyed it. Whether he thereby learned to improvise, is something that I will not swear to.

It may seem strange, that, given such continual struggle, I did not make the decision to devote myself entirely to music, indeed, that I persistently rejected Türk's repeated assertion that I would yet become a musician. But the matter simply fit only too naturally together. In Halle I could have no other vision of the life of a musician beyond that provided to me by a vision of a few organists, piano teachers, municipal musicians and the traveling virtuosi who passed through. All this could not appeal to me. And Türk's career also seemed to promise no satisfaction. The idea, however, of making my living through composition (and the impoverishment of my parents had forced my attention in this direction), seemed to me to be a degradation of the holy art, perhaps as if a pious Christ had seen bodily sustenance in the Last Supper. I thus looked for a vocation that, in addition to the work needed to dutifully fulfill it, might allow as much leisure as possible for that other vocation, music, to have its fair share. That this once again was a serious error, that one cannot serve two masters, and that no worthy success can be expected if one does not focus one's whole strength on a single point: how could the sixteen-year-old, innocent of the world, and entirely unadvised, recognize this?

I dedicated myself to legal study. It seemed full of life, and had already appeared to me as an important side of the life of nations and states. At the same time I had been able to see the Counsels of the City Courts in Halle, at least then, were not overburdened with work. The morning could belong to their civil service, and afternoons and evenings belonged to playing cards, socializing, hunting. For these I felt little attraction, and allowed myself to hope that I could use the ample leisure time for my musical desires. In my sixteenth year I was admitted to the University of Halle.

\

CHAPTER 5

THE THEATER IN WEIMAR

What, moreover, during this entire time, taking in the last semester of school and the first year of university, came to my assistance, stimulating and enriching me, was the appearance of the Court Players from Weimar, which visited my hometown for several summers to give a series of performances. This was the first time that we were able to be present at truly artistic performances, and heard many operas by Paer, Winter, and especially by Mozart. The effect on us young people, entirely unaccustomed to life in a metropolis, was magical. When in Paer's *Kamilla*[1] the husband, tormented by jealousy and thirst for revenge – this was the noble form of Strohmeier, then the leading basso – first appeared on the silent stage, wrote a letter to the outcast and imprisoned wife, took out her portrait, pressed it to his lips, and then smashed it to the ground, and once more moved away angrily: then we all could scarcely breathe, and only felt relieved, when he once more entered the theater, in order to now pour forth his lament in a milder, but more powerful voice. But when finally the moment of liberation approached, one looked to see in which of the underground vaults the unhappy and innocent woman sighed in anticipation of her death by starvation, and the chorus of the household on the stage called to the upper stories, in wide-resounding chords her name, Kamilla! – for a long time, unanswered, and finally guided by a weak sound in the right direction – then you could probably read on our pale faces the same anxiety, that threatened to suffocate everyone there on the stage.

It is the misfortune of large cities that everything is present in excess from the earliest childhood, so that everything is taken in prematurely and indifferently as well, and the powerful appeal of the new and unheard is lost, when the real years of enjoyment and elevation arrive. And it is the unacknowledged benefit of small and middling cities, that the rareness of artistic celebrations means longing desire and undefiled receptivity; — provided there is spiritual inclination on the part of the residents.

There was never a performance of an opera by Gluck. The general favorite was Mozart. For my part, I lived and breathed only for him. The noble enchantment of his tunes, so manifold and yet so inward, so changeable and yet so softly flowing, carried us, like the scarcely moving surface of the sea, softly rocking, to the land of dreams, and to dreamily changing feelings. I remember

---

[1] Ferdinando Paer's *Camilla*, premiered in Vienna in 1799, was a reworking, with added Gothic elements, of an older *opéra comique* by Dalayrac.

very distinctly, that when I opened one of the green volumes of Härtel's edition of Mozart's works at the piano, an entirely individual and sweet scent seemed to waft toward me. This was no intentionally evoked idea, or a created simile, but rather an unmediated feeling, that naturally had its origin simply in the vagaries of power of fantasy. What I felt at the time as Mozart's effect will always be the realm in which he reigns unrivaled, and holds the minds of Germans in a sweet embrace. Another and deeper realm was unknown to me then.

But it was not only the operas that blessed us and elevated us; the performances of tragedies also exercised their power, and not just temporarily, but throughout our lives. Especially the dramas of Schiller had an effect on us young people, who knew them by heart, but had not yet seen them on the stage, with a force that perhaps had a distant connection with the effect of the tragedies of Aeschylus on the youth of Athens. If, in *Wilhelm Tell*, even before the raising of the curtain, the distant sounds of the troops, with the not outstanding, but nevertheless significant music by Romberg removing us from our surroundings, and enchanting us to the faraway highlands, where the shepherd-folk, long-oppressed, but never forgetting their liberty and human rights, wrestled free of the bonds of servitude: how our young hearts beat faster and more powerfully! And in those days the true *Wilhelm Tell* was still performed everywhere, not changed into that most humble Andreas Hofer, or even a hero of Italian opera. And if, once more, the dark Philip of Spain[2], the master of two worlds with all his proud grandees, went on his knees as if struck by lightning when the powerful figure of the Grand Inquisitor, bent under the weight of centuries, was led on by two Dominicans: how we Protestant boys felt in our resisting hearts the superiority of church power, and at the same time the humiliation of the tyrant, who yet had to hear that call "Give them freedom of thought!". These dramas were living history for us! And we felt, without arriving at a clear realization about this, that Schiller's power lay not only in the individual thoughts, but rather, in the creation of great and powerfully gripping scenes. Since Aeschylus and Shakespeare no other poet had understood how to evoke such great pictures, and such elevating spectacles.

However, certain oddities also did not fail to appear, that necessarily belong to the existence of a university city, a city, that by and large lives from the university and the students, and in which the students to some extent play a leading role. So it had become conventional, that during performances of *The Robbers* the entire parquet would fill with students, and then, shortly before the beginning of the overture the seniors from the student nations would file in two by two, all of them "*im Wichs*[3]," namely, in the

---

[2] In Schiller's *Don Carlos*.
[3] A sort of uniform for special occasions. These student 'nations' were fraternities within universities, now mostly obsolete, which grouped together students from particular regions.

festive, if also odd attire, which they would wear for celebratory student gatherings: a tight jacket with sash in the colors of the student nation, white leather breeches, stiff boots that extended up well over the knee, known as cannons, on their heads a high, three-cornered hat, which in my day had already been two-cornered for a long time, with a dangling feather, and on the side the "beater", our dueling-weapon. When a sign was given, all the robbers who were before us in the Bohemian forest pulled out their swords. They were supposed to join in the song "We lead a free life", but remained silent, and instead the whole crew of students stood up and festively sang the entire song with the sound of the trombones and the jubilation of the entire orchestra. Only then could the presentation on the stage continue. Whatever one may think of this confluence of public and performers, once upon a time it was irrefutably a part of theater and student life in Halle. We would have had to have been expelled one by one rather than to omit a single verse. It is also self-evident that on these festive evenings none of the charming daughters of the city were absent from the theater. Indeed, in those days the theater had an entirely different significance than it does today. The twin stars of Schiller and Goethe had risen over Germany from Weimar, and had begun to send out their fiery beams over the fatherland, and far beyond its borders. Each word of these two great figures resounded like a new gospel, and gained entry and residence in the hearts of all those struggling for culture. The power that Schiller's words of decision exercised over the whole German people can scarcely be imagined now that they have for such a long time been all too familiar for every tongue, and are native to every mind. One might boldly claim that Schiller, the longest buried, was the mightiest champion in raising the Germans to a fight for freedom against foreign powers, and that his influence was always expressed and always will be expressed as often as the people are aroused to liberty, that is to higher realization and well-being. Those Weimar players, however, appeared to us as immediate emissaries of the prince of poets; for Schiller and Goethe themselves had trained them, and introduced them to the meaning of the high poetry. The former, who himself is supposed to have read very poorly, and whose home and position stands farther from the theater, probably had an effect only through the sharing of his high thoughts and the power of his mind. Goethe, in contrast, as head of the stages and expert, was the actual director and guide of the artistic union he created. Thus his Olympian peace was more often individually notable, if I am correctly informed by the players. If, during rehearsals, a player did not perform with the right sense, Goethe, who sat at the middle of the stage, would say, with imperturbable equanimity, "Once more a word of explanation or correction to be added." This "Once more!", was repeated, until the right expression was found.

It was often suspected that Goethe spent too much time on the theater; he himself was from time to time amenable to this point of view. If I am permitted to make further conclusions from my experience, then I must contradict this view; I must assume that for anyone who is sensitive, like myself, the effects of the theater created by Goethe like beams of light spread from spirit to spirit over time and continued to be felt, no matter how small the playhouse in Weimar may have been. The content of those poems, the performance on the part of individuals, among whom were highly talented artists, I mention only the names of Pius Alexander Wolf[4] and his spouse, and the collaboration of everyone in the noblest unity, and then also the awareness that that pair of poets had themselves created the presentation, as shortly before it had provided the poems for its people, all still warm from the donating hand, donated to us: the whole became an electrically powerful beam, and radiated undying enthusiasm…

We young people felt and recognized that. But the celebration of the *Satyrspiel* should not have been lacking either; as it happened it found not theater, but the closed breasts of the young people. We knew, as I said, our Schiller by heart. It was he who inspired us, whereas the dramas of Goethe were far from able to transmit to us the same ardor. Now, however, one after another of Schiller's tragedies was performed, and – soon a half-scene was missing here, there a whole scene. Who could have done that? Who touched and maimed our holy poetic temple? — It could not have been anyone but Goethe. We were certain of that, and we even had figured out, in our hot heads, the reason for this herostratic outrage. It was envy! The Courtier — thus it was spoken by our beardless lips – envied the Dramatist! Had the Olympians wandered through our smoky smelling city of salt, I do not know what might have happened. Heaven was gracious, and granted us some time to think, and perhaps to learn something. But at that time the ferment was powerful, and might have led to ostracism in one form or another.

---

[4] German actor and writer, 1782-1828. Married to actress Amalie Wolff-Malcolmi, 1780-1851. Both were credited with pioneering a more naturalistic performing style.

CHAPTER 6

WAR, AGAIN

And ever more wildly the overwhelming waves of public life washed into the small eddies of our private life. It was really a time, this time of Napoleon, that one can barely imagine now, in spite of all the historical evidence. Always and everywhere war, armies from and toward every direction of the compass. Here is the procession of the victorious, there the procession of the prisoners, here the princes, who "have ceased to reign", that Napoleon had summarily removed – there a crowd of new kings and princes, whom he had promoted from being sons of lawyers, and even from being cooks and stable boys, to the throne. The main current remained, however, that from west to east toward Moscow, and then – back! To Paris, until the overthrow of the mighty, whom, truly! not the power of man, but clearly that of a Higher Power had laid low. And all of this whizzed past our little Halle, as the great military highway required.

The harbingers of the reversal were already before our eyes. We already heard the incomprehensible news, after the Peace of Tilsit[1], that "the Prussians are coming", and one night we were woken by the noise of horses' hooves and the back and forth of lively voices in high pitches, and the short and choppy way of speaking that are so characteristic of the sturdy residents of Pomerania and Brandenburg. Riders with bright military outfits rode up and down before our windows; they belonged to Schill[2], whose name had a fine reputation at that time in Germany, and who was generally known as the "Knight of Queen Louise". His daring undertaking and dismal end moved every heart; from Halle as well many capable young men had joined his fine band.

And soon we also heard of the happier platoon of the Duke of Braunschweig-Oels[3]. He also came through Halle, in order to reach the seat of his father and the mouths of the Weser, where the rescuing English ships were waiting for him. His group of cavalry in short black tunics, black felt shakos with white metal skull and crossbones, and above the black horsetail plume— and in their midst the not tall, but powerful figure of the Prince, who, from the

---

[1] July 7, 1807. These two treaties, with Russia and Prussia, formalized French control of central Europe, and sharply diminished the status of the Prussian crown.
[2] Ferdinand Baptista von Schill, 1776 –1809, killed in a premature attempt to liberate Westphalia from French control. Louise of Mecklenburg-Strelitz, the queen of Frederick William III, had interceded with Napoleon at Tilsit, and was a heroine among Prussian nationalists.
[3] Frederick William, Duke of Brunswick-Wolfenbüttel, 1771 –1815, commander of the Braunschweig forces against Napoleon; he was later killed just before Waterloo.

thick curls of his golden-blond hair and beard, boldly and wildly gazed with his bright blue eyes – made a powerful impression on us. Schill had aroused the first stirring of resistance and hate against our oppressor; now the vision of the German warriors, who from the far shore of the Danube fought threw forces twenty times greater than theirs to freedom, for the first time directed the thoughts of us young people toward a common fatherland, toward Germany; and these thoughts would continue.

Later we heard, at first indefinitely, as if from an oracle, and scarcely believed, the news of the defeat at Moscow; and finally, there came the first swarms of Cossacks! We knew them well; from our study of the Greeks we knew them – they were the ancient Scythians, against whom the great Macedonians had fought in vain; if you would like to see them very true to life, look at the ancient mosaic of the battle between Alexander and Darius! The men around the Persian monarch with their long-shafted lances and short whips are the original image of these knout-wielding riders of the steppes, who, on their little steeds, with delicate feet and long manes, riding on a high saddle (they put their booty underneath) trotted past our eyes, first hesitated for no apparent reason, and then rode wildly forth. One fell with his horse before our window, and died immediately; he had broken his neck. One cannot particularly discuss their uniforms. One had a sheepskin, one a blue collar, one a yellowish or gray military tunic, and always with white breeches and a cloth or a close-cut fur cap; their outstanding characteristic, however, was the broad belt, from which usually two or four pistols gleamed, richly decorated with silver — the cavalry had just been facing the Turks in the field, and many carried a costly Turkish sabre; their main weapon, however, was still the lance. The bearded faces looked down at us – amazingly friendly, and then wild once again; I could admire many heads, which greatly resembled my beloved *Transfiguration*. How could one resist looking! How much fear and joy we felt! We saw one, unnoticed, take the nursling from his mother's arms (the Cossacks were, like all people who are close to nature, enthusiastic friends of children), dandled him in the most loving way, and, blessed, gave it back. Then a new group arrived from the Don; suddenly two of those who had arrived first, a youth and a man, leapt from their steeds, and moved, weeping, to one of the new arrivals, an old man with a long, flowing, and snow-white beard. They were a father and son, a thousand miles distant from their motherland, who were greeting their grandfather.— Here and there sparkled the brightly polished armored harnesses of individual Caucasians amidst the groups of cavalry. Then one saw Tatar figures with truly Mongolian features, their eyebrows inclined sharply upwards. And there were Bashkirs with white, pointed felt hats over their beardless, and half-feral grinning faces trotting amidst the group, many of them still provided with bow and arrow. From one I bought an arrow; he seemed to be happy with the price, and shook my hand in a friendly way, so that on the following day I still could not use it properly. In my boyish irritation I was surprised and displeased that I could not, before the handshake, even bear the man's glance; or else I would have been pleased to look at him, eye to eye. Was it the bestial wildness that frightened me off?

Amidst all this, at the head of this or that group, performed by the select group, one heard their martial songs; they had no other music. One scarcely believes this, and yet it is true. These songs often sounded in the major mode (in constrast to many Russian folksongs), and — in canonic duos.

Amidst this uproar was where I saw my venerable Türk for the last time. He had been attracted by the novelty of the sight, and far more by the sound of the national songs, and soon pushed his way into the densest crowd of cavalry, listening, with his head crooked to one side, but then he jumped backward, startled, as soon as a hoof hit the cobblestones. Not long thereafter he had sunk into the deepest silence.

He had once told me: he had mutually given his word along with Kapellmeister Reichardt[4] that whoever should survive the other would write and perform music for the burial of the other. I was, amidst the desolation of all of those in Türk's circle the only one who could remind him of this. Not an acquaintance of Reichardt, although I did know his compositions of Goethe-Lieder, an act from the heroic opera *Brennus*, and the opera *The Tempest* (after Shakespeare), which he had written in competition with Zumsteeg, I went with confidence to the famous man, who had retired from his very busy life to his marvelously beautiful garden in Giebichenstein near Halle. I arrived at the house early in the morning, and was shown through a hallway into the garden, where I would find the man. Excitedly looking about I wandered in and went up the first terraces, until finally by a turning the not large but noble old man stood before me. I bade him in the name of the students of Türk to begin upon the work that he had earlier agreed to. He listened kindly to me and my concern and said: so that we may better talk about this, bring the fruit basket with you, help yourself, and accompany me through the garden. And so I wandered in with the honorable gentleman and answered his sympathetic questions about Türk's final time and my relations to him and to music, very excited, but however, given his mildness, courageously enough. He indicated his willingness regarding the memorial, but doubted whether it was feasible amidst the storm of the busy days. In the event, it could not take place. The unrest without limits, the general desolation that

---

[4] Johann Friedrich Reichardt, 1752-1814, a prominent composer of songs and stage works, was Kapellmeister to the Prussian court during the 1790s. After falling from favour due to his sympathy for the French Revolution, he became director of a salt mine in Halle. His extensive writings, often in the form of letters from Paris or Vienna, are a valuable source for operatic aesthetics around the turn of the century.

had spread over everything that that time, had, in as much as I recall, gotten in the way. I visited the old man once more and he showed me in sketch or piano reduction two overtures that he had written for the victory celebration of the German cause. Whether they were completed and performed, I do not know. It is generally known that instrumental compositions were not his strong point, still less than was the case for his model, Gluck; he had emulated now this, now another old Italian. Had it been imaginable that the recollection and image of the amiable and exalted one could pale after those hours, then his short but quite invaluable explanations of Handel's music would have been powerful enough to arouse all that is forgotten and buried to the most vivid presence. Here spirit spoke to spirit! The discussion was not about notes and envious six/ five chords, but rather the spirit was open, that had created those songs, and continued to live in them. Without any comparison with the contents of the music books of that time they had doubtlessly given me a powerful push in the direction which my own thoughts would later take.

I could certainly not have an inkling of that at the time; my mind was not directed toward activity as a writer – it seemed to me to be directed exclusively toward composition; and here I was facing a composer, a real and celebrated composer!

Why didn't I ask him? Why didn't I fall at his feet, imploring him for advice and assistance? — I was only thinking about him, and forgot about myself.

Still dreaming, I returned to the city. And I was once more surrounded by the rush of life during war-time; for now the bloody game of weapons would come very close to me.

Near Halle there were two groups of Cossacks; from Skeuditz[5], however (on the road from Leipzig) French people were approaching in superior numbers. These were cuirassiers of the Empress (green uniforms, brass cuirasses and helmets) and infantry. The Cossacks retreated slowly, skirmishing along the way; the French pushed their way up to Petersberg[6], and then turned back on their side; they had only wanted to reconnoiter. Along with a few curious people I accompanied the movement; soon we came upon the dying, and heard quite closely the drawn-out whistle, that cut through the air in rapid pulses.

The situation became more serious, when Prussians and Russians (if I am not mistaken, it was the Kleist'sche Corps) took control of the city and occupied the same position at the long bridge that in 1806 had been so weakly defended. Now this position stood the test, for it was taken seriously. In front of the

[5] About 30 km southwest of Halle.
[6] About 13 km north of Halle.

bridge, in the direction of the city, redoubts were thrown up, and provided with artillery. While the thunder of cannon had already begun here, a Russian mounted battery – I can still see the open powder cart galloping by, more in the air than on the pavement – raced over the market back to the city; they had been, apparently, order to the heights by the stone bridge, in order to work from there. Just one spark in the open cart and a whole portion of the city would have been obliterated.

Here I realized for the first time, how the mind of man can be so entirely occupied by an important event that he notices nothing else. — The broad space of the market between the Rathaus und the main watch was dotted with a few soldiers (mostly Russians). I had stopped for a while at this spot, after which I and other meddlers had been sent back from the immediate vicinity of the redoubts. Bored by the monotony of the noise and view I finally returned home.

On the following morning I was congratulated by everyone I met, without knowing why. Finally, I found out the reason. Close by me a stray cannonball had knocked down two of the scattered Russians, and I had had no notion of it, so completely had my attention been distracted from the little events near me by the cannonades and the companies rushing past. Even the whistling of bullets, which was mixed with the deeper sounds of larger shot, had not given us the most remote notion of personal danger, so entirely were our minds focused on the course of the important events around us. I had no perception of that brown-red coloration of the surrounding which Goethe reports to us. This Goethe-related phenomenon perhaps had partial origin in the highly developed color sense of the Master; inner excitement calls forth the corresponding color, it was one of the psychological color phenomena, about which the deep-thinker had so much of importance to report[7]. I had experienced something similar in the vicinity of the Klaustor, where the batteries of both sides carried out their play. The roadway was covered with Prussian soldiers, who had lain down, in order to offer the smallest target to the bullets; I had leaned up against a house. Suddenly I was overwhelmed with a great mass of falling lime and stone debris; a ball had hit close by above me, and caused the debris to pour down, without my being aware of its impact.

The French (I believe it was the corps of Lauriston) pelted the city violently with grenades, and it caught fire in several places. No matter how great the superiority of the French – the Prussian position remained unshaken. And it was, in fact, different soldiers who now defended the position, it was the *Volksheer*.

And finally we heard the artillery thunder from Leipzig. Streets and fields were dotted with people; everyone was curious for the news. Many lay down on

---

[7] Goethe's ideas on optics, which tended to run counter to the Newtonian consensus and argued for the subjectivity of colour perception, were contained in his 1810 treatise *Zur Farbenlehre*.

the ground, in order to hear more clearly. The artillery thunder seemed to come closer. Suddenly the Leipzig road (the Galgstrasse[8]) was filled with a dull roar, heart-rending whimpering, and curses in a foreign tongue. A slow procession of broadly-built wagons approached, to which there appeared to be no end. That unearthly sound of lament was coming from them. These were Russian hospital wagons, on which the poor wounded and mutilated lay closely bedded together, with the head of one by the feet of the next, alternating, on both sides.

I had gone home to rest. In the first glimmerings of morning my father woke me with the words: "Don't be frightened, pull yourself together. All is lost, the Prussians are retreating". In a flash I had reached the gate. There I saw a strange and eerie scene. A long column of Prussian infantry came towards the city from the direction of Leipzig, without the playing of drums, silently and slowly, in small groups and pairs; their faces were blackened with gunpowder and dust, they approached, apparently extremely tired, very serious, and without speaking; and for us as well any word died, and every thought faltered. What was it? The lost battle? No! Riders galloped in, a monstrous scream came from every mouth. The battle had been won! And now the messengers of victory had arrived, the prisoners were brought in, a plundered artillery piece was drawn past by two horses, and many more would follow.

How many from Halle and the vicinity joined those battling for Germany before and after the battle, I do not know. It was not possible for me – I was too young and not strong enough.

I had wanted to make myself useful as an engineer, and had worked for it day and night, but it was in vain. And indeed I presented myself in Halberstadt, for I do not know what commission, but I was rejected. Körner's song: "A German maiden will not kiss you!",[9] which was on all the girls' lips at the time, upset me the least.

---

[8] "Gallows-Street".
[9] A nationalistic song intended to spur young men to join the resistance against the French.

CHAPTER 7

THE UNIVERSITY

Having been a city child I thus became attached to the University of Halle.

There is something unusual about such a university. Just as many advantages flow to universities in great residence-cities[1] – better resources, more famous names, greater power of attracting exceptional teachers in all subjects – one is reserved for university cities: the unmediated effect on the minds and education of those belonging to the university, and those living nearby. What really can a great political figure be worth to the university? The university is an exceptional organization like so many others: like the ministries, like the general [military] staff with its troops of officers, always at an advantage in their fine white uniforms, like the court and its noble following. And what are students, then? Young people, for whom one hopes that they will learn something, and become something. All of these circles, and many more – the judiciary, industry, the clergy – they are generally separate, at least with any necessary internal connection, within the body of residents numbering in the hundreds of thousands. The situation is otherwise in the true university city. For the university city, the university is not simply a distinguished source of income, but also, above all, the source of spiritual life. Thus the entire city, down to the lowest strata of residents, takes on a greater share of the education that is disseminated from the university than would be conceivable in the residence-city. Even in the class of artisans, in my time, every resident knew the outstanding professors. If the frugal, humble, and slightly hunched-over figure of our professor of dogmatics, Knapp[2], crept by, or if the majestic figure of Chancellor Niemeier[3], the pedagogue, his round head held high, with his hat held ever in greeting in his hand, walked down the street, then the burgers of all sorts would be there to respectfully greet them. The professors, in turn, were not far removed from the circles of burghers; and if, on the one side the burghers did everything to honor the professors, if, among other things, the wealthy master smith Uhlich moved his workshop so as not to disturb the scholar (Knapp) living next door, likewise the scholars were happy to carry on stimulating and instructive conversations with the burghers. Thus the whole city was a single broad group of comrades; you had to keep to yourself, if you did not wish to join together in mutual unity. That the clergy, the medical professions, and the bureaucrats were linked to the university is self-evident.

[1] Translator's note: that is, cities where important monarchs and princes reside.
[2] Georg Christian Knapp, 1753-1825. Full professor of theology at Halle beginning in 1782.
[3] August Hermann Niemeier, 1754-1828. Appointed chancellor by Jérome Bonaparte in 1808.

Within the University more than one professor was inclined to open his house to students. Here, however, the touchy pride of the latter would sometimes lead to surprising scenes. A newly arrived student had to bring a letter of recommendation to Geheimrat Schmelzer[4], who taught feudal law and diplomacy, and who maintained a very noble bearing. Schmelzer was so good as to invite the student to dinner with his family. The young man was embarrassed, and finally blurted out: "I do not know if I am permitted to go about with Philistines". Philistine was the name given to anyone who was not a student. Such foolishness was accepted with good humor.

Along with such childish behavior, and considerable conceit, a sense of brotherhood and a devotion to honor was evident among the students, such as is seldom to be found among a crowd of almost unsupervised youths. To the students their "On my word!" was holy. Such a word of honor was not to be broken, and the whole *Kommilitonenschaft* [body of comrades] felt bound by *One for All, All for One*. During my years of study it only happened twice that students left Halle, without paying the debts incurred under their word of honor. The groups of Landsleute behaved likewise, and paid debts to the last penny (not without difficulty), so that no one could say that a "Hallescher Bursch" [lad from Halle] had not kept his word.

How things stood with regard to devotion to study, I cannot say for sure. With respect to myself, I first studied logic. It was presented to us in the broadest and most boring manner. At the first lesson I wrote down conscientiously every word from the salutation "Highly honored gentlemen!" to the concluding "to be continued in the next lesson". At home I realized that every word was already in the compendium. At the second lesson I only noted down a few things that seemed to be particularly interesting; at the third lesson I simply listened and soon that fell away as well. This formal logic provided us with the laws of thinking in such a shadowy way, and nothing transpired that might attract us to philosophy, we, who had already read Plato, Cicero and other ancients, so that my sad behavior was probably shared by the large majority. In general, philosophy was not well-represented at the time; the names of Hegel, Schelling, and Fichte were not heard, and creative or obviously progressive spirits were lacking in this area. In addition the legal faculty had probably not kept up with the important men at other universities – with the likes of Hugo, Savigny and others.

For me all these lacunae were filled in the most marvelous way.

The Romanist Woltär[5] was living in Halle, at a very advanced age. For a long time he had not been training any more collegia, and only participated in

---

[4] Friedrich August Schmelzer, 1759-1842, from 1817 director of the university.
[5] Johann Christian Woltär, 1744-1815.

the legal opinions of the faculty, and the sittings of the *Schöffengericht*. How it happened that I wanted to hear collegia with him, I do not know; simply that I reported to his institutions and entered the auditorium at the appointed, which at the time was at his private residence. There was only one other listener in addition to myself. Finally, Professor Woltär arrived, a pleasant little presence, with a peaceful and yet intelligent face, surrounded by thin silver hair. Entirely at ease he looked over the almost empty room, and said, with winning friendliness "Gentlemen, I am very thankful for the confidence in me that you have demonstrated, and you certainly know the academic saying that "tres faciunt collegium": thus you will not be able to object that the lecture will not take place". At this point he went to the door. Perhaps he had noted embarrassment and regret in my demeanour. Still at the door, he waved to me with his finger, and I followed him. He went up the steps to his study. "Are you really sorry that the lecture is cancelled" he asked me, until then completely unknown to him. I spoke vehemently that for me a great hope had disappeared. "Well, then, I will give the lecture for you alone." The other, an older man, and previously officer with the Polish insurgents, also participated. I do not know how it went for him, but what I related above is accurate down to the conversations. He also left well before the end of the lectures, I do not know when and why.

These lectures, the purest gift of love that I ever received in the spiritual domain, were rather peculiar, and perhaps there was never their like. They stretched over five semesters. They were announced as "institutions", that is, a sort of basis of Roman law, as it was put together and codified under Emperor Justinian as a code of law. Only in these institutions was the most basic consideration of the pandects (the real, detailed code, to which the other laws were added later) and novellas, and additional comprehensive information regarding the history of Roman law included. And how he discussed these! My honorable benefactor – who once happened to mention: he had written out the pandects four times without punctuation, in order base his criticism of the text on the transcripts which were supposed to reproduce the old manuscripts, entirely without deviation from the traditional presentation — in his entirely free lectures first dealt with the introduction of the individual laws (I think that I recall that they numbered in the hundreds of thousands), then he shared the literal content of the law in question and included its interpretation, and whatever was notable regarding it. Not infrequently he would turn to the *Basilica*[6] (the authentic translation of the original Latin text into Greek) and also included them from memory. In general it was rather difficulty to follow the presentation. It certainly would happen that the honorable old man, entirely

---

[6] A law code from the late ninth century, codified in Byzantium.

dedicated to the true content of the lesson, at the conclusion of a presentation would express the complete opposite of what followed from his basic and clear presentation. The calculations that he found it necessary to include as examples in the matter of settling estates, etc. were fatal for him. Here the most amazing errors of calculation appeared one after another, and strangely came out to the most exact result after the most immense egregious compensations. I can assure you that not a single time was the comedy of these errors evident, so much was the listener captured by the seriousness and weight of the matter and its handling.

I did not remain true to a juridical career, a case that my benefactor doubtless had not foreseen; he might well have hoped to train me up as a future worthy Romanist after his model, and in fact I had studied Roman law with great enthusiasm. But the good deed done for me in this way lost none of its weight. Who has accompanied me this far through my variegated occupations and has imagined to themselves how isolated from the world I was in my lonely paternal house, growing up without any kind of advice, will certainly have already said to themselves that I was in danger of losing myself, indeed of dissolving in the fantastical. Logic could not touch me. Now the historical logic of Roman law arrived, now its relentless practice and strict order arrived, and gave me an interruption, which I could no longer avoid, if my life were to have any kind of result.

Only now did I experience in myself a transformation, which could have made me notice the irrationality of a doubled choice of profession, had the possibility only become visible of giving up one or the other vocation. Law was already becoming significant, and attracting me to Woltär's lectures. Alongside law music had not lost the least part of its power with which it had grabbed my mind. At the same time, I was too obstinate to easily give up something decided or begun. I held on jealously to the study of law. But my sense turned rapidly from the pure science to the practical path of life.

CHAPTER 8

EARLY INCENTIVES FOR THE PRACTICE OF LAW

Two experiences from my early years may have contributed to planting the importance, indeed the holiness of the practice of law in my soul, though I was always inclined by nature and upbringing more toward the purely spiritual. If you consider these events to be of little weight, I cannot contradict it. That they, however, were not entirely without influence in the process of development of my soul, is evidenced by the lively recollection, indeed, continuing sensation of these important moments. I could still paint Jakob Aelteste today, if I had the manual dexterity.— In my earliest boyhood I had once found a little table-knife in the garden, and, enchanted, brought it to my father, so that he could enjoy my treasure with me. That was a mistake. Because shortly before a friend of my father's had come to visit, and had now come back, with the question: Might it be that we had found a pocketknife? He had lost his when he had come to visit us. My father became suspicious that I had not found the knife in the garden, but that it was the one that his friend had lost, and that I had lied, in order to keep my possession, and avoid punishment. The friend had already gone away again. My father pressed me to confess, and hit me hard in order to force my confession. I maintained what I had claimed to begin with, and was taken crying to bed by my pitying mother, where, for the first time in my life I could not fall asleep.

My father was extremely disturbed by what had happened and my alleged guilt. Late in the evening he went with the knife I had found to his friend, and the friend gave him the news: his knife had been found – it had slipped out through a hole in his pocket into the inner lining. Both men went back to our house (after ten p.m.); they declared my innocence, and everything that was possible to make it up to me took place. In vain. It was not the pain of the punishment, but rather the powerful injustice that had been done to me, that I could not get over. I recognize that for many long years I could not think of this without bitterness.

A second incident (when I was ten to twelve years old) gave me a view of solemn old-fashioned justice.

Across from us lived a doctor, Hofrath Senff, who often took care of mentally ill patients in his house. Now and then we would see one of these going in and out more often. He was a quiet, introverted young man, dressed partly like a peasant, partly like a city-dweller. He was the son of the rich innkeeper in Ostrau, a few miles from Halle. Soon the young man had gone back to his father.

We had half forgotten him, when the news came: an execution would take place in Ostrau. My father decided to attend it with a friend, and took me along. We got out at the large inn, and listened to the sad story. The condemned, known as Jakob Aelteste, had been a quiet, moderate and good man for his whole life long, and had served as a servant in the village. As an aspiring man in his twenties, he had become engaged with a young farm girl; both were poor and virtuous. His fidelity was unshakable, but it was an imperative necessity that the marriage should follow immediately, or else the maiden would lose her honor; and just then it happened that the unhappy young man had the fate to become a soldier. In vain he implored the magistrate (Ostrau belonged to Saxony) to be released from his responsibility; and the decision was that he could only be released through the payment of a sum of thirty thalers. Where could he manage to raise this sum? —Completely without prospects, and despairing about the misfortune of his fiancée, Aelteste went Sunday morning after church to the house of a wealthy man, who lived nearby, probably with the intention of asking him for help. But he saw the man going out of his house to the church – and the time in which he could be released was quickly running out. And so he thought that he could break in, take the money and – this he asserted with vow after vow – work it off in order to replace it, so as to purify himself. He went into the house through the open door, picked up a hatchet lying in the hall, in order to break into the writing desk, where the money was kept. He was successful in everything. Unseen he entered the chamber of the absent man; broke into the writing desk (the house seemed to be entirely empty of people), and counted out the necessary thirty thalers from a much larger sum that was lying there. Now as he turned to leave the room, there was the young maidservant of the homeowner before him, who had either come back, or had remained unnoticed in the house, and who called out: "Aelteste! What are you doing there! Help!" Aelteste, out of his sense from the fright at the unhealthy surprise, swung the hatchet – and the unhappy woman lay dead at his feet.

There was no witness to the frightful deed, no one, since the maid had been killed, witness to the burglary. Aelteste hastened unnoticed from the house, unnoticed from the spot, where he could not stay, into the open. The next day he went back, turned himself in, and became his own accuser. The conscience of the hitherto guiltless man had forced him to it. He was sentenced to death by the sword. The execution would take place the next day.

My father had gotten permission to visit the condemned man that same day. It was a beautiful bright day. We were shown to the house where Jakob Aelteste was in custody. A door led from the wide village street into a corridor, a second corridor on the left into a medium-sized chamber, in which gendarmes were sitting as guards. A real post for guarding the prisoner had not been set up.

From this room we went through an open door into a long but narrow room, only lit by the window. Here sat Aelteste. He was left to his solitary thoughts, and opposite him there stood an old heavy wall-clock, which counted out the few moments of his life, soon to run out, with its loud tocks, one after another. He was not tall, but was a healthy-seeming figure holding up his head and its melancholy but peaceful countenance. This seemed to be its usual expression; it probably had seldom been brightened by more lively joy and feelings of happiness. When we came in he sat up and with a quick motion tossed his flowing brown hair out of his face. He answered my father's questions quietly and modestly, mostly with words from the Bible and verses from the hymnal. Resignation, yes, even the desire to atone for his crime was to be seen in his words and his manner, and without any acting. My father was able to arrange it so that at the same time he was putting him to sleep and took his pulse. He told us afterwards that the pulse was entirely moderate, only beating a little dully, but his brow was damp with cold sweat. We left him and went back to the inn.

On the following morning, as I have said, the execution was to take place, but before this the *hochnotpeinliche Halsgericht* would be done. This *Halsgericht* was a form that had been retained in Saxony and other states as a holdover from the former "*Geschwornen*" or lay judges. The investigation was led by the judge appointed by the state, and the closed files sent to the upper *Spruchkollegium* for repetition of the verdict. Now, however, this form of justice, which only remained as a form, and yet was so important and shocking, came into actual legal practice. There is a court of twelve *Schöffen*, men from the people, who are to find or "create" what is just, announce it in the open before all the people, and its finding is to be valid as the final decision.

During the night the numerous visitors, who had found themselves together in the inn, were woken from their sleep by an unearthly din and cries of woe. Two reports made their way to us. Later the previous evening Aelteste, needing fresh air to breathe, had left his room, and had gone into the open through the anteroom, past the sleeping gendarmes, and out through the corridors and courtyard – all the doors having been standing open. A half-hour from there was the border, the night was mild, and the moonlight bright, there were no observers nearby; he reached the border, and nothing stood in his way, so he was free. He walked out, looked around, breathed the refreshing air, and the peace of the night – and went back to his prison. "He wanted his justice!", as the people's expression goes.

The other report was more serious. In that same fateful night, the son of the innkeeper – the very same young man, whom we had seen with mental illness in the care of Hofrat Senff, lost his life in a terrifying way; he had cut through his neck with a dull woodsaw, and before doing it, had called out: he had to hurry before Jakob Aelteste, to accuse him before the Throne of God. Now we learned for the first time that the murdered maid had been the beloved of the son of the rich innkeeper, and had carried a pledge of his love under her heart.

Early in the morning we went to the place where the *hochnothpeinliche Halsgericht* was supposed to be held. It was a rather wide bridge, made of stone, which led over a moat into the courtyard of the Castle Ostrau.

In the absence of the military, the surrounding villages had supplied hundreds of young men and youths, who instead of weapons carried long stout staves in their hands, and lent the whole thing a solemn air. A part of these surrounded the prisoner as a watch-band, the great majority formed a guard, within which the prisoner found a free way through the thousands of onlookers, who filled the broad and even space before the entrance to the bridge.

We managed to get onto the bridge itself, and were opposite the *Schöffen*. An old man in a black garment, with a broad and serious figure, presided; the other eleven were wearing the usual Sunday dress of the peasantry. To the side of the *Schöffengericht* the judge and his clerk had found their seats. The clerk read a short report regarding the criminal investigation that had taken place, and asked the *Schöffengericht* to carry out its duty. A breathless silence and motionlessness reigned over the thousands who were tightly packed together.

Now the old man presiding rose slowly and apparently with effort. It was our innkeeper, the father of the young man who had put such a terrible end to his life only a few hours before, and who had called out that he had to precede Aelteste in order to accuse him before the Throne of God. With a monotonous voice, often breaking off, the old man spoke the appropriate formula: you, the *Schöffen* of the area, are come together under God's free heaven and in the eyes of the entire people there invited, in order to defend justice and punish crime and see that it is atoned. Whoever has a complaint to raise, let him come forward. Aelteste was dressed in what was supposed to be his dying garments —bib and breeches of white linen bordered with black, and held together with black bows, the same sort of cap on his head – and led forward and place opposite the man presiding. It was obvious that he had no clear awareness of what was going on.

The questions from the chief *Schöffen* remained unanswered. They were repeated, and repeated once more. Then finally resounded, from behind Aelteste, in a loud, hard voice: "I accuse." A shudder went through everyone – it was a large, strong man, in a long flowing robe, that had spoken – it was the executioner. At the first words Aelteste turned to look at his accuser with a dying glance; it was his first and last sign of life.

Now the charge of robbery and murder against Aelteste was spoken in sharp, hard-hitting words. He was shown the ax, and he acknowledged it with guilt. Next came the death sentence and the white sticks that signify the soon to be broken body, and the irrevocability of the sentence. The sound of the breaking wood had perhaps a sharper effect on the nerves of all of us, than on those of the condemned man, who since his glance at his accuser showed little sign of awareness.

Now the procession started to move from the bridge to the place of execution, rather distant. First went the school children of all the surrounding villages, with singing of songs of death, which resounded far over the still corridor, illuminated by the light of the morning sun. After them followed – singing along – the condemned man, before or after them the court. The moment has remained terribly in my memory when the head, with a light stroke of the broad, thin sword of judgment, fell, and the people, having pressed in close for the successful blow, clapped their approval.

CHAPTER 9

THE PRACTITIONER OF LAW

My honorable teacher Woltär had departed this life. Although he often lived in discord and resentment with his wife, he was nevertheless unable to survive her death, and followed her into the grave almost immediately. I had striven to follow his footsteps and make myself at home in Roman law, and was considered a good Romanist – naturally, in as much as one can say this about a young student. This was to lead me into a rather dangerous adventure.

I had found a warm reception at the house of Schwarz, the *Land-und Stadtgerichtsdirektors* at that time. Now my examination was to take place *zur Auskultatur* [first stage of training for young jurists – oral examination] and indeed, before two *Räten* [lawyer/civil servant]. Schwarz, a very good-natured, witty, and only occasionally thoughtless *bon vivant* asked me whether I were not afraid. This seemed, given my ambition at that time, to be an attack on my dignity as a twenty-year-old. "To the contrary", I replied impertinently, "I am hoping to have a rather difficult examination". Schwarz, without the slightest evil intention, said to my examiners: "Watch out for this one, he will give you something to think about." Naturally such a jest for these worthy men, regarding a boy, was not well-received, and so it may have been the case, that the first *Examinator* (a certain *Justizrat* Niewandt, who later proved very kind to me) did not wish to make the test in Roman law any easier for me. "Mr. Candidate," he asked first, "what is the content of the *Lex Julia Papia Popaea?*" Such a *lex* is well known to contain several, often many, legal provisions, which are arranged without any particular order relating to the various branches of law. This is especially the case with regard to the above-mentioned law, in which hundreds (if I am not mistaken) of provisions from the law of inheritance, criminal law, etc. come together in a complete mish-mash. I had studied this section of law very seriously, and was well prepared for an examination on it. But, as often happens, at the moment he asked that question I could not immediately come up with the relevant answer. Naturally, I could not at any price, not even through a momentary stammer, reveal any weakness. In order to play for time, I began without delay: "Heineccius (a legal scholar of the 18th century) counts 33 chapters in this Lex"." This effort may have seemed dubious; the *Examinator* interrupted me, and went immediately to other questions. If he had had a minute more patience, I don't know what more I could have done. This can serve as consolation and a hint for examinees who understandably are well prepared.

I passed the exam successfully, and thus attained the initial rank in the juridical career, that of *Auscultator* — I will avoid going into detail regarding the sorrows and joys of this career. The concept, the idea of the law, and in contrast, its immeasurably broad application, these are twofold. I probably realized early on, that my true reward would only last as long as new perspectives and a new opportunity to learn something presented themselves, and that the reward of the practitioner of the practicing lawyer must not remain at this level, but rather the unending practice of the learned must grow. This, however, is so much the more difficult in that the great majority of legal cases remain in a very narrow circle – debts, inheritance, divorce – in which the same tasks repeat themselves with only changes in names and amounts. I, and many of my young colleagues, had a doubly heavy burden on our shoulders: my work as a civil servant, and along with this the other work which I had to take over for the *Rechtsanwälte* in order to earn my living. What, on the other hand, stimulated my enthusiasm was the automatic assignment of the more reliable ones among us, which was a benefit to me in Halle and later at the Oberlandesgericht in Naumburg. We were entrusted with reporting on the progress of pending cases and presentations further decision (*Dezernat*), as well as independent investigation (instruction) regarding cases, without the participation of a counselor. This ran against the provisions of procedure, especially since we, following the model of the counselors, allowed ourselves, in public presentations, simply to label the acceptable versions as "acceptable" without further discussion. But the legal civil servants, at least in the so-called colleges, were at that time so overburdened with work that they could hardly dispense with our assistance. At any rate, this set up was invaluable for us; it provided us with self-respect and thus the greatest enthusiasm and conscientiousness, in order to justify the confidence that had been placed in us. At that time we had such a high regard for the dignity of a Prussian jurist, that we certainly would have demanded a bloody accounting from someone who had declared a perversion of justice to the benefit of a minister or his system with the name of a Prussian civil servant to be acceptable.

The private tasks that I had to take over from the justice-commissioner, were a second burden, and not at all minor; for I had not only to look after myself, but it had also become necessary for me to support my parents. But these jobs were enriched for me by the related tasks that they provided me, and provided spiritual refreshment as well. I will only mention the defense of a young country girl (13 to 15 years old), which I had taken over for Justice-Commissar Räpprich, and under his name. Several fires had broken out one after another in the district where the girl lived, which obviously pointed at arson. Anonymous reports, and finally apprehension *in flagrante* indicated the young girl as the culprit. No doubt was possible, although any indication regarding her motives was lacking. I no longer know which track I followed; to be brief,

I said, based on medical authorities: "The guilty party is driven, against her will, by the impulses of a monomania (called pathological arson), which sometimes, although rarely, appears in the adolescent years." The *Physikat* rejected my assumption. I however (that is, Räpprich) continued to sustain it; the opinion of the *Ober - Medizinal – Kollegium* in Berlin was solicited, and it held in my favor. The unfortunate girl was rescued; I know nothing about her subsequent fate.

The last case that I worked on in Halle provided a very individual view into the way in which many men, curiously enough, seem destined to fall.

In Halle there lived a French language teacher, Nicolas Douel, a born Frenchman. I had met him in the house of my friend Schwarz; we had become closer through our common liking for music.

This Douel had been a postulant in his youth at a French monastery. The monastery was dissolved as a consequence of the Revolution, and the postulant joined a new regiment as a clarinetist. When the regiment was supposed to depart for Belgium, the prospect of battlefields was highly unattractive to the former monastic; he may have thought, along with Schiller (though unaware of it): "*Macht man dem Tode hier Musik?*" [Does one make music here for Death?]" In short, he deserted to Holland. Not long thereafter, when the Republican armies retreated, he had to escape from one point to another, then to move to Westphalia, and to flee from the spread of French troops here as well. For several years he was driven from place to place, fleeing before the French troops, by the danger of being recognized and punished as a deserter. Finally he had arrived in Halle. Here he was able to feel secure, and his conditions took on the most desirable form, at least given his modest needs. He gave remunerative private lessons, and even found a position at a school.

But now his Gallic nature led him to ruin.

With respect to one of his private students, an underage young woman, he allowed himself impermissible demonstrations of love. The matter came, I do not know how, to the attention of the police. As a consequence, a criminal investigation was initiated, and Douel was sentenced to eight years in prison. He chose to appeal, and selected me to defend him. I took on the petition, the documents of the case were provided to me, and I was allowed to visit the appellant in his prison cell. After I had thought the matter through, I went to him, finding him deeply bent over, and explained to him, that I had hope of gaining his freedom. For non-legal readers I should note here, that it is the professional duty of the defender to cause everything that can, legally, and with respect to the documents of the case, speak in favor of the defendant, to be taken into account with respect to his benefit.

–

My grounds for the defense were simple, but as I still believe today, undeniable. Such crimes, namely, as the one that took place here, whose publication damages the honor of an offended party, should, according to law, only come to the attention of the courts through the express request of the offended party or their natural guardian. Such a request was not made; rather, the parents of the young woman had amicably declared in the course of the investigation: they wished, as Christians, to forgive the unfortunate defendant and did not want him to be punished. Consequently – I further conclude – the investigation should not have ever been opened, it was unjustly opened and carried out, and could for this reason be based on no valid claim of justice. Even today, I confess, this final conclusion seems untouchable. I proposed a complete acquittal. Soon after the delivery of my defense motion, I had to go to the *Oberlandesgericht* in Naumburg, in order to take my second examination (the *Referendariatsexamen*) and await a later offer of employment. But first, a truly French turn would be added to this legal case.

One day, namely, legal papers were sent me, and when I opened the package, I found, beautifully written:

Douze valses, composées et dediées a M. Marx par Nicolas Douel. The peculiar character had composed the waltzes in prison; how they found their way into the trial papers, and then to me, I do not know.

In the first session at which I was present in Naumburg, the case came to its verdict. The Referent explained that according to his opinion acquittal on the grounds that I had stated was obligatory, but that to come to this conclusion after the crime had already come to be considered by the court, was a true nuisance. For a long time the matter was argued, and finally we believed that a solution could be found, that classified the crime from the point of view of punishing immorality by the police. However – and I must still thus object today – this was not a police matter [i.e. misdemeanor], but rather a criminal case [felony]! And the punishment for immoralities, that is, those committed in public, which become a nuisance for the public, is indeed incomparably less. Howsoever that may be, the sentence was reduced to four years of house arrest. Here, and many other times, I had had to learn how one's own convictions have to yield to the decisions of the majority. He was sent to Magdeburg to serve his sentence; but in the order through a terrible oversight the word "*Festungshaft* [house arrest]" was replaced by the word "*Festungsstrafe* [prison term]." When he pushed the cart for the first time next to the deep water of the moat, he threw himself in, and ended his life.

CHAPTER 10

FROM HALLE TO NAUMBURG

The geographical separation between Naumburg und Halle is little, five small miles; but the distance between the two places was, for me, a bit farther. Halle, the university-city, was shot through in all its veins with spiritual life; Naumburg was a commercial city, and especially a producer of wine. It lies within a three and fourfold girdle of hills with vineyards, each one crowned with a cozy country or winery-house, in which, especially during the period of the grape harvest the most comfortable and most hospitable life pulses, and half the nights are bustling with drinking sprees, country dances and fireworks. One might have imagined that one had been moved to the Rhine, if only the hills with vineyards had not been so tiny, and the wine so bitter and chalky, and if the imposing chain of Rhinish towns, and the greater independence and freedom of thought of those living near the Rhine had not been lacking. But the merchants of Naumburg were still a very highly honorable class of inhabitant. In contrast them stood the numerous officials of the *Oberlandgericht*, full of that stiff bureaucratic pride which is so easily embedded in Prussian state bureaucrats. Where this world of civil servants formed a closed system, or at least claimed precedence, even the most harmless pleasures were colored according to its very individual ways. How often I could observe that at the balls a considerable number of officials and lawyers, well-off men in their forties, with notable "embonpoint", mixing into the crowds of younger dancers, each, naturally with his young dance-partner! And on this side and that, what did one hear about? — This highly interesting case, that entirely incomprehensible decision – and similar delicacies from the moldy old legal proceedings. The interns for better or worse had to play along with their elders, at least from time to time. And the beautiful young ladies had to participate as well.

This may all have been very nice for those who enjoy this sort of thing; for my part, easygoing temperaments were lacking, and in terms of wit (which I include among the former) I found not a trace. In particular, my music seemed to have atrophied; I had not a single instrument at my disposal. There was nothing to rent, even if I had had money to spend on it. My life had stagnated, and only the legal vein still had a pulse.

Now, however, a rather odd personality came to my rescue. Johann Gottlieb Schulz! Your name should not be forgotten, when my life is being discussed.

Schulz was the son of a poor farmer in Lausitz, and as a young boy he had to lead his father's little flock out to field and pasture. But soon he had enjoyed more instruction from the schoolmaster of the village than is usually considered advisable for peasant children, especially poor ones. Stimulated by this, he managed to get his hands on a book, the only one that he could find there. It was – a Latin grammar. It was his companion in his loneliness in field and meadow. Then, one day, a noble gentleman happened to come by, on horse or wagon; it was the rector of the Gymnasium in Sorau. "What kind of book do you have there, my son?" Schulz, very nervous, handed him the book, trembling. The foreign gentleman was astounded to find a ragged shepherd boy with a Latin grammar. He examined him, and the boy demonstrated a very good understanding. "Why don't you go to the school in the town?" Schulz turned pale, blushed, it was as if he had been struck by lightning; and finally, he, in the midst of a stream of tears, said that would be the dream of his life, but that it was quite impossible, since his father was too poor. The impossible, however, often becomes possible. The worthy Rector took the boy to Sorau, gave him a free place at the Gymnasium, and some material support. As soon as Schulz was feeling at home at the Gymnasium, he began to give instruction to his fellow students, in order to earn the support he needed. Gradually he found opportunities for larger earnings by giving lessons in the city. Schulz was gradually able to acquire a library that by the time of his move to Naumburg had grown to several hundred volumes. At the same time he had saved a couple hundred thalers while still in Sorau with which he planned to attend a university.

In the meantime, however, a younger brother, who had his mind set on becoming an apothecary, had grown old enough that he could start studying. But he also was lacking the financial means. My friend Schulz gave the hard-earned money that was intended to pay for his university study to his brother, and - has never attended a university. He led a sort of peripatetic life, in which he worked here and there as teacher and private tutor. Carrying his growing library around with him, as a snail carries its shell, studying day and night, he continues to work. On what? That is hard to say; for he had no defined goal. Studying and thinking, in order to study and think, that was the content of his life. If one reminded him, that this is usually only half of a life's task, and the other part is work: then he would reply, reassured, that where there is force, then the effect will not be absent; there must be forces, that work in a particular direction, and others, which work sporadically, first here, then there, but nothing is lost. That a force could also fall to bits was something that he simply did not want to acknowledge in the spiritual realm. Here I stood facing a true polyhistor, like my father would have liked to make out of me. He knew the classical languages, as well as Italian, French, a little Spanish, and basic Hebrew (as I heard from experts).

For this latter language he was accustomed to give me a curious stimulus for a much later time. To hear him talk about it, and its power and depth, was inspiring. He would occasionally become blunt in this area. If it happened to come up in conversation that I was of Hebrew descent and yet was entirely incompetent in the language, he scolded: "Children, how dumb you are!" — And I was happy to be scolded, for he then would share elevating information about the language, about which he noted that he considered it to be the highest probably oldest of languages. The fact that rather than using adjectives it places noun next to noun he called *urmächtig* [full of ancient power]. He was happy to cite as example the word *bathkoll*, literally "daughter of the voice", meaning prophecy; the thunder that rolls through the heavens, is the voice of God, and the meaning, which the Most High conveys therein, is the "daughter of the voice". For my ear, always listening everywhere, just the sound of the words of Hebrew in his pronunciation was music. "What does" he said, "your little spark: and there was light! mean? Is this the way that the voice of the Creator must have sounded? *vayehi 'or*! He called, and a World flamed from the Ocean of Light! Infinite flames blew and rose up audibly[1] — What on earth do you mean with your little bitty light."

With such a sense he read to me the Psalm 137, with its ancient power. At the exclamation: *aru! aru! ad chajesot ba*! (raze it! raze it! To its foundation!) his voice rolled with an Old Testament fervor. Much later, when in Berlin I had to compose the *Song of Retribution of the Captives in Babylon*, I could not help remembering this. However, it was lacking in the gentleness and humility of the songs of Löwe, who joined song and the chorales of the church.

Along with his language studies he also had a serious involvement with natural sciences, which was provided to him by an ongoing correspondence with the brilliant natural scientist Oken[2] in nearby Jena.

Significant for his general aspirations, and the same time, for his constant lack of means was that he, sitting in the middle between Jena, Halle and Leipzig, worked for honoraria to improve dissertations for candidates needing help for the Master's or the Doctorate at all four faculties.

In addition to this, he still found time for teaching in schools and privately, and regardless of many oddities in appearance and behavior, was very much sought after, yes, even in poetry (a little volume of poetry, titled *Maja*, was published in Naumburg) and by the editors of the *Naumburger Weekly*, in which I also saw my first poem (on Don Juan) appear in print.

Schulz, thus, had erred. His activities, supported by no official position, could not provide lasting security. Through my departure for Berlin he lost

---

[1] And did not our Goethe have this same view, when, in his Faust, says "Ungeheures Getöse verkündet das Herannahen der Sonne [A monstrous roar announces the arrival of the Sun]"
[2] Lorenz Oken, 1779-1851, a specialist in the classification of fauna.

the only friend with whom he might feel a spiritual affinity; his letters bore witness to this, without giving any importance to the fact. I was able to offer him a position as a teacher in Berlin with an acceptable honorarium. He joyfully accepted, but for an indefinite date in the future; because first he guaranteed his help to a school colleague in need of assistance in founding a boarding school. Later, I happened to return home in the evening darkness, and went to my room without a light. Then a figure stood up from the sofa: "Are you Marx?", said a tired and deep voice, "I am Schulz." First taken aback, and then happy, I received him without being able to provide immediately a secure position for him. After a few days he left Berlin in order to return to Sorau. There he must have found a dismal end to the exhaustion of his life.

It may then be that the destiny assigned to him, and his early lack of advice had let him founder on the wrong paths; he had been helper and friend to many. Including myself. In his vicinity, in exile in Naumburg, I became the man that I had never been in Halle, as the effete offspring of a Jewish family, effete, in spite of fencing, in my corporal development, warped in my spiritual development, because everything that I yearned for came without effort. But I had achieved a certain municipal reputation in Halle with my painting and my music! But I had there in the last years been able to gather two *Singvereine* about myself, one for opera performances, and the other for church music. The latter, with which I performed Mozart's *Requiem*, and Handel's *Messiah*, among other works, were performed, was quite unique. There were only four singers, who performed these works in the silent salon of the Staatsrat von Jakob. Opposite us hung original paintings by Francesco di Francia and other masters. One of the listeners was the second daughter of the household, Therese, who had become known under the name of Talvy through novellas and the masterful translation of Serbian folksongs, and who later had married Professor Robinson from America[3]. Among the singers there was Löwe as an incomparable tenor, and Julie, the youngest daughter of the household, later to be his spouse. I no longer recall how we managed for the five-voiced movements of *Messiah*. Even at that time it was clear to us that Handel's choruses in particular require massed voices. We could easily have managed a large ensemble, since the *Opernverein* had forty members. It was simply that our idea was fixed on restricting ourselves to only what was absolutely necessary, so that the only participants in our artistic devotion would be those who would join in with heart and soul. We thus sought through the most proper attention to details to replace what we had given up through our lack of massed voices.

---

[13] Therese Albertine Luise von Jakob-Robinson, 1797-1870, took the name Talvy as a version of her initials.

All this, and many intimate relationships were now sacrificed and gone. In Naumburg I found many excellent men, and much ambition among the *Themisjüngern* [disciples of the Greek Titaness Themis, personification of law], but only with respect to their future vocation as civil servants. The only freer spirit was Schulz. His more solid manliness was a strong contrast to my softheartedness. He even directed one of his poems (in that collection) toward me. Thus:

"Geliebter Freund, nur keine Trenodien!

Das ganze Glück ist keiner Throne werth;

Laß, was nicht dauern mag, entfliehen:

Was gilt dem Glück, der Ewiges begehrt!"

"Dear friend, please, no threnodies!

All of happiness is not worth a throne;

Let that, which may not last, pass away:

Yearn for the happiness of the eternal!"

the poem began; what had a more powerful effect on me was his immovable and unstoppable motion forward against any adversity of destiny. This became evident above all in a beneficial way in a significant transformation of my character.

In Halle no wish of mine remained unfulfilled; even the appetites proper to youth my over-good mother tried to satisfy as much as she could. Now, everything that I loved was gone. Indeed, I passed the first winter in a real state of need; due to the situation of the city and my budget I could only have warm food to eat two or three times a week. For the other days I had bread (I allowed it to get a few days old, in order not to consume more than was necessary), with which I added in alternation a little butter, or cheese, or a pickle. Ah, and that painful line of verse: "The singer's drink is Wiesenquell" now became reality, and for myself. The last week of the month I had to work lying in bed, because I had run out of money for heat.

And with these Lucullian meals, which I celebrated behind closed doors, my character immediately changed. Until then I was weak, covetous, rarely satisfied with the externalities. Now, thrown back on my own devices, wedged into the tiniest closet, I found an elasticity of the soul, a defiant courage, and the cheerfulness that has, until today, through good days and bad days, remained the basic tone of my life. I felt that the door was closed, and was so secure, and so self-sufficient! I had become a man.

And finally music would no longer be neglected. I gave instruction in piano to the son of a household which felt benevolently toward me (I had already tried my hand at this in Halle); and since I had already amused him considerably with the stories of "Nutcracker and Mouseking" by E. T. A. Hoffmann, I also wrote for his delectation my own "Nutcracker and Mouseking", a grand battle scene for piano in the vein of the "Battles of Austerlitz, Jena" etc., in which the Quick March (Grenadier-March) of the Mice and the grand triumphal march of the troops stood out; — at least this was the unshakable judgment of all the boys who played and listened; I also remember a Canzona which was written in the Italian manner to fantastically constructed words with a sound that was half-Italian, half-Spanish (Friend Schulz had helped). I must have grabbed at the strange mode of expression; for I would not have set a real Italian text, and would not have understood one.

In addition, I got to know a young colleague from Berlin, who soon became dearer to me than all the rest. This was Gustav Nikolai[4], who later became known for his *Travels to Italy*, his *Cantor von Fichtenhagen,* a comic novel about music, etc. He was in the possession of the only piano that could be borrowed, had brought with him a large collection of overtures for piano four hands, and was overflowing with enthusiasm for Cherubini, and particularly for Spontini, of whom I had not yet gotten to know anything.

Even more important for me was a more intimate acquaintance with Gluck.[5] I had already gotten to know a few of his compositions while still in Halle. It was just that, sunken in Mozart's sweet romanticism, and entirely a stranger to the concepts of musical drama, I had been unable to develop a taste for these compositions, so unlike lesser compositions in terms of pure musical relationships. Now I got my hands on *Iphigenie auf Tauris*, and it was for the longest time my only musical possession. I played; I became completely devoted. How often I wandered in the lonely beech forests, recited the dark Thoas, the scenes of despair of Orestes, pursued by the Erinyes! Anyone listening to me must have thought I was crazy, or more charitably, taken me for an eccentric hero of the stage, so much did I overflow, freed from all consideration and moderation, with that powerful sound; I played with the greatest passion, and threw myself to the ground when the storm of despair broke over the unhappy hero. An observer might have smiled or laughed; so what! Thus I gained an understanding of the great tragedian. First I had an inkling, and then I realized it: that he did not make the melody for the words, but that much more the

[4] Gustav Nikolai, 1795-1865, who also had some success in song composition.
[5] It might be noted that the works of Christoph Willibald Gluck, 1714-1787, having been wholly dominant across Europe during the 1770s and 1780s, had fallen heavily out of favour around the turn of the century.

words became song for him, and that this song was nothing else than heightened speech, the direct expression of what was going on in each moment, in every word, in every syllable – yes, that in the music itself every movement, all of the acting of the characters taking on life, was depicted. Without knowing it, I had – at least, this is my serious opinion now – managed to capture the deep-thinking Master exactly from that point, which is the only point in which is power and significance can be understood. I can probably say that in those beech forests the basic lines for my much later work *Gluck and the Opera*[6] were laid out. Just as certainly as I have never sought to emulate Gluck in my compositions, yet his noble example shone forth over my entire artistic career.

---

[6] *Gluck und Die Oper*, Berlin, 1863.

Alexanderplatz, Berlin, around 1800

CHAPTER 11

TO BERLIN

One thing had to become clear to me in Naumburg: that I would not find a satisfying life in small cities. Among them Naumburg would perhaps have been the most pleasant. One must see this little city on its festival days, during the Hussite-Festival or Cherry-Festival, in order to properly evaluate it. The well-known saga has been too widely spread by Kotzebue's almighty theatrical hand. The Hussite leader Procopius is supposed to have advanced with his troops against the defense Naumburg, and the quarter-master Wolf, leading all the children of the city, dressed in funeral clothing, approached him, to beg for mercy, which he then granted to the fearful population. This is given as the reason for the festival.

In the early morning the drums with hollow sound march through all the streets. Under the direction of their teacher there are processions of all the little girls, shining in their blue or red dresses, and even more beautifully adorned with silken ribbons, to the *Schützenwiese* [guard-meadow]. This offers a broad space, surrounded in the manner of an amphitheater by some little hills, and closed off by the Guardhouse. There, many steins are emptied and there is dancing in the evenings. Around the meadow, however, pleasure tents are put up, which families gather socially, and enjoy the merry crowd of children who are playing and dancing. I can still hear the refrain of the children's song

Ei ja freilich, Wie ich bin, so bleil' ich, Bleil' ich, wie ich bin, Ein gutes Kin(d)!

(the modification of some words — *bleil'* instead of *bleib'*, *Kin* instead of *Kind*, is authentic).

The charming festival, the graceful, almost romantic vicinity, the Saale river, which I already knew from Halle with much more flow, the merry life of wine and wineries — all this was unable, as soon as the excitement of novelty was past, to make me forget the more spiritual life of the university city; over all these little cities my yearning flew to Halle, the highest goal to which I had yet aspired. I had certainly already heard many scathing opinions: the civil servant, and especially the jurist, must take his satisfaction in his work alone. But I had also already realized that this opinion was a deception. The most dutiful of works did not fail to also take part in every enjoyment in life that was accessible to them, and appropriate. The pleasure of parties, of the glass, of the rich hunting around Naumburg – all of this was enjoyed to the fullest. Ah! For me, for my particular way of thinking, these joys could have no meaning – I remained far from them. I probably appeared to be a foreigner to the others, particularly to the members of the collegium. I did not really feel that way at the time; only later, looking back with tranquility, I had to admit it to myself, and was able to assign the guilt, if one can talk about guilt here, to myself alone.

A division was evident – scarcely noticeable, but it was there. — I no longer belonged to my chosen vocation, since I felt driven to decline the majority of the positions that he offered me. And I still did not know that our President, Freiherr von Gärtner[1], fundamentally, though not without exception, as would soon be evident, did not prefer to give anyone a position in his native city; that would easily lead to disturbing relations, or ones that might provoke suspicion.

If there was no guilt here, yet it was not out of the question that I, on the other side, had invited considerable blame. Above all, the work of assistant to the commissars of justice, which quite a number of my young colleagues shared with me here and elsewhere, was not at all according to the law; the Presidium nevertheless knew about it and simply let it take place, because we, without means and without salary, were forced into it out of need. Or was service as judge to be accessible only to those with means?

If these additional tasks had a considerable claim to my time and energy, music nevertheless, I cannot deny it, also had its share. Many things were written along with the cases, among other things my first symphonic movement – so inexperienced and foreign to form, that it was only Löwe's later reminder that impelled me to add the repeat. Löwe implored me to indulge him in this – the symphony seemed to him like a giant who was missing an arm. Ah, the poor little giant!

Why had I not filled in this gap on my own, given that every sonata, every symphony or overture presented me with the model of the form? — The reason was to be found in a particularity of my character. It had always been almost impossible for me to create my compositions unless from my own deepest inner feelings, from the deepest inner conviction – models, examples, authority, even that of the most important names, were worth nothing at all. And also at the time Löwe's encouragement had not really taught and convinced me, but rather I was much more won over by the warm approval that spoke from inside me.

To be sure, if these additional tasks had pushed my official ones into the background, I should have sought guidance on this. Thus I received a written warning from the president to quickly complete the overdue work. Guilty, as I had to admit to myself, and truly saddened, because I highly respected the president, and he had always shown himself to be well disposed towards me, I worked for three nights and the days in between, packed up the completed work

---

[1] Gustav Wilhelm Freiherr con Gärtner, 1775-1840.

to send to the president, and sank unconscious from [into?] my chair. After sleeping for twenty-four hours I could once more get up again, without any noticeable damage. But I have never tried do the same again.

Oddly, much innocence was connected to the guilty. Thus I had once the larger part of the work of an assessor who had been called away, including having to take over a bankruptcy case. After a few days the assessor unexpectedly returned to his position, and the president decreed that his work be given back to him. Eager to learn, as I was regarding each new task, I wrote to the president: I had, according to his decision, sent the work back, but asked him to be so good as to be permitted to retain the bankruptcy case, since I had not yet worked on such a case. The president waved at me during the session and said: "the bankruptcy case must be given back to the assessor, but you will have work." Apparently he had misunderstood my request, and written it off as my displaying my eagerness. Now an overload of work rained down on one already doing the work of three. — How could I catch up with it all?

Among my tasks was a case, for which numerous of those involved had to prove their standing (*legitimatio ad causam*); the point of legitimation was extremely burdensome to argue. I, as *Instruent*, arranged for appointment after appointment, and even suggested to the three attorneys to hold two appointments a day. In spite of this no end could be seen. The president was absent; the vice-president, an excellent man, who had just left Saxon service, opined that the case was not being moved forward with enough dispatch. He issued a decree calling on me to schedule more appointments and to not fail to move things forward from here on. The accusation, no matter how undeserved it was, I would have accepted in silence. Unfortunately, in the decree there was the proviso: copy to the parties! Thus the reference shared with me would come into the hands of numerous parties, that is, the public; and that would happen even if the reference were deserved, not allowed. I thus requested a withdrawal of the injunction and included with my justification the written explanation of the lawyer, that they ought to have opposed the scheduling of overloaded appointments in consideration of their other activities.

It was precisely now that the President returned. The withdrawal of a presidential decree which I had sought seemed to him to be quite inconsistent with the dignity of the court, and he declared: that despite everything presented the default of the process was my responsibility.

Immediately after this event a judgeship in Halle became open in Halle. Not this position, but a lesser one was supposed to be coming to me, while that one would go to a son of Mayor Streiber in Halle, a younger intern, who had not worked in Naumburg at all, but rather with the *Oberlandesgericht* of Magdeburg. I was at the time on the commission for the representation of a council member in Halle. Undaunted, I directed my complaint to the Justice minister, and provided him with a theoretical discussion supporting my position, which sought, in opposition to Savigny's essay "On the vocation of our age in legislation"[2], to show that every age is called and must be called to the necessary legislation for its own day. The Ministerium decided in my favor: I should receive the next open position as a judge. I returned to Naumburg and tried to persuade the President that my step was driven by necessity. The President offered me a judgeship in Wittenberg; I held it to be advisable, to gratefully accept it. Returning from there to my residential district, I found my father, who had hurried after me with the news that a second position in Halle had been made available. Now I was decided. I wrote immediately to the President, turned down Wittenberg, and asked for the position in Halle. Thus however, my position in Naumburg, at least in relation to my wish to have a position in Halle, had become pointless. I appeared (or was depicted) in the light of someone not satisfied with a position; and now the decision regarding my position was taken from the Ministry and given in absolute secrecy to the President. I submitted my resignation in order to move from Naumberg to the Kammergericht.

---

[2] Friedrich Carl von Savigny's *Vom Beruf Unserer Zeit für Gesetzgebung und Rechtswissenschaft* was published in 1814, and was a highly influential contribution to the creation of a new legal framework after the dismantling of the Holy Roman Empire.

CHAPTER 12

BERLIN

For me, moving to Berlin was no small thing. I had never visited any city larger than Halle; and now Berlin was waiting for me, which I did not even know through contemporary depictions[1]. And the biting witticisms of Lessing and Jean Paul were still unknown to me; one was known to have called Berlin a house of forced labor, and the other a galley of criminals. I knew and had enjoyed Goethe's *Muses and Graces in the Mark*, without it awaking any further considerations on my part. For me, and all more distant scholars remained only in the light that "old Fritz", and before him, the great Elector[2] had poured upon it — a fatal favor, if their successors allowed themselves to be misguided, and not to stride strongly and heroically forward, as those had done in their time. Then, too, this Berlin was also the capital of Prussia, and Prussia for me, as for all was the protective power under whose leadership Germany would find itself united as the "State of Intelligence", in which spiritual life had to find its freest development and most propitious encouragement. And thus there was the prospect of approaching the rich artistic institutions and the working circles of so many exceptional men.

I considered it essential to create the means for myself that would make access possible. Twenty-four letters of recommendation, not more, not less, were my endowment; along with fifty thalers, which a generous supporter had loaned me. The basis of my fortune thus amounted to: negative 50 thalers. The costliest item however, was a patronage that I would receive that the conclusion of my stay in Halle.

At that time the renowned Hendel-Schütz[3] lived in Halle as the spouse of Professor Schütz[4]. She was known in a somewhat earlier period to have been one of the leading ornaments of the German stage. While our queens of the stage generally still in later years tried, with desperate zeal tried to hang on to the roles of young lovers, she had, in the brilliance of her highest youthful beauty, preferred to choose older roles, for example, the mother of Coriolanus. Later,

---

[1] Berlin at this time had a population of only around 200,000, but was in the midst of a period of rapid growth that would see it double in size by 1848.
[2] References to Frederick II of Prussia, reigned 1740-1786, and his great-grandfather, Frederick William, elector of Brandenburg 1640-1688; these two men were most credited with the rapid rise of Prussia into a dominant European monarchy by the late eighteenth century.
[3] Johanne Henriette Rosine Hendel-Schütz, 1772-1849, actress and pantomime.
[4] Friedrich Karl Julius Schütz, 1779-1844, historian.

she became the artistic companion and successor of the wondrously beautiful Lady Hamilton, and introduced "tableaux vivants" to Germany[5]. Now she was resting from her stormy career, so full of achievements and experiences. In the house of her father-in-law, the philologist Hofrat Schütz[6], very highly regarded at the time, she had a stately apartment, which let onto a garden of unusual beauty. The latter was a part of the city wall, the former fortifications. On one side it bordered the wall, now beautifully overgrown with trees and shrubs; a piece of the broad city wall closed it off, but still bore on its imposing back an airy gazebo and the path leading there.

I was introduced to this Lady by the mathematician, Professor Mensing[7]. She strode from the first chamber, where she had received us, to the adjoining one, and led me into the following rooms. Captivated by the view of a marvelous marble bust, I dallied. She turned, and once again invited me to follow her. "I beg your pardon," I said, and asked, still delaying, "Is this a Diana, or the head of a nymph?"

"This is my likeness," she replied, "from earlier years, of course." She felt that I had in no wise wanted to utter a gallantry, but rather that I had wondered in all seriousness, and had asked. We became close friends, naturally, she as the spirit-bestowing patroness, and I eager for the spiritual gift. Soon the animated conversation closed the circle that had formed around her and her intellectual spouse, soon people were improvising poetry, and formed a court of love in the manner of the troubadours, soon she was relating previous experiences, or led us, glad to follow her, out into the garden, which she jestingly liked to call her "hanging garden". Often, while we were wandering there below, there appeared up above a wonderfully beautiful head, half-Greek, half-Roman in its form, with brown flowing air. It was Sappho, her fifteen-year-old daughter, on whose shoulder a splendid parrot would sometime rest. I do not know whether she wrote poetry; but she seemed poetical, and that is probably the most charming vocation of feminine youth.

When my departure for Berlin was imminent, my worthy female friend said to me: "Now I would like to give you your furniture for your residence according to my fashion". And she told about the great ballets that she had seen in Copenhagen (this may have been at the end of the previous century). Perhaps she had also participated, since for a long time she had been a member of the singing chorus and the ballet, simply in order to entirely train her voice

---

[5] This practice, most associated with Emma Hamilton but widely disseminated around the turn of the eighteenth and nineteenth centuries, has been much studied; for an overview, see Carrie Preston, *Modernism's Mythic Pose: Gender, Genre, Solo Performance*, Oxford, 2011.
[6] Christian Gottfried Schütz, 1747-1832.
[7] Johann Gottlieb Wilhelm Mensing, 1792-1864.

and her posture on the stage. These were unforgettable hours, and with an effect for much longer throughout my life, which opened for me a view into the departed and probably never to return, past. For those ballets were something entirely other than those of French origin which appear in our day. There was something similar to the spirit of the ancient pantomime, in as much as matter and performance with some reference to antiquity remained. Galeotti was the creator of this ballet, which I now got to know; Schall[8] written the music. At a little piano I had to sit down in front of Schall's music and play. She sat relating the story and describing it to me. At every moment of the action that excited her she arose and presented what was happening in pantomime. In the familiar living room, with the small and not at al powerful instrument, she mostly in her dark-colored housedress – one saw that there could be no talk of any kind of illusion. And yet the impression was more powerful and more sustained. I only got to know two of the pantomimes.

The first was -- *Romeo and Juliet*, modeled after Shakespeare. For this high poetry to be transformed into a pantomime, for all the high and heart-wrenching words of the poet to be choked off, so that the entirely inspired characters became mute, was perhaps a step farther away from the life of the people according to its poets, than the cutting up of this tragedy and others even more elevated for operas by Gleissner[9]. But even this mistake shows how much higher the aspirations were in comparison to the childish and hence extremely unattractive ballets which the following period until the present day has taken over from the French. If one approved of the subject matter, then the performance was entirely worthy of praise. The drama began, appropriately for a ballet, with an evening ball in the palace of the Capulets, a truly large-scale and pleasingly-seriously written dance (C minor, similar to our slow waltzes) led the long row of dancing couples through the perimeter of the hall; Juliet, Romeo and the other more closely-involved persons developed in pantomime the details of the plot: the glance, the flight, the finding of the loved ones, the spying suspicion of Paris, and forth. While I followed the dance, with eyes flying back and forth, it presented the main events of the action in pantomime. Her acting almost made my heart stop when, in the later --scene the good-hearted Friar Laurence says, brooding: perhaps there is still time. She rested both trembling hands on my arm, and gave a glance with her powerful eyes, that seemed to drink my soul away from my breast.

---

[8] Vincenzo Galeotti, 1733-1816; Claus Nielsen Schall, 1757- 1835. The two worked together in Copenhagen.
[9] Franz Gleissner, 1759-1818, was a court musician in Munich and composed, among many other works, thirteen operas, none of which was on a Shakespearean theme..

That was her. Galeotti appeared more creative to me in the second ballet, *Bluebeard*. This was the well-known story; Sir Bluebeard, as a punishment for their curiosity killed his wives one after the other, until retribution overtakes him with the last one. When the curtain rises, one is looking at the bedchamber of the knight, with princely decorations. In the middle is the broad and splendid bed. The knight lies, deeply asleep covered with a costly purple blanket; the scene is shrouded in darkness. Then, the spirit of the first to be murdered appears in trailing shroud, and lifts, threateningly, her corpse-pale hand against the slumbering man, who seems to be tormented by horrible dreams. And then comes the second, and the third of the murdered women; the long series of apparitions circle the place in a solemn and threatening round dance. The tormented man seems to want to get up – and everything disappears; his sleep becomes quiet, like rigor mortis.

Now, suddenly, in ghostly half-light, all seven spirits return together. They entice, they push an eighth airy image towards the slumbering man. It is the image of the newcomer; the hatchet, calling for blood, which waits for her, floats before her eyes. In renewed and terrible torture, the sleeping man turns. Then he awakes. A moment of paralysis, one of slumber – and he throws off the purple blanket, gets up and calls the servants, to prepare his bridal procession.

This was the preparation to which I owe the unforgettable. — A coachman had the honor of driving me to the residence. Until the Elbe I was so engaged with the Fata Morgana of what was before me so as not to see anything. Finally the wagon, decidedly not equipped with wings, dragged itself through the incalculably uniform flatland of the Mark. I, coming from the soft meadows of my native city, in which the wanderer disappears behind the waving wheat fields, I who, was accustomed to see the friendly garland of the hills of grapes in Naumburg and the more rugged fells of Halle around me, thus made a furrowed brow for this vicinity, which, as it seemed to me, seemed to be cut according to a rule, these needy fields, these scrawny nags, which went by with their farm wagons made from thin staves — so far away from the heavy farm wagons and stately steeds of the Magdeburger and Thuringian lands. That this Mark also had charming and fruitful spots, was hidden from me at that time. But the wretchedness of the view did not particularly bother me – I only had the destination in mind. For the moment I revenged myself on the area through a marvelous image. I drew it – the road and the view, the endless rows of poplars and the easily countable stalks of corn, wagons, horses and even, in my exuberance, the people, entirely on the line. For in fact, the straight line ruled everything like an idée fixe.

Our direction of travel and chance worked teasingly to heighten my extravagant expectations. First we arrived at Potsdam. The first row of columns

CHAPTER 15

THE BERLIN OPERA AT ITS PEAK

When I made the decision to move to Berlin, I said to myself: I will not enter the opera house there until it presents an opera by Gluck. And what do you know? On the very first evening the ticket read "Gluck's *Alceste*".

I had already seen the opera house. On the night of my arrival I had been so excited by the expectation of all that was before me that I could not immediately rest. Once again I wandered through the moon-drenched streets by the castle, past the armory, only saw now for the first time the strange but entirely magnificent construction of the University buildings[1], with no inkling that not long after a position for me would be founded there. From there I looked to the left; and there it was before me, the Opera House! — One might think find the comparison not entirely appropriate when I say that the slim construction, stretched out in a line, appeared to me to be one of the sphinxes that Egypt stored up thousands of years ago for our astonished eyes.

On the following evening, I wandered in with my ticket, already acquired in the early morning, and found my seat in the still almost empty parquet. Next to me a woman in her middle years sat down, naturally someone unknown to me. The house became full.

Here I must confess a weakness regarding which many of my colleagues will laugh. In fact, I enjoy listening to the instruments tune up. For most these unrelated and content-less tones are annoying; it ruins their illusion, as they say.

It has a different effect on me. The tuning of the instruments tunes me at the same time, the spirits of the tones are beautifully awoken in my inmost parts as if from fragrant slumber, my anticipation is wound up more and more, and the first chord already finds me in an elevated mood.

Never before had I had such an orchestra before me! Seven or nine contrabasses, twenty-four violins, if not more, I am not entirely sure of the numbers, had gathered; their first tremolo gripped me with frightful force. Still under the might strides of the overture the curtain rose, and there, before the palace, gathered in mourning and grief for the beloved king, on bended knees, opened hands gesturing toward the seat of the Gods, was the Hellenic people,

---

[1] [ABM]: It is well-known that old Fritz had said of this building, in those days the palace of Prince Heinrich that the parterre seemed like a fortress, the main floor, a church, and the upper floor a powder-magazine.

and its call, transfixed by the mighty sound of the trombones of the orchestra, rose up to the cruelly indifferent Olympians.

Naturally Gluck's work was present for me note for note; it lived in me just as I had inspired me from the score. It was not long until a movement somewhere seemed not lively enough, seemed to drag, and almost unaware I beat the time at a more rapid pace, in secret, of course. Soon this happened again for the second, and then the third time, and now I became aware that the same had to be happening for the woman next to me; she, as well, beat time in secret, but more mournfully. Between the acts I dared to talk to her, and she regarded me, not in an unfriendly, but a questioning way. I repeated my statement, and now a strange male voice spoke French to me: his spouse did not understand German – I had to speak French to her. Rapidly my glance flew to the one addressing me, and whom did I see? – it was Napoleon's countenance, quite memorable to me from Halle, that met my glance. Napoleon's countenance – so would the majority of all those have seen him have said to me; only through a longer look would the imperceptible difference in expression between the countenance of the Emperor and the face of nevertheless honorable mortal from an entirely different sphere become perceptible. The two foreigners exchanged a few words, of which I only understood their sotto voce expression: "Il écoute bien". He then kindly invited me to tea the next day, and I, without, in my haste, waiting for him to speak his name, declined, with regret: the next day I had to hear the renowned Boucher. "Mais Boucher, c'est moi!" It was the famous violinist Alexandre Boucher[2], who, at that time, because of his resemblance to Napoleon, found it hard to appear in Paris under Bourbon rule. And the lady was the just as renowned harpist and pianist[3]. Naturally the invitation was understood to be on the French schedule, after the concert.

It is not my intent to follow the elevated poetry and its representation at the time. I would like to simply think of a moment that is particularly present for me: it belongs to the ballet, which I saw here for the first time. The news of the wondrously quick recovery of the King had spread and - with the swinging tunes of the great painter of life the crowd of servants and connections flew in happy animation, the corps de ballet in wide floating steps, more in the air, rather than touching the earth. That was a dance of

[2] Alexandre Boucher, 1778-1861, violinist and composer. His likeness to Napoleon was much remarked upon, and was cited by him as the reason for his avoidance of France for much of his career.
[3] Céleste Gallyot, d. 1841. She was Boucher's wife.

joy, a poetic impulse of motion and appearance! Then came the solo dances with their artistic pieces, with their almost impossible contortions, with their rectangular elevations, the legs and arms in straight lines, the tortures, entirely contrary to nature, of the French ballet! O, my patroness and teacher! How differently you had appeared to me in Halle! I may have become unruly, or even loud; because the Parisian woman next to me whispered to me: "Mais ils dansent aussi bien!" She had not seen it any differently in Paris – and our high-minded Gluck had not been able to put down the misbehavior there either.

It was a good omen that my desire for a Gluck opera immediately came true. I had really arrived in Berlin at a good moment. The theater still had a significance that it later would not achieve again; one could still feel the effects of Iffland's direction and training[4], it still numbered in its rank more than disciple of that man, who we may judge not for his writing for the stage, but for his personal accomplishments on the boards. In that regard very recently the noble couple of artists, Wolf and his spouse, had appeared unforgettably, he as Hamlet, she as Lady Macbeth. Along with them was Devrient, the only incomparable artist among all the actors that I have seen.

Three Devrients have achieved the high approbation of the public. One, Emil[5], the ornament of the Dresden Theater; the other, Eduard[6], of outstanding merit through his dramaturgical writings (*History of the German Theater*, etc.). The one that I am speaking about is generally known as the old or the great Devrient[7].

The actor works without mediation through the appearance and activity of his person; his creation is indissolubly linked to it. Thus Devrient has probably found emulators and imitators, and some of them highly talented ones. What he was however, has remained without equal, and must remain so; for it was determined by his entirely incomparable personality. Already at the beginning of his career he was significantly different from the great majority of the actors of time; he had not belonged to any real school, had not grown up among the models which the great stages offer. His first activities and his schooling came in the relaxed circle of a traveling troupe (or at least it was seen that way at the time), and thus it was decreed that he himself had to be

[4] August Wilhelm Iffland, 1759-1814, was director of the Prussian national theater from 1796, and was instrumental in forging a mastery of the classics of the German stage.
[5] Gustav Emil Devrient, 1803-1872, a tragedian.
[6] Eduard Devrient, 1801–1877, brother of the former, was best known as a baritone singer
[7] Ludwig Devrient, 1784–1832, uncle of the former, and best known for Shakespearean and other classic roles. The Devrient family produced many other notable performers.

his one and all. This absolute ego he had, by the time when I saw him, allowed to grow into a truly demonical force, to a force, which I only met twice more, but in an entirely different field, in Paganini und Liszt.

Devrient's figure, on the smaller side of middling, slender, and capable of any movement, had nothing of that which one usually calls winning or noble. His face, with not large, but burning eyes, bore the stamp, which Klopstock assigns to those angels who are blasted to hell by the thunderbolts of the Almighty, and marked for eternity. It was in fact the reflection of that demonic artistic force, which prevailed in him, and struggled incessantly, not without torment, to break forth; for he became and was, what he had to represent. And that then came forth from him bodily, without one being able comprehend, how he, with his hoarse and not very sonorous voice, with his hands contracted, like claws, by gout, might make it possible. And this figure, marked by the unextinguishable stamp, was able to present the most various figures. He was the convict escaped from the galleys, hunted by minions to his death; in the "*Drillingen*[8]" he played the three brothers – the ship captain, brutally hardened, who leaves the salt water behind; in contrast to him, the youngest, blond, the eternal child; and I have forgotten the third brother. Jubilation and pleasure awoke his Falstaff. Here there was nothing of the music hall, nothing common; he was and remained throughout a knight, a gentleman, even where he when condescended to Mistress Quickly and the cronies. At the words: "So I lie, and so I lead my blade!" he was an entirely proper and elegant fencer; we did not laugh at his shapeless obesity, we regretted it, as if it were only disfiguring clothing that did not belong to him at all. He gave incomparable performances of the thrice-changing scene, in which, exchanging roles with Heinz, first represented the King and then the Prince perfectly. For the latter he took the last grand Hofmannian garment off, so that only the profligacy was left – the naked essence of the Prince – as he was at that time. The King was acted by the excellent Lemm, no longer young, and who had become somewhat stout; there could be hardly any greater contrast than that between his and Devrient's appearance. And see, in that scene it was Devrient before our eyes, by speech, movement and form, Lemm incarnate.

Beyond comprehension, so that I almost resist writing down the truth, was his acting in two moments of *Richard III*. In that scene, where the ghosts

[8] There was a potpourri in four acts by this title, for which the arias and songs were published in Frankfurt am Main, 1812.

of the murdered appeared between the sleeping places of the two rivals, and call out to Richard their eternal "Despair and die!" the murderer is gripped by horror on his high pillows. In a circling motion – I can find no appropriate simile, beside the children's game, in which a short stick is twirled about its center – he twirls, as if without will and unable to resist invisible forces, down to the floor, awakes, and remains stretched out as if dead, while his eyes look all about, full of terror. And then, when he, abandoned by all, except for the awareness of his power as hero and ruler, calls out those despairing words "My kingdom for a horse!", he hurries, limping, over the battlefield, as boys do, when the imitate the horse's gallop. The clever, and impartial reader may smile, may barely hold back a "How childish!" For those of us who saw him it was deadly serious, and fearful, and chilling.

For me the pinnacle of all the performances of the great actor was that moment in *King Lear*, where the poor old man, through his own fault and the heinous guilt of his neighbor, is being hunted in the forest, in the unforgiving night storm, into madness. At the beginning he is only desperate, not insane. When, then, does madness seize him? Shakespeare does not give the answer, but he found his interpreter in Devrient. Suffering the pain of despair, which is evident in his voice and gesture, a moment of stiffness and deathly stillness appear. How many thousands of voices in a single minute have in a tangled interweaving whispered their desires to him, and breathed imperceptible orders! – And now the old man stares out into the empty air, into the space of the spectators, and in frightening haste begins to pour forth a stream of incomprehensible meaningless words into the empty air! – this is Madness.

Here I have only mentioned two masterpieces. But that time was close enough to the great German poets for them to have taken a lively part in it, as well as the following period – at least with respect to the theater. Goethe's dramas, and particular Schiller's, still met with general approval, and were performed much more frequently than later, and now. In this regard, however, the character of the "Court Theater" and the love for show which the Berliner had adopted from them was evident, the pleasure in pageantry often making a rather odd effect. The coronation procession in the *Maid of Orleans*, lasted, with its inclusion of all those princes and knights, dignitaries and hangers-on, children, maidens, spirituals confraternities, and whatever all else, an amazingly long time (it was claimed that it was a half-hour) and thus became the main event of the drama, at least for a large portion of the public; and also for the Count Brühl[9], General Intendant at the time. This excellent, educated, and truly noble man of the court had namely his main eye directed at costume. Everything was to appear with the greatest possible historical accuracy, and with a stateliness, and a level of wealth that was fitting for the court. He would never have forgiven using an already existing costume of the thirteenth century for one of the twelfth or the fourteenth century, and would have thought it a crime against Schiller's ghost, if each group that the poet indicates or that tradition has handed down were not brought in the worthiest way to appear on the stage. In this respect there was lacking, and this was not his fault, the coordination of all the performers that had made the performances in Weimar so effective. And there was lacking that lively, impossible to hide, and willing participation of the audience, which I had met in Halle. For those of us from small towns (I have mentioned this above) theater was a rarity, and therefore a feast, a celebration, almost as it was for the Greeks with their dionysia. For those in large cities the theater is open all year long; what value does today's performance have, when tomorrow the same performance, or another one, is to be had?

Along with the great dramas, as is evident, there was lighter fare and ballet. The opera was the most richly considered, however. Along with the masterworks of Gluck and Mozart, during the course of the year operas by Cherubini, Méhul, Winter and many others were given. Rossini and Auber were tried, but found no especial response, and could not, just like Meyerbeer with his *Crociato* und *Emma von Roxburg*, find a continuing place in the repertory. The "Purely Musical" had a warmer response for Spohr, whose always soft and flowing melodies, whose clean interweaving of the voices, like the continual weaving of the silkworm's cocoon, whose chromatic sliding through all the keys, particularly charmed the quartet-players, and allowed one to overlook the lack of dramatic firmness and color.

The darling of Berlin opera lovers, however, was at that time Karl Maria von Weber. Through his war songs, and especially through the men's choruses, for which Theodor Körner had written poetry for "*Lützow's wilde verwegene Jagd*"[10] he had become a Prussian citizen, and had become the lapchild of the Berliners; quite naturally, for Prussia's people had, more so than all the rest of Germany's tribes, given all to the struggle against the oppressors, and staked its best blood to the effort. Its volunteers and people's army were called out

---

[9] Carl von Brühl, 1772-1837, succeeded Iffland as controller of the Prussian theater.
[10] Inspired by the *Königlich Preußisches Freikorps von Lützow*, a corps of volunteers founded in 1813 to fight against Napoleon.

by Weber's military songs; something like this is not forgotten. Now it was, however, shortly before I came in Berlin that Weber had appeared there with his *Freischütz*. The opera was based on German legend, aroused the romantic streak native to us Germans, and took place throughout in the sphere of the life of the people. And all this had been made so clearly perceptible to the Germans by Weber together with his poet, and had successfully used easily comprehensible song forms, that soon his melodies were heard from every voice. When I happened to talk to him later about the opera and its extraordinary success, he said, in a bad temper, almost wistfully, "Don't talk to me about this success! That which has no musical value, these little songs, is what people praise; and where I exerted my strength, is ignored." At that point I did not venture a reply; but he was incorrect. Those "little songs" had like a little golden magic key opened the hearts of all, and the larger movements had been appreciated as well. He quickly understood, more quickly than Spontini, more quickly than Beethoven, for he was more intimate with the German people, than with the Imperial people, and was closer to it, and more comprehensible than the last of our musical heroes, who from his heavens and with his visions did not descend to bourgeois earthly life, but beckoned us upwards, up there, where the ideals of this life celebrate their immortal dance. Weber himself did not understand that composer, as his sarcasm (for example, against his symphonies) show.

The burning point of operatic activity, however, was Carnival. This had continued from the old Fritz to the time that I am telling about. In those days in Berlin one looked forward to the time of Carnival with more excited and higher-flying expectations than today. Of course, the real luxuriously foaming pleasure in Carnival of the Catholic and southern lands, the wantonness of Paris, the more naïve drunkenness of the Romans and Neapolitans could find no place here; we found the more richly garlanded goblet of spiritual pleasure more appropriate. And for that reason the opera house opened its broad space.

The House itself (we may be permitted the recollection on behalf of the young) was different; only the exterior walls have remained. The comfortable corridors, the pleasant satin seats were not there; lacking were the hundreds of triangles and rectangles, medallions and other sort of curved decorations, which with the carved and painted gold now border curtain and ceiling in a sort of Hotel-garni for all sorts of cherubs, medieval personalities, water sprites and artists in gallant bourgeois dress. Also lacking was the splendor of the broad proscenium boxes with their watch of cold goddesses, behind which the festive decoration of the stage shyly and humbly pushes back. At that time surrounded by a slimly vaulted proscenium box on the right, with another on the left, with the galleries in beautifully curved Moorish arches, the broad auditorium sat opposite the equally wide stage, which single-mindedly offered in a tranquil immense unfolding a single great image, the gods of Greece, with priests sacrificing before the altars. This, the one, was what had been wanted, not this or that, anything and everything.

Thus the creation of Frederick the Great and its modern transformation, even in view of the establishment and decoration of a playhouse, stood in contrast to each other, with notable characteristics of both.

The second of my drafts was "Otto III", which I had planned for an opera.

It was to start with the storming of Rome by the young Emperor. The scene is, at the rise of the curtain, in Rome itself, bounded in the background by a section of the fortress wall; the leader of the Romans is Crescentius, the husband of that Constance, who is to ruin the young hero. The calls and noise of wars penetrate from outside; in vain the Romans resist, in vain is the Pope carried by on his high seat in order to bolster their courage. The besiegers force their way in; the first is Otto, in the glow of battle he orders Crescentius to be put to death, and does not listen to Constance, who implores for the life of her spouse at his feet. Only when it is too late does he agree and feels his young heart irretrievably smitten by the glance of the beautiful and despairing woman. She, however, swears death to him, and will revenge her spouse on the besieger through slow-acting poison. I had great expectations for the portrait of the hero, who with German father, and born to a Greek mother, strives for Roman lordship; especially, I hoped for a great effect from the fact that the action began in the noise of the storm of battle, with the back and forth of the double choruses of the besiegers and defenders, with the depiction of the battle between the highest powers on Earth – the Emperor and the Pope, but finally concluded in the spooky stillness of the sickbed of the dying Emperor, with only Constance nearby in his final moments, who, now that rescue is no longer possible, makes known to him her vow of revenge and the completed deed[6].

I certainly know, that the same material had been handled by more than one poet, and not always happily. But, I thought (and I still have the same belief) that it was material that was absolutely suited for opera and not for a purely poetic drama; Otto and Inez del Castro (which had been handled several times, and never by Gluck) seemed to me to belong to this category. The frightful end could only be made bearable by opera and not by spoken drama, I thought. Whether I was aware at the time, that Goethe in his *Egmont* also withdraws from the noise and bustle of the happiest life into the stillness of the prison, out of which the hero has only one exit, to the scaffold, is something that I do not recall.

I cannot turn away from this look back on former plans without including a few fleeting considerations.

The first has to do with the distinction made above regarding the missions of the spoken and sung drama. Why is Otto suited for opera, and not for spoken-word drama? Which persons and which actions necessarily belong to one or another genre – one sees that these are questions which can only be

---

[6] Marx's account of this episode is highly fanciful. It might be noted that Crescentius II's wife was seemingly named Stefania, and not Constance.

answered from the essence of the neighboring arts or artistic genres. Lessing has already spoken unforgettably in his *Laocoon* regarding the boundaries and affiliations of the arts. I myself have reason, in my "Gluck", to express, how the same material – the Eumenides – must be shaped in three different ways in the hands of the sculptor, the spirit of the poet, and in the mood of the musician. Now this basic question returns; if I am not mistaken, with weightier importance, if badly neglected up until now.

The basis of the decision can, as said above, only lie in the essence of the artistic genres.

The spoken word, in comparison to the word which has been both melted into the melody and veiled by it, has much great definition and also much quicker and more powerful comprehension. Two words of the poet (I love, - I hate) express an entire mood, while singing must spread out a wide web of tones, in order to suck the souls of the listeners, and thus enchant their moods, and finally their understanding and experience. To compensate music is able to spread out the entire fullness of the life of the soul and pour into the soul of the listener to be jointly consumed. Poetry gives the hardened kernel; music releases it for gas-like fluidity and volatility.

If what is hinted at here has been given a basis, thus it follows that: all that is kernel-like and requiring a quicker decision necessarily demands pure words; music will not only limit and veil the word, but also the pressing personality and action.

Characters and actions, which in themselves are not kernel-like, not arranged for a quick active decision, do not merely tolerate, but require the wavering, rising and sinking element of music, like waves. Now then! Otto is born to be hero and ruler, but never becomes these. The flexibility of the youth, the Greek mother, the all too quick victory, the blazing passion, all unites with the hero in order to kill him, before the poison draft brings the final decision through the secretly approaching deed, not springing forward with a powerful blow. This same character imbues all the people and situations in the drama.

If we want an example for the other side, let us look at Wallenstein.

The other consideration has to do with the intended plot for Otto, and the same basis in Goethe's *Egmont*.

The direction which the poet gives to his drama is by no means arbitrary; it is immutably determined through the content and basic notion of the poem. This is not necessary to prove to anyone who sees artistic work as more than fantasy play, anyone who recognizes in it the commanding power of the idea – and sees the poet or artists as the true servant of this idea.

Both of the subjects mentioned have in common that the hero, not having grown to his task, is forced away from the scene of action of the deed he has undertaken, and now, free of every purpose, remains alone with himself and his death. This is the frightful judgment which is imposed on both heroes, and which moves our soul to the deepest sympathy.

For the musician, who is only too happy to work from the whole, in order to shake mind and spirit, the reverse, to sing from double choruses and powerful orchestra to the silence of solo song, is certainly not unthinkable. Gluck dared it in his *Armida*.

Johanne Henriette Rosine Hendel-Schütz, née Schüler, (1772–1849)

CHAPTER 14

Personal relationships

But where had my letters of recommendation gone?

One, from Hendel-Schütz, had been addressed to the noble artistic couple Wolf [sic]. I had already admired them in Halle; at that time they belonged to the Weimaraner, and now they were attached to the stage in Berlin. Yes, I had already had a personal relationship with them in Halle, as could only take place in the atmosphere of the university there.

The broadly admired artist, who so often delighted everyone, and who had in return received the warmest of tributes, once – whether correctly or incorrectly – decided that she had been neglected by the public in some role. The next evening she nevertheless appeared according to the call of duty, but performed without any commitment whatsoever; and so on the next night as well. This was more than her hot-blooded brother Studio could bear; he decided, should she appear in such a lackluster fashion once again to solemnly – pound her. Another such decision to receive her in the same way I had averted with the help of my friends. She appeared without any inkling of the decision and played ice-cold. With utmost effort it was possible to once again hinder the outbreak. Now, however, I hastened to the theater, and sought frantically to speak to the artist. Astounded, and somewhat annoyed, she admitted me, and I made her swear, before I revealed the situation to her, to change her manner of acting, and to give back to all of us, even to the indignant, who had been her greatest devotees, the great artist once again. I do not know what she answered; but I can still see the tragic glance of Niobe which her dark eyes sent upwards. She performed incomparably and showered with the loudest homage. She had learned my name; the adventure had no further consequences.

Now I visited the artistic pair with a recommendation, was kindly received, and asked repeatedly about my address. I very clearly lettered out street and house-number; that one, on such occasions, hands over one's card with the address noted on it, was something that I knew nothing about as yet. The natural result was that I did not receive any invitation. A second letter, from Director Schwarz, led me to the famed E. T. A. Hoffmann, at the time *Kammergerichtsrat*. I found that he was not at home, and delivered my letter. At the next session, he waved me aside and asked me whether I wanted to take a position in Prussian Poland. I thanked him and explained that my plans for the time being were not at all directed to a position, but rather towards the realization of certain artistic and scientific plans. He looked at me with astonishment, and kindly invited me to visit. But as often as I asked after him at his residence, I received the reply that he was not at home. Finally Häring explained to me: "You must not look for him at his house," he said, "but instead with Lutter and Wegener in the wine-room, which is where he spends his free time". I resisted, and I never saw him again; at any rate he was taken by his final illness and death a short time later[1].

I had better success with Generalin von Helwig[2]. Previously she had lived as Amalie von Imhoff in Weimar, where as a young poet she earned popularity and fame, and, as I can report more from the utterances of others than her own, there had enjoyed the goodwill of Goethe. Now, in her middle years, mingling the beauty of youth with the dignity of riper age in one noble picture, she lived at the side of the highly honored General, to whom one attributed great service with his weapon, and she taking a lively interest in all the beauties offered by the arts, and he inclining less to this side, than to mathematics and other strictly scientific undertakings, infrequently and generally only joining the circle that she gathered around her later. To this circle belonged the sculptor Rauch[3] and along with him, General Gneisenau[4]. Younger artists, painters, and sculptors joined. I as well, the only one who knew music, was allowed to enter. The happiest hours for me, however, were those which I was able to spend with the worthy lady and her enticing young blonde niece, happy with their enriching and animating contributions.

I recall one such evening, during which she presented me a series of paintings done by an Indian artist: the execution seems to be half gouache, half fluid watercolor. I had never seen anything of the sort before, or since.

The pictures were of the size of a half-sheet of writing paper. This already distinguished them from other painting, in that the frame (or, if you like, the edge) was already made by the artist. For some of these the edge, almost an inch wide, was filled with a crowed of the tiniest bright flowers and buds; elsewhere the edge was covered with a deep blue, from which countless golden stars twinkled forth, some singly, others ordered into constellations. The most precious and most amazing things, however, were the paintings themselves; one can gather from the descriptions that follow, that the individual figures barely

---

[1] Ernst Theodor Amadeus Hoffmann died in 1822, at the age of 46.
[2] Anna Amalia von Helvig, 1776-1831, was principally resident in Sweden, where she was a prominent figure in the arts.
[3] Christian Daniel Rauch, 1777-1857, an exceptionally successful artist who acquired a near-monopoly of major public sculpture in Prussia during the first half of the century.
[4] August Neidhardt von Gneisenau, 1760-1831, personally led the capture of Napoleon at Waterloo and was later governor of Berlin.

reached the height of two inches. On one of these pictures one noted the nearby foreground separated with chalky cliffs. Here, on the left of the viewer, a man looking anxiously about, to judge by his clothing and posture, poor and common, is hiding behind rocks and brush. On the other side a horse, richly apparisoned, is hidden. What was going on here? — The middle ground of the picture visible over the rocky peaks gave no information about this. There a murdered man lay slain, stretched out in his blood; one became aware of the deadly wounds by looking at the exposed head. The man hidden in the foreground had attacked him, and led his horse away. But the slain man was not forsaken; around him some young women had gathered, and one thought to recognize in a despairing figure his beloved spouse, who would follow the corpse onto the pyre. Over this principal group the eye could make out in the background a city with carelessly open doors. It was also in peace that a criminal act had been carried out by a murderous hand.

Another page showed a round dance of naked female figures. Bodies, members, the head, all were presented in the most charming way; I expressed my pleasure more or less in these terms. "But you do not see!" the Generalin told me. I looked, rather taken aback, at the page once more, and now discovered, that the big toe of the naked, tender little foot was decorated with gold bangles, from which little green or red stones glittered; I mentioned this. "But you do not see!" resounded for the second time – and now, for the first time, with a sharper look I found that the dancing figures were not at all naked, but draped with white linen veils, almost as transparent as air, which could only be seen more where they formed a fold in the breeze, and the material turned back upon itself two or three times; in general they provided a view of the delicate bodies.

My favorite picture was of quite another sort once again. It showed a meadow in the background, closely and tightly enclosed by tender shrubs, that allowed no view into the distance; above was the deep blue sky, spotted with little white clouds. It seemed like the most tranquil and peaceful refuge, untouched by the noise and bustle of the busy outside world. In the middle of the meadow sat a noble maiden, here arms and hands outstretched, playing tenderly. And at her feet lay tiger and lion, lamb and deer stretched out next to each other in peaceful concord.

Who gave the creatures this peace? Who guaranteed for the tender and defenseless unthreatened life and existence next to the violent? — Then one notices, in the deepest darkness, in the middle of the branches, scarcely visible in the shadows, a wondrously strange bird, resting, and looking down with erect head at the maiden and the circle of creatures around her. —

Is this magic? One of the wondrous creatures from Brahminic poetry? I do not know; I only relate what I have seen.

The good woman, to whom I owed the view into an unimagined magical world, had received the pictures from her great uncle, who had been governor in an Indian province. She told of its splendor and the hundreds of slaves, which he had solely to attend to his needs; one imagined that one had been transported into one of the tales from the "Arabian Nights". Just the gentleman's tobacco pipe kept twenty slaves busy.

It was during one of these beautiful evenings, when I had just sat down at the piano, that Bettina (Frau von Arnim[5]) was announced. I had not met her yet, and knew nothing about her, but I immediately left the piano. The Generalin went up to her, and the usual exchange of intimate greetings flowed, without my paying attention to it. Suddenly I could hear, all the way from the door to where I was, Bettina's voice saying: "Oh!, you must be ...., who made those beautiful songs!" I had in fact occasionally sung a couple of newly written songs for the Generalin. Perhaps the remark of the woman (later so well-known) should have been flattering. But since I was still awkward in matters of art, I found the unexpected address of a stranger to be highly unpleasant. I bowed dutifully, and my mouth remained closed. The witty liveliness of Bettina and the soft friendliness of our hostess helped to make up for the dissonance of this first meeting. Bettina presented her drawing, in which she had sketched a memorial for Goethe; it was the well-known figure of Zeus in the style of Phidias, on which the head – unfortunately somewhat aged – of Goethe was placed. Goethe's head was even in old age noble and handsome; he could never have grown the head of a Zeus. There was likewise much that was praiseworthy regarding intent and talented execution.

Now she turned once more to me with the words: "Now I would like to sing a song of mine for you." And she sang with a strangely beautiful voice. Had she stopped after the first or second strophe, I would have been able to say many pleasant things about her. But strophe followed strophe, strophe on strophe, and I had already stopped paying attention, when suddenly I was woken by the question: "Are you quite bored?" "Oh, not at all!" I gasped. What could one say, even with the best of intentions, about a little melody repeated endlessly with each strophe? Only the basic tone of the mood can, if lucky, sound through in such a treatment; deepening and presentation of particularly states of the soul are not permitted by this form.

---

[5] Elisabeth Catharina Ludovica Magdalena Brentano, Countess von Arnim, 1785-1859, was related to and acquainted with all major cultural figures of the time, and was a gifted musician, writer and artist in her own right.

Bettina had invited me to visit her; I did, and she sang solo settings with a peculiarly appealing delivery, especially recitatives from the Psalms of Benedetto Marcello. I knew them already, but followed the spirited presentation with new and warm interest.

More often had I not visited the ladies. At her house, and much more at that of the renowned Rahel (Frau Varnhagen[6]), whom I got to know later, I resisted the well-known ways of so many of the female "greats" of Berlin. These ladies – who combine intelletual abilities with education, but principally are nourished by what they cull in interactions in society with intellectually and truly instructed men, and in relying upon the respect and protection owed to their gender now and then launch a pert word or a bold statement, without allowing the sparks emitted to grow together into a creative flame – very easily take on the appearance and sound of the superior and patronizing. And indeed I found this to be intolerably degrading to men. They survive on our crumbs, I said – truly not thinking of myself, but rather of well-traveled and highly capable men – and they want to wrap themselves in the gleam, as if all what they had snatched originated with them? — Before and after I had been acquainted with truly formative and creative power in entirely other women – first in Staël, later in George Sand (given their national/French point of view), when she so boldly struggled to bring the female gender to greater worthiness, and likewise in the great poem "*Von Geschlecht zu Geschlecht*" by Frau Fanny Lewald-Stahr[7]. These are spirits at work.

Another circle of acquaintances opened for me at the house of the poet Stieglitz.

Heinrich Stieglitz, as poet of Greek songs very well-regarded at the time by the friends of the Hellenic liberation struggle, and beloved in wider circles as well, had a position at a gymnasium in Berlin, and also held the position of a keeper of the Royal Library. His primary activity was directed, however, to his poetic work, such as his *Pictures of the Orient*, which appeared in the early years of our acquaintance. He was supported by the great generosity of his uncle, the rich banker Stieglitz, in Petersburg. But precisely an excess of luck, was, as often happens, his undoing.

Because he was no poet! He was only an extremely talented, always ready verse-artist. As a poet he was lacking in nothing but matter, comprehensible substance. How often did I see him, with his small, but youthful and powerful

---

[6] Rahel Antonie Friederike Varnhagen, 1771-1831, best known for her voluminous correspondence, returned to the Prussian capital in 1819.
[7] Fanny Lewald, 1811-1889. The work in question is a novel in eight volumes, published 1863-1865.

figure, with his brown curly locks, wildly and weirdly haloing his head, his glowing eyes darting here and there, in order to grasp and capture the wickedly fleeting mental images! How often did he snatch up a suggestion from myself or other friends and present it in stately verses before our amazed eyes! Many of these products were incorporated into the *Pictures of the Orient*; from them I made *Nahid and Omar*, a musical novella, a dramatic presentation, not intended to be performed on the stage, but captured in its lyric chief moment, which have an inner connection to each other, and thus form an interdependent whole.

Stieglitz had, along with all his worldly goods, gained for himself the most precious of all, a woman, whose charm was only the reflection of a deeply moved mind and a bright spirit. Brightly this spirit gazed out of soulful eyes; only in one respect was she blind and had gone astray. She believed that her beloved spouse was a poet. And poetry, the more passionately that Stieglitz tried to struggle with it and violently grasp it, yet the more brittle and frightfully escaped from him; it seemed to veil the darkly glowing countenance of the poor man as madness; and then his wife could no longer bear it, and could live no longer.

At that time Stieglitz had surrounded himself with poisons, daggers, and fire-arms, was entirely inactive and with nothing to do, had given up his positions, had sunken into gloomy brooding, often appeared absent-minded, played thoughtlessly with his weapons, and also let slip occasional hints pointing at suicide or some sort of approaching end of life. At this time Doctor Mundt, later Professor, the director of the General Hospital, L. von Voss[8], and myself were the closest associates of the couple. We were happy to do what we could to relieve his anxieties; but nothing had any more effect. So on a fine summer evening we three went with the couple to the Brandenburg Gate, to relax in the open air; for all of our hearts were very heavy. Mundt went ahead with Charlotte Stieglitz; we followed, with the visibly sick man between us. We soon went back, for he staggered and turned first to the right and then to the left, carrying on a common conversation with each of us. Once, when he had turned away from us, I pointed secretly at him and said quietly to Voss "he is dying!" "No! she is dying!" he replied. The hollow and powerful voice, despite all restraint, of the excellent man shook me more than any lightning bolt could have done; I instantly saw clearly, as if during a flash of lightning in the night. For I already knew the wonderful man, if only from stories. In wider circles he was already well-known at the time for his *Ahnungen und Lichtblicke*.

Voss served in the artillery during the Rhine campaign. The battery, to which he belonged as the youngest officer, was pointed at a high point over which the

---

[8] Arnold Christian Ludwig von Voss, 1775-1835.

state road ran. This led to a low point in the terrain, where the ground sank, and then went up once more; at the low point it was surrounded by bushes. Through a mental error the battery was not camouflaged, and there were not even lookouts in the direction of the enemy. The officers had gathered and were conversing quietly about the worries of the position, when from the near side Major Blücher[9], the later field-marshal rode up with a small troop of hussars, and was amazed to find the twelve-pounder there. He immediately left the whole troop to cover the artillery (quite inadequately), and rode alone down to the dip in the road to reconnoiter. And in fact, as soon as he had gone down, French jumped out of the bushes on either side, who obviously had been targeting the battery, and surrounded Blücher.

And then the young Voss went to those in command and asked: "Captain, may I?" Hardly was the question asked, and the answer not yet ended, and he aimed his weapon directly at Blücher's person, fired. The shot thunders over, Blücher sits high on his horse, the French dive to either side, and the battery is saved for now.

"Who did that shot?" thundered Blücher's voice, still in the distance, as he leaps back to the battery. The captain hesitates for a moment in answering, for in truth, Voss's deed was doubly questionable. How easily his shot could have knocked down the Prussian officer. How easily, even if this did not happen, could it arouse suspicion of extreme recklessness or even treason! The young man stepped up to Blücher, and said, while saluting: "Herr Major, it was I who shot." "I will never forget this!" answered Blücher, glowing with joy. And he kept his word. This deed was the impetus to Voss's successful career.

And this heroically steadfast man had the most delicate mind, open to the finest secret emotions. Even before the days in question he had planned an investigation of the strange gaze with which the poor poet Stieglitz was endowed. Stieglitz had not brought his Charlotte home, and lived by himself in Berlin; but the young lady was waiting with her mother in Leipzig. Both had undertaken a little trip to a nearby spot. This much Stieglitz knew. But now the letters he expected were long delayed; he felt very uncomfortable, and complained of this to his old friends. Voss looked at him, and into the distance at the same time, and spoke in phrases: "Your Lotte is on a trip – she has caught a fever – but there is no danger. They are staying at a village inn. Your Lotte is a in a bed with this sort of drapery (description). The landlady is just preparing a tea of....it will put the sick woman back on her feet...."

---

[9] Gebhard Leberecht von Blücher, Fürst von Wahlstatt, 1742-1819, leader of the victorious Prussian forces at the battles of Leipzig and Waterloo.

And on the second or third day the letter arrived that confirmed what Voss had prophesied.

You may ask me, is this true? I have reported it exactly as Stieglitz and his spouse told me several times. You may ask me, do I really believe it? Naturally, such events can be pure invention, or rest on self-delusion. But, no matter how often this is the case, such reports are found from all periods, from all peoples and all levels of culture. Can they all be nothing but delusion and invention? Do we know so much about the boundaries of the spirit's power in humans that we can assert: this is possible for the spirit, and this other thing absolutely not? Is plain, that is, groundless disbelief, more warranted than just as plain superstition? Or in the end is one more dangerous than the other?

You may ask, whether I myself believe in such perceptions. What weight does the belief or unbelief of a single individual have? However, I will say certainly: yes, I consider them to be possible; I must. For I myself have experienced the like more than once, and strangely enough, never with respect to myself, but rather as an impartial witness to the experiences of others. I will only mention two cases here.

My childhood friend Schwarz had a cousin Heinrich, whom I knew well, but with whom I had no closer relationship. Heinrich had a lung disease, his death seemed unavoidable and close at hand; at that time he lived in retirement at Gräfentonna in Thuringia; there had been no news of him for some time. Late in the evening I was sitting with Schwarz on a low sofa, opposite his folding writing desk, which supported a bookshelf with a row of orderly books, all pressed up against each other in order. We were alone, conversing quietly; if I am not mistaken, Schwarz mentioned his sick cousin. The deepest quiet was present in the chamber, in the entire house, on the street. Suddenly a book fell off the shelf, hit the tabletop, and fell at Schwarz's feet. Schwarz, whose courage had been proven by dueling, and who had always shown himself to be unshakable, colored and blurted out a few incomprehensible words. I jumped up first and went immediately to the bookshelf; neither here nor elsewhere was there a clue to the event. I picked up the book, and it was a Horace, that Heinrich had given to his cousin, and inscribed with the words "as a remembrance", etc. In falling it had opened to the ode

Linquenda tellus ....

(You must leave your meadow and your house and your pleasing spouse...) I concealed the impression that the strange occurrence had made on me, and sought to help Schwartz in this regard. –A few days a letter arrived from Gräfintonna with the news that Heinrich had died on that day at that very hour (between 9 and 10 at night).

And also in Berlin I found a close relative, Sophie Gossmann, a talented and sensitive woman. Her mother lived in Dessau, and just then was seriously ill; the daughter was very concerned, and only with difficulty did her spouse and myself manage to convince her to take a walk in a little-visited garden. Happily just then a detailed letter from her mother's hand had arrived, which reported on the illness and also that she had seen considerable improvement, and was even close to recovery. Cheerful and entirely tranquil, Sophie started to walk with us. But in the garden she became quieter, turned in on herself, and finally moved to the strongest feelings. Ripping her green scarf from her head with the words "I must not wear green, I must wear clothes of mourning", she broke out in loud lamenting; we had to return home. At that very hour (as a letter reported several days later), the woman who was apparently recovering had died.

Now you can imagine the impression those words "Not he, but she will die!" had made on me. And they came terribly true.

On one of the subsequent mornings a common acquaintance, the bookdealer Lehseldt, with whom I had no closer connection at that time, came into my room, bide me to greet with composure the sad news that he had to impart, and said: "Doctor Stieglitz had ended his life, had ended his life through suicide. "You are saying", I cried, "Doctor Stieglitz is dead!" "No", was the answer, "not him, she gave herself death."

And so it was. Without hope of rescue she saw her beloved spouse sink ever deeper into the night of spiritual powerlessness, and stagger toward the grave. Then she had a mad notion, which lying and self-deception should never have permitted to enter her soul: a terrible blow could shock the unhappy man with electric power, and newly animate him. She may also have had the thought that if this measure were also in vain, life would only be a burden. She managed to get him and the serving girl out of the residence, put on a white nightgown, laid herself down in her bed, and pressed the dagger she had carried with her so quietly and surely into her heart, that only a few drops of blood made their way outside. Then she wrapped herself modestly in the coverlet.

Thus she was found not long thereafter by her husband returning home from the theater – already passed away, but not yet cold.

Theodor Mundt gave Charlotte Stieglitz a noble and touching memorial in his *Lebensbilde* [Portraits from life][10].

I wrote my *Nahid and Omar*[11] for her gracious voice, for her most noble singing, full of soul. She was the first and best singer for Nahid, though I heard it beautifully later from famed singers.

---

[10] *Charlotte Stieglitz, ein Denkmal*, Berlin, 1835.

[11] A music drama or song cycle, written by Marx around 1834; originally with orchestral accompaniment, it was also arranged for voice and piano

I will return once more to Theodor Mundt. At that time I and all the friends of the unfortunate Charlotte felt thankful to him, and bowed to the deeply moved biographer. Later he made himself known through the most varied of directions, occupied with his history of literature[12], his Machiavelli, and many other works. Over many years, until the end of his life, I continued to have friendly interactions with him. Along with him and his spouse, faithful until death, Clara Mühlbach-Mundt[13], I was in contact with the spirited Gutzkow[14], the talented dramatist Laube[15], the novelist Mügge[16], the elegant writer Feodor Wehl[17], and others. I also got to know Mundt's physician, Dr. Schlemm[18], who handled me in my severe illness with truly friendly support and the happiest of results.

At about this same time I met Adolf Stahr[19], tirelessly searching and successfully struggling for truth and beauty, and his spouse Fanny Lewald-Stahr, who recently in her biography along with the most valuable content has given a depiction of everything with truly heroic sincerity and truthfulness. Between the two of them and my spouse and I there later came to be a bond of the most cordial association.

[12] *Geschichte der Literatur der Gegenwart*, 1853.
[13] Luise Mühlbach, pseudonym for Clara Mundt, 1814-1873.
[14] Karl Gutzkow, 1811-1878.
[15] Heinrich Laube, 1806-1884.
[16] Theodor Mügge, 1802-1861.
[17] Feodor von Wehl, 1821-1890. Wehl and the other writers mentioned here were associated with the Young Germany movement, a group of young literary figures who opposed absolutism, advocated religious and gender emancipation, and argued for a greater engagement of cultural figures with the realities of daily life.
[18] Friedrich Schlemm, 1795-1858.
[19] Adolf Stahr, 1805-1876, the husband of Fanny Lewald, whose *Meine Lebensgeschichte*, Berlin, 1861-1862, is an invaluable source for this period.

CHAPTER 15

THE BERLIN OPERA AT ITS PEAK

When I made the decision to move to Berlin, I said to myself: I will not enter the opera house there until it presents an opera by Gluck. And what do you know? On the very first evening the ticket read "Gluck's *Alceste*".

I had already seen the opera house. On the night of my arrival I had been so excited by the expectation of all that was before me that I could not immediately rest. Once again I wandered through the moon-drenched streets by the castle, past the armory, only saw now for the first time the strange but entirely magnificent construction of the University buildings[10], with no inkling that not long after a position for me would be founded there. From there I looked to the left; and there it was before me, the Opera House! — One might think find the comparison not entirely appropriate when I say that the slim construction, stretched out in a line, appeared to me to be one of the sphinxes that Egypt stored up thousands of years ago for our astonished eyes.

On the following evening, I wandered in with my ticket, already acquired in the early morning, and found my seat in the still almost empty parquet. Next to me a woman in her middle years sat down, naturally someone unknown to me. The house became full.

Here I must confess a weakness regarding which many of my colleagues will laugh. In fact, I enjoy listening to the instruments tune up. For most these unrelated and content-less tones are annoying; it ruins their illusion, as they say.

It has a different effect on me. The tuning of the instruments tunes me at the same time, the spirits of the tones are beautifully awoken in my inmost parts as if from fragrant slumber, my anticipation is wound up more and more, and the first chord already finds me in an elevated mood.

Never before had I had such an orchestra before me! Seven or nine contrabasses, twenty-four violins, if not more, I am not entirely sure of the numbers, had gathered; their first tremolo gripped me with frightful force. Still under the might strides of the overture the curtain rose, and there, before the palace, gathered in mourning and grief for the beloved king, on bended knees, opened hands gesturing toward the seat of the Gods, was the Hellenic people,

---

[1] [ABM]: It is well-known that old Fritz had said of this building, in those days the palace of Prince Heinrich that the parterre seemed like a fortress, the main floor, a church, and the upper floor a powder-magazine.

and its call, transfixed by the mighty sound of the trombones of the orchestra, rose up to the cruelly indifferent Olympians.

Naturally Gluck's work was present for me note for note; it lived in me just as I had inspired me from the score. It was not long until a movement somewhere seemed not lively enough, seemed to drag, and almost unaware I beat the time at a more rapid pace, in secret, of course. Soon this happened again for the second, and then the third time, and now I became aware that the same had to be happening for the woman next to me; she, as well, beat time in secret, but more mournfully. Between the acts I dared to talk to her, and she regarded me, not in an unfriendly, but a questioning way. I repeated my statement, and now a strange male voice spoke French to me: his spouse did not understand German – I had to speak French to her. Rapidly my glance flew to the one addressing me, and whom did I see? – it was Napoleon's countenance, quite memorable to me from Halle, that met my glance. Napoleon's countenance – so would the majority of all those have seen him have said to me; only through a longer look would the imperceptible difference in expression between the countenance of the Emperor and the face of nevertheless honorable mortal from an entirely different sphere become perceptible. The two foreigners exchanged a few words, of which I only understood their sotto voce expression: "Il écoute bien". He then kindly invited me to tea the next day, and I, without, in my haste, waiting for him to speak his name, declined, with regret: the next day I had to hear the renowned Boucher. "Mais Boucher, c'est moi!" It was the famous violinist Alexandre Boucher[2], who, at that time, because of his resemblance to Napoleon, found it hard to appear in Paris under Bourbon rule. And the lady was the just as renowned harpist and pianist[3]. Naturally the invitation was understood to be on the French schedule, after the concert.

It is not my intent to follow the elevated poetry and its representation at the time. I would like to simply think of a moment that is particularly present for me: it belongs to the ballet, which I saw here for the first time. The news of the wondrously quick recovery of the King had spread and - with the swinging tunes of the great painter of life the crowd of servants and connections flew in happy animation, the corps de ballet in wide floating steps, more in the air, rather than touching the earth. That was a dance of

[2] Alexandre Boucher, 1778-1861, violinist and composer. His likeness to Napoleon was much remarked upon, and was cited by him as the reason for his avoidance of France for much of his career.
[3] Céleste Gallyot, d. 1841. She was Boucher's wife.

joy, a poetic impulse of motion and appearance! Then came the solo dances with their artistic pieces, with their almost impossible contortions, with their rectangular elevations, the legs and arms in straight lines, the tortures, entirely contrary to nature, of the French ballet! O, my patroness and teacher! How differently you had appeared to me in Halle! I may have become unruly, or even loud; because the Parisian woman next to me whispered to me: "Mais ils dansent aussi bien!" She had not seen it any differently in Paris – and our high-minded Gluck had not been able to put down the misbehavior there either.

It was a good omen that my desire for a Gluck opera immediately came true. I had really arrived in Berlin at a good moment. The theater still had a significance that it later would not achieve again; one could still feel the effects of Iffland's direction and training[4], it still numbered in its rank more than disciple of that man, who we may judge not for his writing for the stage, but for his personal accomplishments on the boards. In that regard very recently the noble couple of artists, Wolf and his spouse, had appeared unforgettably, he as Hamlet, she as Lady Macbeth. Along with them was Devrient, the only incomparable artist among all the actors that I have seen.

Three Devrients have achieved the high approbation of the public. One, Emil[5], the ornament of the Dresden Theater; the other, Eduard[6], of outstanding merit through his dramaturgical writings (*History of the German Theater*, etc.). The one that I am speaking about is generally known as the old or the great Devrient[7].

The actor works without mediation through the appearance and activity of his person; his creation is indissolubly linked to it. Thus Devrient has probably found emulators and imitators, and some of them highly talented ones. What he was however, has remained without equal, and must remain so; for it was determined by his entirely incomparable personality. Already at the beginning of his career he was significantly different from the great majority of the actors of time; he had not belonged to any real school, had not grown up among the models which the great stages offer. His first activities and his schooling came in the relaxed circle of a traveling troupe (or at least it was seen that way at the time), and thus it was decreed that he himself had to be

---

[4] August Wilhelm Iffland, 1759-1814, was director of the Prussian national theater from 1796, and was instrumental in forging a mastery of the classics of the German stage.
[5] Gustav Emil Devrient, 1803-1872, a tragedian.
[6] Eduard Devrient, 1801 –1877, brother of the former, was best known as a baritone singer
[7] Ludwig Devrient, 1784 –1832, uncle of the former, and best known for Shakespearean and other classic roles. The Devrient family produced many other notable performers.

his one and all. This absolute ego he had, by the time when I saw him, allowed to grow into a truly demonical force, to a force, which I only met twice more, but in an entirely different field, in Paganini und Liszt.

Devrient's figure, on the smaller side of middling, slender, and capable of any movement, had nothing of that which one usually calls winning or noble. His face, with not large, but burning eyes, bore the stamp, which Klopstock assigns to those angels who are blasted to hell by the thunderbolts of the Almighty, and marked for eternity. It was in fact the reflection of that demonic artistic force, which prevailed in him, and struggled incessantly, not without torment, to break forth; for he became and was, what he had to represent. And that then came forth from him bodily, without one being able comprehend, how he, with his hoarse and not very sonorous voice, with his hands contracted, like claws, by gout, might make it possible. And this figure, marked by the unextinguishable stamp, was able to present the most various figures. He was the convict escaped from the galleys, hunted by minions to his death; in the "*Drillingen*[8]" he played the three brothers – the ship captain, brutally hardened, who leaves the salt water behind; in contrast to him, the youngest, blond, the eternal child; and I have forgotten the third brother. Jubilation and pleasure awoke his Falstaff. Here there was nothing of the music hall, nothing common; he was and remained throughout a knight, a gentleman, even where he when condescended to Mistress Quickly and the cronies. At the words: "So I lie, and so I lead my blade!" he was an entirely proper and elegant fencer; we did not laugh at his shapeless obesity, we regretted it, as if it were only disfiguring clothing that did not belong to him at all. He gave incomparable performances of the thrice-changing scene, in which, exchanging roles with Heinz, first represented the King and then the Prince perfectly. For the latter he took the last grand Hofmannian garment off, so that only the profligacy was left – the naked essence of the Prince – as he was at that time. The King was acted by the excellent Lemm, no longer young, and who had become somewhat stout; there could be hardly any greater contrast than that between his and Devrient's appearance. And see, in that scene it was Devrient before our eyes, by speech, movement and form, Lemm incarnate.

Beyond comprehension, so that I almost resist writing down the truth, was his acting in two moments of *Richard III*. In that scene, where the ghosts

---

[8] There was a potpourri in four acts by this title, for which the arias and songs were published in Frankfurt am Main, 1812.

call out to Richard their eternal "Despair and die!" the murderer is gripped by horror on his high pillows. In a circling motion – I can find no appropriate simile, beside the children's game, in which a short stick is twirled about its center – he twirls, as if without will and unable to resist invisible forces, down to the floor, awakes, and remains stretched out as if dead, while his eyes look all about, full of terror. And then, when he, abandoned by all, except for the awareness of his power as hero and ruler, calls out those despairing words "My kingdom for a horse!", he hurries, limping, over the battlefield, as boys do, when the imitate the horse's gallop. The clever, and impartial reader may smile, may barely hold back a "How childish!" For those of us who saw him it was deadly serious, and fearful, and chilling.

For me the pinnacle of all the performances of the great actor was that moment in *King Lear*, where the poor old man, through his own fault and the heinous guilt of his neighbor, is being hunted in the forest, in the unforgiving night storm, into madness. At the beginning he is only desperate, not insane. When, then, does madness seize him? Shakespeare does not give the answer, but he found his interpreter in Devrient. Suffering the pain of despair, which is evident in his voice and gesture, a moment of stiffness and deathly stillness appear. How many thousands of voices in a single minute have in a tangled interweaving whispered their desires to him, and breathed imperceptible orders! – And now the old man stares out into the empty air, into the space of the spectators, and in frightening haste begins to pour forth a stream of incomprehensible meaningless words into the empty air! – this is Madness.

Here I have only mentioned two masterpieces. But that time was close enough to the great German poets for them to have taken a lively part in it, as well as the following period – at least with respect to the theater. Goethe's dramas, and particular Schiller's, still met with general approval, and were performed much more frequently than later, and now. In this regard, however, the character of the "Court Theater" and the love for show which the Berliner had adopted from them was evident, the pleasure in pageantry often making a rather odd effect. The coronation procession in the *Maid of Orleans*, lasted, with its inclusion of all those princes and knights, dignitaries and hangers-on, children, maidens, spirituals confraternities, and whatever all else, an amazingly long time (it was claimed that it was a half-hour) and thus became the main event of the drama, at least for a large portion of the public; and also for the Count Brühl[9], General Intendant at the time. This excellent, educated, and truly noble man of the court had namely his main

---

[9] Carl von Brühl, 1772-1837, succeeded Iffland as controller of the Prussian theater.

eye directed at costume. Everything was to appear with the greatest possible historical accuracy, and with a stateliness, and a level of wealth that was fitting for the court. He would never have forgiven using an already existing costume of the thirteenth century for one of the twelfth or the fourteenth century, and would have thought it a crime against Schiller's ghost, if each group that the poet indicates or that tradition has handed down were not brought in the worthiest way to appear on the stage. In this respect there was lacking, and this was not his fault, the coordination of all the performers that had made the performances in Weimar so effective. And there was lacking that lively, impossible to hide, and willing participation of the audience, which I had met in Halle. For those of us from small towns (I have mentioned this above) theater was a rarity, and therefore a feast, a celebration, almost as it was for the Greeks with their dionysia. For those in large cities the theater is open all year long; what value does today's performance have, when tomorrow the same performance, or another one, is to be had?

Along with the great dramas, as is evident, there was lighter fare and ballet. The opera was the most richly considered, however. Along with the masterworks of Gluck and Mozart, during the course of the year operas by Cherubini, Méhul, Winter and many others were given. Rossini and Auber were tried, but found no especial response, and could not, just like Meyerbeer with his *Crociato* und *Emma von Roxburg*, find a continuing place in the repertory. The "Purely Musical" had a warmer response for Spohr, whose always soft and flowing melodies, whose clean interweaving of the voices, like the continual weaving of the silkworm's cocoon, whose chromatic sliding through all the keys, particularly charmed the quartet-players, and allowed one to overlook the lack of dramatic firmness and color.

The darling of Berlin opera lovers, however, was at that time Karl Maria von Weber. Through his war songs, and especially through the men's choruses, for which Theodor Körner had written poetry for "*Lützow's wilde verwegene Jagd*"[10] he had become a Prussian citizen, and had become the lapchild of the Berliners; quite naturally, for Prussia's people had, more so than all the rest of Germany's tribes, given all to the struggle against the oppressors, and staked its best blood to the effort. Its volunteers and people's army were called out by Weber's military songs; something like this is not forgotten. Now it was, however, shortly before I came in Berlin that Weber had appeared there with his *Freischütz*. The opera was based on German legend, aroused the romantic

---

[10] Inspired by the *Königlich Preußisches Freikorps von Lützow*, a corps of volunteers founded in 1813 to fight against Napoleon.

streak native to us Germans, and took place throughout in the sphere of the life of the people. And all this had been made so clearly perceptible to the Germans by Weber together with his poet, and had successfully used easily comprehensible song forms, that soon his melodies were heard from every voice. When I happened to talk to him later about the opera and its extraordinary success, he said, in a bad temper, almost wistfully, "Don't talk to me about this success! That which has no musical value, these little songs, is what people praise; and where I exerted my strength, is ignored." At that point I did not venture a reply; but he was incorrect. Those "little songs" had like a little golden magic key opened the hearts of all, and the larger movements had been appreciated as well. He quickly understood, more quickly than Spontini, more quickly than Beethoven, for he was more intimate with the German people, than with the Imperial people, and was closer to it, and more comprehensible than the last of our musical heroes, who from his heavens and with his visions did not descend to bourgeois earthly life, but beckoned us upwards, up there, where the ideals of this life celebrate their immortal dance. Weber himself did not understand that composer, as his sarcasm (for example, against his symphonies) show.

The burning point of operatic activity, however, was Carnival. This had continued from the old Fritz to the time that I am telling about. In those days in Berlin one looked forward to the time of Carnival with more excited and higher-flying expectations than today. Of course, the real luxuriously foaming pleasure in Carnival of the Catholic and southern lands, the wantonness of Paris, the more naïve drunkenness of the Romans and Neapolitans could find no place here; we found the more richly garlanded goblet of spiritual pleasure more appropriate. And for that reason the opera house opened its broad space.

The House itself (we may be permitted the recollection on behalf of the young) was different; only the exterior walls have remained. The comfortable corridors, the pleasant satin seats were not there; lacking were the hundreds of triangles and rectangles, medallions and other sort of curved decorations, which with the carved and painted gold now border curtain and ceiling in a sort of Hotel-garni for all sorts of cherubs, medieval personalities, water sprites and artists in gallant bourgeois dress. Also lacking was the splendor of the broad proscenium boxes with their watch of cold goddesses, behind which the festive decoration of the stage shyly and humbly pushes back. At that time surrounded by a slimly vaulted proscenium box on the right, with another on the left, with the galleries in beautifully curved Moorish arches, the broad auditorium sat opposite the equally wide stage, which single-mindedly offered in a tranquil immense unfolding a single great image, the gods of Greece, with priests sacrificing before the altars. This, the one, was what had been wanted, not this or that, anything and everything.

Thus the creation of Frederick the Great and its modern transformation, even in view of the establishment and decoration of a playhouse, stood in contrast to each other, with notable characteristics of both.

CHAPTER 16

SPONTINI

At the pinnacle of opera at that time was the Italian Gaspardo [sic] Spontini[1]. With him, the fickleness of fortune became visible for the first time for me. Within a short span of time I would be witness of the most extravagant admiration and the most shameful denigration, both from the very same persons, heaped upon the very same head, with irrepressible excitement. Is it possible for such fiery enthusiasm, if it is authentic, to change into such irate criticism? For the first time I could really see the meaning of the fateful tag-line of the Berliners: "*Man so duhn!*"[2]. The jubilation with they had so often greeted Spontini, had been no real enthusiasm, no enduring glow of amazement and love, like that which discerning spirits offer to the leading spirit; it was the straw-fire of fleeting excitement, which quickly flares up and just as quickly chokes to death in thick smoke. At that time no voice was raised in complaint; I myself had used my words and my name in favor of Spontini. A quarter of a century, and more, has flowed by since those events; everyone can know look back upon them calmly - — and the deceased can at least have the last word on the matter: his recognition, what he was, and what he provided Berlin. More than many, I think that I, from the beginning to the end enjoyed and could boast of his friendship and his artistic assistance.

I mentioned above that Spontini was at the pinnacle of the opera. The peak of the opera and Spontini's activity was Carnival time. Here opera was foremost. Next to those of Mozart and Beethoven there were, as said above, the musical works of Gluck and Cherubini, but more favored than all the rest, by the number of performances, were those of Spontini. These were the real festival operas, which – namely in *Nurmahal*[3], *Alcindor*[4], *Agnes von Hohenstaufen*[5], proper court operas - opened the court festivities to the broader public.

The leader and center of these staged marvels was now Spontini. When, with the house full-to-bursting, his fine, not overlarge figure, with an entirely courtly, and almost brittle posture, he appeared quickly and quietly in the orchestra pit, with his slim, high head, his wavy hair most carefully coiffured, his dark, moss-

---

[1] Gaspare Spontini, 1774-1851, was resident in Berlin from 1820 until 1842 after a dazzling career under Napoleon and a more troubled attempt to establish himself in Restoration Paris.
[2] "So it goes".
[3] Premiered in Berlin, 1822.
[4] Premiered in Berlin, 1825.
[5] Premiered in Berlin, 1827.

green tailcoat adorned with a very small wreath (which he gave much importance to), then the orchestra stood motionless, all the bows on the strings, all the mouthpieces by the lips, waiting for his gesture. For, even though many were individually rebellious in secret, at that time, before unfavorable constellations proved themselves to be effective beneath, at that time his entirely Napoleonic-absolutist leadership was strong and unquestionable. When, immediately after he stepped onto the podium, his darkly flashing eyes quickly turning from left to right took in a view of everything, his arm with the baton rose, stretched, and resting a while, seemed to turn to bronze: then everyone senses that his will, necessarily and exclusively, made all those participating into his organs; all together they were one body, and he was that body's animating principle. Next to him and after him we have come to know a finer, freer, perhaps more spiritual direction, but not one creating decisively from one single cast.

What gave the man this power of direction? Was it his position, his fame? Both of these contributed, but neither was the deciding factor; the man makes his fame and gives his position meaning.

Spontini's power of direction lay in his personality. Even in this it was evident that he – very differently from the majority of German opera composers – embraced all the moments of the drama in his spirit, not only the composition and music direction, and firmly grasped the reins of a hundred interacting forces with a firm hand and directed. Even the uninitiated viewer immediately sensed this.

I was often able to observe how even non-musicians observed his direction with lively participation, and likewise captured the spirit of the composition from him.

Much more attractive and instructive for me was his activity at the rehearsals for his operas, to which I was soon granted admission. Such a rehearsal was at the same time a touchstone for the power of the participation, which the visitor brought with him. While the performance of a drama seeks to increase the illusion of the viewer to its highest level, it is the nature of the rehearsal to similarly defy any illusion. At such a rehearsal one enters the theater, almost entirely buried in darkness, with only the desks of the orchestra fully lit, the curtain halfway up, the stage irregularly let by a few lamps, at the front a lighted desk for the director, another for the prompter, if such is needed – and suddenly one resounds from above, or from beneath the stage the orders of the machine-master and his assistants: "raise the soffits!" – No. 4 (the fourth coulisse) is falling already!" Now Spontini has appeared in the background as well – sometimes he also goes to a proscenium box in order to get a better overview. From all sides first this one and then that one appears with questions and reports; his attention, however, is directed above all at the arrangement of the scene, in which he misses nothing, and nothing unimportant appears. In the meantime the stage personnel has gotten together, the widow of Alexander (Statyra, Miss Milder[6]) in a luxurious sable fur, the passionate Schulz[7], or the beautiful Seidler[8] in women's hats. How Milder performs her exalted solo, Schulz sings through her passionate scene, close by or behind her turn male or female dancers, the men in linen jackets or greatcoats, the ladies in light and not at all costly morning dress; they practice their *entrechats* and their twirls on one foot with the other raised at a perpendicular. In the middle of all this sounds the "encore!" of the director. It is a charivari to the eye and ear, as if one were to take the comprehensible actions of many persons, chop them up, and mix them all together. Above it all reigned unmoved and undisturbed the will of the One. He would not rest until every bow-stroke, every breath of the winds and singers, every movement on the stage entirely corresponded to his intention, and the whole stood before him like a body cast in bronze and animated through magic.

No greater contrast could be found than that between Spontini's and Weber's direction, which I was able to later observe during his *Euryanthe*. Spontini was everything, word and gesture and look, absolute command, the orchestra was his tool; every player contributed his will and feelings to the will of the conductor. Weber, who had had long experience as a director (while Spontini had first taken over personal direction in Berlin), led his orchestra in a reliably human and yet completely secure way, in the way that a thoroughly talented and spirited player improvises at the piano. Thus the manners of the two men and their works were also reflected in their directing.

I have already remarked, that the high point for Spontini's activity was Carnival, and that his operas had been the true festival operas. Beethoven's *Fidelio*, or what this immortal might still have been able to create for the stage, -- Weber's operas with all their excellent qualities would have been far from so appropriate for the taste of the court at that time, direct toward brilliance and the strictness of military parades and exercises as were the heroic images that Spontini unrolled before us. Amazingly, his entire life prior to this point had prepared him for this, even created him for it.

Certainly he came from the high school of drama, from Paris. In Italy he had (I have studied the scores myself) practiced all the arts of the creator of the new Italian opera long before Rossini did) – what can one offer to the fatherland-less Italians, beyond sweet oblivion? In France he found a nation

---

[6] Anna Milder-Hauptmann, 1785-1838, operatic soprano resident in Berlin from 1815. The work being performed is Spontini's *Olimpie*.
[7] Josephine Schulz, 1791-1880, a soprano much associated with Italian repertoire.
[8] Caroline Seidler-Wranitzky, 1794-1872.

that is certainly the busiest and most active, and consequently the most qualified for the drama, a people already dramatic in nature, and a people created for the stage in that sense. This had long been evident in its tragedies in strong, simple, always recurring forms, unseduced by the fantastic breadth, the richness of ideas, the depth of feeling of the Germans and Britons - and had thus created favorable bases for the operas of Lully, Gluck and Spontini; for the fickle art of tones requires a firm foundation for it not to become incoherent or pointless on the stage. And this nation of the stage was at that time entirely full of Napoleon; the late offspring of the Roman Caesars had irresistibly impressed his mark on all of life.

Thus was Spontini's path laid out. The Roman Empire, impressed on the French through its Napoleonic renewal, military and courtly brilliance in exhaustible splendor, heroism, *la gloire de la grande nation*, rulers and conspiracies and court intrigues, the prince's daughter or other high-born lover paired with the hero, or offered as a prize – let us say *l'amante*, for it was not what we Germans call love, it was a union of convenience, *tendresse* and perfumed grace, in comparison to the natural and vigorous love of the German or British poets as the graces of a ballet dancer would be to a Grecian Hebe[9]. If one were to add, as well, an acting order of high priests, and the accessory of the always admiring people, change the scene occasionally (as the ancient Romans loved to do as well) to the fabulous Orient, and agree, that these French in general are only able to see and transplant themselves: thus one has the entire content of Spontini's dramas before one; therein he lived; the age, his first and his second fatherlands had not been able to offer him anything higher, and have until this moment not achieved anything higher. Thus his task was taken on by Spontini with fire, with evident power, with Italian/musical naturalness and complete French-Napoleonic vehemence. His marches, his warriors' choruses had a world-conquering stride, and entered every army even without the world being conquered, his ballets endlessly shimmered and swayed, just like Napoleonic court festivals, back and forth with coquettish allure and military bravado, his clergy (no matter which religion) solemnized the *sacred rite* with all the anointing and courtliness and stealthy exaltation, that the artist observed in the life around him. The hero, the priest, *l'amante*, — these were the characters that were so firmly pronounced for the composer that each one was already clearly marked in the first measures of the overture. Throughout everything however – in the beat of the march, in the sharply measured dance rhythms, in the biting *sforzatos* in the violas, in the loud cries of the piccolos and brass, in the impetuous unremitting recitatives between the movements – drove the constant "en avant!" of the Napoleonic army on the field of war. We Germans,

---

[9] The goddess of youth.

who had broken the yoke, were still able to bear the echo for a long time, while the French had to overcome the comfortable bed of the Restoration opera.

Such a one had Spontini become, and he was it entirely. One cannot say that he was true to his task – he was one with it – it was the content of his life and spirit, it alone, and it entirely.

That it might have taken entirely different directions, perhaps with much deeper content, was just as incomprehensible to him as it was at the bottom of the hearts of all the French.

In Paris he was favored by Josephine, and commissioned by Napoleon to compose *Fernand Cortez*, the Spanish were to be elevated, during the entry of a Napoleonic dynasty with recollections of their old heroic age, a thought, which was quickly abandoned as soon as they themselves rose to a new one. When Josephine had to make way for the new wife, and move back to Malmaison, Spontini dared, against the will of the Emperor, to want to show his true faithfulness to her. Suddenly (as he told me several times) Napoleon came from a side door into the waiting room, where Spontini was waiting by himself. "*Que faites vous ici?*" he shouted; "*Sire,*" answered Spontini, "*Que faites vous ici?*" Napoleon turned away at the mention of his own unquenchable feelings. — Even if the story was only the fantasy of the composers, even so it remains characteristic.

Such preparations for his effects corresponded to the situation here in the most desirable way. He found here a rich orchestra, which in his hands soon achieved the power and unity that were indispensable for his works and benefited others; the theater chorus, mostly made up of singers with musical talent and good training, was just as superior to the Paris Opera chorus as German choral composition is to the French. Then, however, a ring of the most important male and female singers gathered around him, which was more richly useful, since the individuals were strongly differentiated one from another. Among the men, the tenor Bader[10] towered over the others; a voice at once powerful and insinuating like the sound of silver, made for heroic roles, and through deep feeling warmed and inclined to every mood. In addition there was a play and power in facial expressions and gestures that would have honored an actor of the first rank, but was without peer among singers. I saw him first, when he was in full possession of his vocal powers, in *Ferdinand Cortez*. He masterfully performed this first of Spontini's heroic roles. When he addressed the mutinous soldiers, who all wanted to return home from a strange and foreign land, when he finally shouted, with a lion's pride and resounding power of tenfold trumpets the famous

"Ich bleibe hier!',

---

[10] Carl Adam Bader, 1789-1870.

everyone felt that all these warriors should rather fall at his feet and die, rather than abandon him. — Decades later I saw him once again in the same role, the power of youth was broken, the voice had lost its power, it could no longer make the melody effective in its entirety, but only in a few moments; in the stormy moments, where the warrior-chorus interrupts it blow by blow, one was unable to hear it. And yet the performance was gripping; his acting, his gestures filled out for our fantasy what was missing for our ears, we felt and believed that we had taken in everything. That is the mark of a truly artistic character, that his spirit completes what material strength is unable to provide.

The most prominent among the women was Milder, a sublime figure modeled after the antique model, with a voice that joined the power of marble with her sweet gentleness; she unmistakably owed the high points of her artistic achievements to Spontini. One may call this singer, without doing her injustice, Spontini's creation. True, she had been already generally beloved and admired in Vienna prior to her move to Berlin. But in which roles? In *The Swiss Family*[11] and *Fidelis* [i.e. *Fidelio*][12]– both operas which, their musical content put aside, especially the latter one, were little designed to allow the dramatic power of the singer to come forward. True, she was admired in Gluck's parts, and often brought out deep effects in them, but she did not penetrate to the souls of the great Germans. She created individual moments – these were the peak moments of passion and dramatic decision – with great power; here she was shattering, ravishing, entirely worthy of the great master. But for Gluck the individual moment is never the main thing, but each part, through the whole scene, indeed, through the entire drama is a single, entirely indivisible effusion, each individual moment only making its impression within the flow of the whole. And that she never achieved; between that high point and the next, she descended to rhetorical rest; only her means, the wonderful voice and her antique-sculptural posture and movement, ennobled these intermediate moments as well. That highlighting, however, is once more Spontini's own, in the Romanesque nature and manner; one imagined that one felt its effect and instructions throughout. It was different in Spontini's role. One needed to have seen here in Olympia, in the temple scene in Ephesus. The broad space of the temple (created by Schinkel[13] after what has come down from antiquity) gradually filled with the crowd of the people, the sacrificial virgins, the consecrating priests, circling around twenty blazing altars. The troops of warriors in brass of Prince Cassander and

[11] *Die Schweizer Familie*, an 1809 *Singspiel* by Joseph Weigl.
[12] Beethoven wrote the part of Leonore in *Fidelio* for Milder.
[13] Karl Friedrich Schinkel, 1781 – 1841, was an architect as well as stage designer, and was largely responsible for redesigning and rebuilding Berlin and other Prussian towns after the Napoleonic Wars..

Antigonus, preparing for war, march in with weapons clanging, everything gleamed and echoed with the sacrificial dances, with the processions, with the threatening troops of warriors, with the powerful singing of the choruses marching toward each other; the whole stage, which was much more spacious than now, was filled with these troops. Then the high priest comes forth and announces: the seer (the still unrecognized widow of Alexander, Statyra – for her, and for all, Cassander erroneously is held to be the murderer of Alexander) must be brought forth from the hidden vaults of the temple to consecrate the union of Olympia, the daughter of Alexander. Now one hears in the distance the long-drawn-out lamenting and the sad question of Statyra: Who calls her forth from the night of her mourning to the hated light? Involuntarily a path forms through the onlooking crowd which fills the stage, extending diagonally from the background to the altar in the foreground, giving space for the seer to slowly progress to where the priest and the lovers await her. The singing of the choruses, the great orchestra have sunken to softly whispered tones, and to a breathless stillness. Then the harsh words of the high priest break the stillness: you are summoned, to consecrate the union of Olympia and the Prince – Cassander!

"Cassander" and once again "Cassander!!" Statyra calls with the tones of the angriest horror – and with the call the whole chorus breaks into the fiercely angry exclamation "Cassander!" and the entire over-full orchestra boils over, filled with anger and untamed. But one only hears her, only perceives her cry, as it penetrates the deadly silence. And the figure of the seer, although once bent in scorn and horror, has become enormous. — This was no longer the classic-tranquil Milder, it was the glowing breath of Spontini, which breathed from her mouth at the shaken listeners. And in this most passionate of outbreaks no violence, no forcing of the vocal organ was perceptible; the voice preserved its full euphony, but transformed from feminine mildness to demonic force. It was not corporal, but spiritual, the highest excitement.

Just as Spontini had a conditioning and shaping effect on his orchestra, and on his singers, so also on the scenic presentation of his operas. In this regard Schinkel, the painter of the Temple at Ephesus, was of invaluable assistance. Schinkel's constructions, along with their incomparable traits, demonstrate a very questionable feature. The artist has often permitted more to his free-ranging fantasy than the architect is allowed: he has sometimes put the goal of construction, usefulness, second to appearance – beauty; he has built from outside to inside, rather than from inside to outside. Nature has taken the wiser way with her creations: she first determines the essence of each creation, this essence determines the necessary structure, and it is this that leads to the external appearance. Schinkel, spiritually intoxicated by the beauty of

Hellenic and Roman architecture, deviated more often than is proper from the prescription shared with us by Nature, in the imitation of those forms which are illuminating for all ages. This was generally not actual imitation or repetition of forms, but much more a striving after the same effect of the beautiful in the beautiful. One might thus call his architecture, where this deviation appears, decorative. What must seem problematic for the architect, stood in good stead, where the purpose was decoration, for operatic works – and more so than for operas in general, those by Spontini, which in an entirely Roman vein chose classical antiquity and the East for their settings, and external magnificence and splendor as their garb, so that it could not miss. Here Schinkel's creative fantasy was very helpful. Spontini's operas gave him the richest opportunity for display; and once again, Spontini found in him assistance which was indispensable, and truly invaluable.

Simple brilliance, and the familiar gold spread over walls and ceilings did not do this; even simply external brilliance can and must have poetry, so that it is the reflection of inner majesty. Thus it was displayed in the temple, imbued with soft moonlight, where the solemn song of the vestals was intoned; thus, in the Temple of Diana at Ephesus, where the pomp of Asia is moderated by Greek grace; thus, in the residence of the genius-king in *Alcidor*[14]. It was built upon the clouds; a vast circle of columns of living fire surrounded the stage in the heavens, and took up rising genii, while from the distance the stars shone mildly in.

Most intimately fused were the fairy-like brilliance and intimately poetic music in *Nurmahal*. The princess is separate from her beloved spouse due to jealousy, and precisely at this moment their kingdom of Kashmir is celebrating the annual Rose Festival. The couple reign widely separated from each other, he upon the dais built of shields and pieces of weapons, she, opposite him, on the throne surrounded by roses. Between the two is the noise of the drunken pleasures of the people, singing and dancing, merry and richly adorned. Next it becomes gradually quieter in the choruses and the sparkling orchestra; have they noticed the separation of the beloved monarchs? And even the dance stumbles and sinks into a quiet rocking back and forth. Then, finally, one hears the half-stifled noise of the inner woe and heart-rending lament from the lips of the far-separated spouses. Now that chorus and orchestra are entirely mute, the words of both shake on a continuously sounding seventh (e-d) which is the interval of painful longing that cannot be hushed. But what cares the crowed for the sorrow of the lonely rulers? In a new upsurge, the joyful pleasure of the festival dance sounds once more, and buries the sighs of painful love. No German composer

---

[14] Premiered in Berlin, 1825.

(not to mention from abroad) could have expressed this moment more deeply and inwardly! I mention this point out of personal preference for it. However, it is far from the only one that presents a tender and inward spiritual life. But the basic character of Spontini does not lie in these moments, but rather in those that contain heroism, the brilliance of rulers, and the conventional French traits of celebration, priestliness, and tenderness. Thus, one must recognize, that Frederick William III with his love for military brilliance and his desire to have festival operas that were shimmering with magnificence and richly provided with ballet could have made no better choice for the purpose than Spontini. For the friends of pure music, however, many wishes remained unfulfilled. It was impossible for the Italian Spontini to replace or complete Gluck, who was unforgettable for the Germans, and even for those who responded to Spontini's essence, without making comparisons, the inclusion of endless masses of Ballet (for example, in Cortez), which from a formal point of view obliterated the previous portion of the drama, was disturbing and off-putting.

Thus Spontini was called to Berlin. It must seem strange to those familiar with Prussian practices that he did not serve as a true civil servant in the service of the King, but rather in a strictly contractual relationship. The agreement was arranged by the then-Minister of War v. Witzleben[15].

In this beginning of Spontini's relationship lay the hidden seeds for those disagreements which awaited the artist in Berlin, and which finally had to lead to his being the target of the most shameful slander. If his much-envied reputation, his high position, his sizeable salary and his often imperial bearing had to provoke dissension and hatred, so it soon happened that his official position contained an insurmountable contradiction. He was chief of the opera without restriction – but this opera belonged to the Royal theater, which also included theater and ballet; and this whole was controlled by a general intendant – thus, one chief set against the other. For according to his appointment and his experiences in Paris, where he had been familiar with opera and theater as entirely separate institutions, Spontini could scarcely view himself as anything else than the unrestricted arbiter for the opera; the general intendant however, likewise had to see himself as director of the whole, and thus also of Spontini. From this arose endless disputes between Spontini and the general intendants, (first Count Brühl, later Count Redern[16]) which could not remain hidden from the public, and which had to lead to dissension, and even hatred.

---

[15] Karl Ernst Job-Wilhelm von Witzleben, 1783–1837, Prussian minister of war; Witzleben's otherwise entirely military career gave no hint of any artistic leanings.
[16] Friedrich Wilhelm von Redern, 1802-1883, took over control of the theaters from Brühl in 1832.

At the outset, however, the seeds of this division remained unnoticed. King Frederick William III remained the most ardent friend and admirer of the operas of Spontini; he was never or rarely absent during their performances, was often present at the dress rehearsals, seen on the stage amidst the chorus of vocalists, and applauded warmly. The court, at least in general, joined in; boxes and pit were filled evening after evening with enthusiastic listeners; that part of the public, which was less satisfied with the music, and preferred German masterworks (particularly those of Gluck), was attracted by the brilliance of the productions and the shimmer of Spontini's ballets. Theses performance served, during the entire period of the King's reign, as real festival operas in the place of those brilliant court festivals to which people were accustomed in Vienna, Paris, and other royal capitals; and in fact, they were, by virtue of their splendor, precisely more appropriate than other works that might be deeper in their content.

Despite all this the pleasure in the music of Spontini was still not enough. No battalion could march in Berlin, and perhaps in the entire kingdom, without music by Spontini; every melody from his operas had, if it were at all possible, to converted into a march. And the balls as well, particularly the court balls, rustled with tunes by Spontini.

There was an individual sign of this widespread participation in Spontini's compositions, at least for those movements that were in any way appropriate. The music publisher Adolf Martin Schlesinger[17], then (and still today) the most active music publisher in Berlin and one of the most well-respected in Germany, busied himself in publishing all the Spontini operas, even the later ones, which visibly did not achieve as much success as their predecessors, for Schlesinger, who was unjustly considered to be simply a speculative businessman, cherished and preserved for the master, until the last moment, a truly enthusiastic friendship, I might even say a tenderness, in which not even the famous lovers' quarrels were not lacking. Now it was not enough, however, for the publisher to issue the piano reductions of the operas; the most accessible movements – overtures, marches, ballets – were issued in every possible arrangement: for orchestra, wind ensemble, quartet, etc. I was present when a chamber musician with an accompanist walked into Schlesinger's establishment and offered him the overture to *Olimpie*, at that time the most popular piece of music: arranged for two flutes. Schlesinger, who could be extraordinarily cranky, and probably thought of the request as an insult to Spontini, had already given the customer a very black look, when I suggested that we could certainly hear the arrangement. And so it was played (the visitors had brought their flutes with them); the old

---

[17] Schlesinger, 1769-1838, published many of Beethoven's works, as well as music by Weber, Mendelssohn, Cherubini, Hummel and Löwe.

gentleman nodded his head on the measure with a friendly grin, and the overture to *Olimpie* and the Diadochi appeared, arranged for two flutes.

However, from very early on nearby observers could have become disconcerted that, alongside all this support and admiration there was growing resistance, increasingly sharp and persistent, hatred, and ever more prominent and undisguised hostility, for which there were many occasions, none of them significant individually, but threatening due to their number. People envied Spontini's reputation, and did not hesitate to spread the story: the *Vestale* – his first work to be a success in Paris – did not belong to him at all, but was instead from the pen of young Italian, who had perhaps created it at Spontini's side, before he had become well-known. This foolish fable found not a few believers. Where the other works came from, which are so intellectually similar to that first one, as one Gluck or one Mozart opera is to another by the same author – was not considered.

The poor, sweet child of pain, this *Vestale*! Thus it was supposed to have been plagiarized! And upon its appearance the musicians of Paris (including Cherubini) did everything to dispute the prize for the composer. The masters of music theory noted I don't know how many technical errors; the connoisseurs claimed that his style was unheard of. For in general the dear children of men always yearn insatiably for the new and original – the world cannot live and exist without it. But when the truly original appears before our foolish eyes, then it is misunderstood and if possible avoided, just as the favorite child Elpore is misunderstood and rejected by its father Epimetheus in Goethe's *Pandora*[18], as soon as it comes closer to its yearning desire.

It is certain, and Spontini told me several times with grateful words, that only Napoleon's personal intervention was responsible for the awarding of the prize, and that thus the great warrior and emperor was responsible for the basis of his artistic reputation.

But at the time many thought it unacceptable for a foreigner, a Frenchman, as people were happy to call Spontini in those circumstances, at the top of a German musical institution.*[19]* Some would have preferred Weber, others Spohr,

---

[18] A fragmentary play by Goethe, published in 1810.

[19] The fact that Spontini's status as a foreigner led to certain discomforts in his performance of his position cannot be denied. They had do with the fact that the Maestro was not fluent in the German language; but how many French and Italians are? More than once I heard Spontini's communication with the orchestra during rehearsals. He wanted to speak German; but can we always have what we want? "Meine Erren! (he began) il faut rémarquer, dass der forte doit être; , . ," and then he went on in a classical mixture of Italian and French; Spontini thought that he had been speaking excellent German; the excellent concertmaster Möser, father of the now-famous violinist, explained and interpreted what Spontini had and had not said. But what do such trivialities mean? Never was a German-speaking director better understood and followed.

many now forgotten would have preferred themselves in this post. It must be admitted that Spontini had not penetrated as deeply into the spirit of German music as one might have wished. But at the same time one could not have named in his time a single Italian or French who had penetrated more deeply, or even as deeply as Spontini did. The only one, who had modeled himself on the Germans, had been Cherubini; but he at that time had retired from his more important activities, and had, through continual references to other musicians, first Haydn, then Gluck, and finally his own student Auber, who had been little valued by him up until that time, lost so much of the energy of his original work, that it was impossible for him to stand next to Spontini, no matter how much he surpassed the latter in compositional skill. However that may be, this foreigner administered the Berlin Opera with noble non-partisanship. Along with his operas, which claimed priority, there was not a season that did not include performances of four or five operas by Gluck, three or four operas by Mozart, Beethoven's *Fidelio*, Cherubini's *Wasserträger* and *Lodoiska*, and one or two works by other composers. It is evident that Weber and Spohr were not lacking either. Spontini had stronger resistance against less talented Germans and foreigners, indeed, in this area he committed thoughtless acts of rudeness; such as that which he threw against a young singer, who wished to appear in one of these works: *que voulez-vous de ces cochonneries- là!* Such generally thoughtless expressions – but, it is important to note, used in intimate conversation and counting on official reticence, were, however, not simply taken by those affected as insult towards their work, but rather understood and more broadly spread around, in a blacker interpretation by the entirely non-partisan as vilification of German music (—!—).

And also outside his official activities there was no lack of expression, which though honorable, and even spoken with good intentions, had dissension as their consequences. When the young Mendelssohn brought Spontini his opera, *Die Hochzeit des Camacho*, for examination (it was accepted and performed, but soon after was dropped again), Spontini, who lived on the Gensd'armenmarkt opposite one of the churches which had been built by Frederick the Great after Roman models, took the young composer [20] by the hand, led him to the window, and said, pointing to the church tower: *"Mon ami, il vous faut des idées, grandes comme cette coupole!"* He wanted to give the young man incentive, but his family, which from the beginning had belonged to the enlightened opponents of the composer, only were deeply insulted, and the great following of this house shared the opinion. If Spontini had certainly judged without ill will and with

---

[20] He told me about it himself immediately after the interaction.

objectivity, then the incapacity of the French or Italian to recognize German art and give it is true worth showed otherwise. Thus it was impossible for him, who had grown up with the strict divisions between forms of the Roman school, where the mixture of grand opera and operetta (*opera seria*, and *opera buffa*) had never been understood and recognized, to comprehend the essence of German romantic opera, and thus the style of C. M. Weber. Weber's operas were performed under Spontini, but never were fully appreciated by him. In this respect yet another adverse circumstance entered the picture. The opponents of Spontini gathered instinctively around the name of Weber, although not he, but rather Gluck, or if need be Cherubini, belonging to the same type of opera as Spontini could have been used. But, a popular and contemporary composer was needed; and so it had to be Weber. Weber had long understood the situation. He himself said that the success of his *Freischütz* was partially owing to the opposition against Spontini; indeed, he appeared laudably in public newspapers against those who were zealous to praise at the cost of Spontini. Along with all these adversaries there was also the crowd of "connoisseurs" whose only measure for opera was Mozart and Mozart alone, for whom neither national style and the nature of the Italians, nor the entirely divergent direction of Mozart came into consideration. They wanted music - and thought, as far as they could, of drama. They yearned for Mozartian refinement and inwardness— and he, very like Napoleon – required outward material might.

Thus it was particularly the loudness, the noise of Spontini's music, which caused irritation. Those innocent ones! They had not yet experienced *Les Huguenots* and Wagner.

The one, however, who gave popular expression to this critique of the superfluous, was Zelter. As he, as the story went, came out of some opera of Spontini, the curfew had just passed. "Praise God!" he is supposed to have exclaimed, "now I can hear soft music once more."

What was involved was the ill-fated influence of Spontini's character, as it must unavoidably have been constructed in Italy and Paris. Alongside the elevated self-regard of the artist, which sometimes degenerated into the strangest exaggeration, an irritability and suspiciousness was at work in him, incited by the sight of Parisian games of partisanship and intrigue, which must often have embittered both him and others. He had found an opponent in the critic Rellstab[21], and had transformed him, through successful complaining about his judgment, into a deadly enemy. In vain were the encouragement and advice of this writer and other friends for him to let the efforts of the critic pass

[21] Ludwig Rellstab, 1799-1860, the most influential, and at times provocative, critical voice of the mid-nineteenth century.

over unnoticed; slander and insults will disappear by themselves, or cause no damage, if you can manage to ignore them. These truths were ignored, and the highly placed Spontini continually bled from the waspish stings of the petty, to whom he had to bow so far that only the sting could reach him.

Along with this inconsiderate irritability there was a suspicion, already inoculated and grown large in Paris, which, without particular choice and consideration turned against the first and best, against friends, against associates, and injured many, probably turning them into enemies. I myself was a target of this, when I handed him my first work *"The Art of Song*[22]*"* as a token of pure appreciation. In the consideration of the most important vocal composer, which this book contains, I had labeled him according to my view of the time (which continues unchanged) as a son of Napoleon. I immediately received a reply, which expressed his thanks, but then he asked: what did this reference to Napoleon mean? *Serait-ce par allusion à la fin désastreuse de ce grand homme?* I cannot say that the unexpected question was hurtful, since it did not have the slightest influence on my convictions or beliefs. Much later, through evidence of truly friendly support on the part of Spontini, I was convinced that for him as well this wariness on his part was only a passing mood .

Indeed, a strange incident proved to me that this suspicious inclination was only something imposed and foreign to his original nature, which was a childish and indeed unthinking trust that was the fundamental tone of this unique man. When he, in the course of his official duties, had once prepared Gluck's *Armida* with great care, the thought came to him, unquestionably out of good intentions, to strengthen Gluck's instrumentation, which in general is so well-considered, so chaste and appropriate to its purpose, through the addition of new instruments. To my concerns he gave the answer: "Gluck would have orchestrated it thus, if he had been writing today". The Crown Prince at the time, later Frederick William IV, who had a particular sense and understanding for German music, and particularly for Gluck, had a different point of view. Spontini presented to me an autograph letter, written in French, from the Crown Prince, unmistakably very satisfied with it, and not hurt, but finding himself praised. And what had the Crown Prince written? He had pressingly requested the Maestro to leave Gluck's instrumentation alone, and not to mix in anything foreign, no contribution of his own. "Beryl", he said literally, "is a very fine stone; but one takes care not to set it next to diamonds." The obvious recognition that these words contained only a reprimand, and not flattery, had not been able to penetrate Spontini's otherwise keen mind due to his confident assumption that the Crown Prince would have only wanted to flatter him.

---

[22] *Die Kunst des Gesanges, Theoretisch-Praktisch*, Berlin, 1826.

Now that Frederick William III had entered, Spontini's strongest position was breached. Now all the firing lines of long-nourished hatred flowed together. All that was lacking was a single spark to set things ablaze. And that did not take long.

During one of these disagreements between the head of the theater and the head of the opera Spontini was shown by the latter to have been in his cabinets, and this reproof, already very damaging to the highly placed man in itself, found its way into the newspapers as well, in the guise of an official announcement. Spontini believed that he had been forced to make an official reply, and claimed that he was in the right with the expression that this had to be the case, or "the sacred word of two Kings of Prussia" [23] would be forgotten. This public statement by Spontini was viewed as *lèse-majesté*, and was to be subject to criminal investigation.

It was Alexander von Humboldt[24], who was responsible for quashing the investigation, before it had taken formal shape. He caused it to be obvious that a even a possible acquittal of a complaint, a judgment, the imposition of a prison sentence of the world-famous man, whom the grace of the previous King had called to Berlin, and given such a high position, would be an embarrassment. For Spontini could not, given his pride, ask for a pardon, and enforcement of a sentence would not correspond to the disposition of the reigning king, nor could it be seen by the eyes of a watchful Europe with anything other than painful astonishment.

It was not so easy to appease the mood of the public, once it had been aroused from all sides. Parties hostile to Spontini immediately seized the opportunity; they claimed to be zealous for the respect owed to the King, and wanted to make the artist in his official position repent for what he ostensibly had committed against the King – a deed, that was immeasurably far from Spontini's way of thinking, which was royalist through and through; only the defense of his right and the rejection of an injustice, as he viewed the matter, which he had to find completely unacceptable for his artistic and official dignity, had driven him in this direction.

But the untamable hostility towards him ended in a different way.

When Spontini had ascended to the podium to direct Don Juan (which did not belong to his official duties at all, but had been taken on by him simply out of respect for the work and the public), he was met by such a furious din of

---

[23] The words in parentheses have no claim to exactness; the precise words used have escaped me.
[24] Humboldt, 1769-1859, a world-famous naturalist and explorer, enjoyed a pension from the Prussian crown and, although not often in the country before the end of the 1820s, considerable influence at court.

stamping, whistling, and shouting, that the opera house seem to shake all the way to its foundations, and the beginning of the overture was entirely drowned out. The repeated attempt to be heard was in vain; they finally began (perhaps the most embittered were afraid that the master might still be able to be heard, or that the excited crowed might still have a moment of sense) to throw things at his head. He had to leave his seat and escape the outbreaks of rage via the passageway that leads from the orchestra into the spaces under the stage. He had to leave both his position and Berlin.

His later life was empty of deeds, for his power was broken. His proud heart cannot have been accustomed to reproach. That he later was granted the rank of a count by the Pope, and even took on a new name along with this, may have been occasioned by ambition, but perhaps by something entirely different. It is enough, that he was buried as he descended from his seat.

We were able to topple him. Were we able to replace him? The history of music will give the answer.

We were able to topple him! Him, not his works. Have our German musical comrades at least learned from him?

Wagner, whom he had once warned against as strange, certainly. According to his own free admission he intentionally modeled his Rienzi after the Spontinian manner; that is, not imitated or borrowed, but rather as one artist is the successor to another, as Mozart was the successor to Haydn, and Beethoven the successor to both; each learning from the other, each preserving his own manner. That which was closest to day: the fuller, often over-full instrumentation, the frequent overbalancing of the material, the heightened brilliance and splendor of the scenery and costumes; all this could not go unnoticed, and seen over and over again, made its effect, and asked to be heightened further.

Only two things remained unstriven for, or unattained, and lie in the distance. One is the refinement that belongs to all of Spontini's creations, and is not denied for a moment. Throughout we have princeliness, heroism, warriorlike brilliance, the magnificent rule of spirituality as a strongly established and highly placed power in the state; even love does not appear in his passionate guise, but conditioned by the attitude and moderation of princely status; even the conspirator always appears with his brilliant followers in a princely and elevated way. The composition corresponds to this throughout. True, it only seldom reaches the hidden depths of the human breast; but it knows how to set the brilliant exterior to music that is always appropriate and often highly vivid.

What a difference between him – or his great predecessor Gluck as well, whom he named as his teacher many times in my presence, and whom he tried to follow in as much as it was possible for the Italians and French in comparison to the faithful and true Germans – and for the majority of German opera composers before and after those two!

For the German, as things are today, great dramatic life, that is, the demands of the scene, comes after their beloved music. It is easy for reality, with its demands and conditions, to seem too raw and terrible for him; lovingly and soon he years for sounds of strings, which seduces him away from all that, and lulls him into sweet, if empty, dreams. And because things are – in general! – that way, thus even for the opera composer acting, or drama, the scene, or unyielding reality disappears from his mind, he practices writing fugues and canons, plays endless string quartets, pours out his private feelings in maudlin songs, - and thus believes, in God's name, to be completely prepared for the opera, and for the drama!

May God improve matters! And he will – we will improve things! The hour of renewed and higher existence for our people brings fresh life into all our veins, and even to those of the drama and the opera.

END OF VOLUME ONE

VOLUME II

Gaspare Luigi Pacifico Spontini (14 November 1774 – 24 January 1851)

CHAPTER 1

MY RELATION TO SPONTINI

Until my move to Berlin I had not gotten to know anything by Spontini beyond the overtures for *La Vestale* and *Fernand Cortez*, and three duets from the latter opera; that is, I still did not know him at all. For, just as is the case with Gluck, likewise with Spontini, one can only comprehend his music in its proper place, on the stage. For him as well, the real task was already no longer the music, but the drama – the dramatic effect. Now his opera began to have an effect on me, beginning with Cortez.

It was at this time, 1823 I believe, that I was introduced to Spontini. From the salon, decorated in the Parisian taste, I was led into his workroom. I was introduced to him as a friend of music. He met me in a friendly way in his usual house-wear of light white fabric. Naturally, I soon led the conversation to *Fernand Cortez*, which I had seen shortly before. I spoke to him of the impressions that were entirely new to me. "However", I added, "at least the situation on the stage was not new to me. We Germans have an opera of similar bent in Winter's *Unterbrochnes Opferfest;*[1] it is just that that one takes place among the weaponless Peruvians, while your Cortez plays instead in the glittering Mexico in the battle against the warlike group of Indians. One is sure, that Winter belongs to a now peaceful people, but you, in contrast, worked under Napoleon's eyes." This turn of phrase seems to have pleased him. He told me, as mentioned earlier, that Napoleon himself had commissioned him for a composition that would arouse new heroic feelings in the Spanish, "who belong to France", as he still said in 1823 in an entirely Napoleonic way. – "For", he added, "Napoleon's mission was not, as people always claim, conquering; that was only the means for his end. His mission was to awake the sleepy and backward peoples to new life and progress." I felt that I did not have the right to answer in a contradictory way, and underlined the observation that they served Napoleon's goals only against their wills, and only so. From this first visit on I remained in unbroken contact with Spontini, and was presented to his wife and into the circles of the most well-known, or drawn into the friends of the house.

In this house I met many attractive and important personalities. But it is understandable that none of these had so much power of attraction for me as

---

[1] Peter von Winter's *Das Verbrochene Opferfest*, premiered Vienna, June 1796, and set in conquistador-era Inca Peru.

did Spontini himself. Even the sound of his voice, and especially his singing, when he would now and then let one hear a little passage be heard in order to clarify something which particularly moved him, did not fail to animate me in a lively and sympathetic way. His voice was a high tenor, extraordinarily soft and ingratiating, with a metallic ring like a softly-blown trumpet (*cantabile dolcissimo*) at the same time. His pronunciation of French was not at all pure, as I had learned before and after from highly-educated French and Polish; it gave evidence of the fact that he was Italian, but his diction also had something that was entirely departing from the social way of speaking. I once dared to remark to him: that his speech gave me an impression of the manner of speaking of Talma,[2] the hero of the old French tragedy. This did not seem to displease him, but he replied, without making a direct reference to the comparison, that I would find the best evidence for the manner of French tragedy in Gluck's recitatives, which he himself had studied and which he sought to emulate, naturally without giving up his own individuality.

I should not omit mention that I also was once guilty of a small perfidy towards him.

Spontini had chosen Handel's *Messiah* for one of his *Penitential-Day* concerts, which had been performed not long before then by the Singakademie. I tried to get him to choose the Alexander's Feast instead, and he paid me little attention. Now came the first rehearsal, and one remembers the wonderful chorus *Weck' ihn auf aus seinem Schlummer!* [*Wake him from his sleep!*], that chorus, which according to Reichardt's spirited words is well suited to wake princes from their beds of heavy sleep. The basses from the orchestra, supported by the waking stroke of the timpani, and all the other instruments that can be added, repeat incessantly (this is a so-called basso ostinato), a short figure, which continually plays tonic, dominant and subdominant D…A….D…G ….Here one uses according to old habit two timpani on D, A; for the bass tone G one then strikes the timpani truly across the head of the D once again. Spontini easily recognized, on my observation, that it would produce a purer effect to use a third timpani on G. He immediately gave the order to get a third timpani. This, however, may have seemed uncomfortable for Kapellmeister Seidel;[3] he came forward and noted that there is no word about a third timpani in the score; the score, however, was taken from the engraved English edition. I could not so easily let my suggestion be ignored, for I thought it was good, and still today am of the same opinion. At the same time, I realized that explanations based on the meaning of the

---

[2] François-Joseph Talma, 1763-1826.
[3] Friedrich Ludwig Seidel, 1765-1831, organist and opera conductor, became court Kapellmeister in 1822.

work would not be acceptable, and thus only noted entirely in cold blood: if the Kapellmeister would like to see in the original score, he would already find the third timpani. Spontini looked at me, and decided that he had to have a third timpani. Whether and where the original score might be, was something I did not know then, and still do not know.

When I founded the *Berliner Allgemeine Musikalische Zeitung* in 1824, Spontini supported me by sending tickets to his operas and concerts, and provided me with free admission to the rehearsals. Here it was where I could observe him during his directing activities and get a closer idea of his intentions. Without question, a closer acquaintance and interaction with Spontini, along with the increasingly deep study of Gluck, contributed significantly to giving me a distinct view of the dramatic.

Whether in general Spontini really supported that critical undertaking, I do not know. Probably, however, he was in no way indifferent to what the journal reported about his work. He had, since he was not entirely fluent in German, each article read and translated by friends. I still recall, that I once at his request undertook to translate an appraisal of *Olimpie* that I had written into French. Thus I had to experience how difficult it is to translate something going deeply into a subject from German into the infinitely poorer French, without substantively affecting the content or the presentation. I was rather competent in French, but nevertheless had to call on one helper after the other – and it all remained deficient, and clumsy. We all were unsatisfied – except for Spontini. He thought, probably more out of politeness than sincerity, that he should manage from this "piano arrangement" to "decipher" my score.

Finally, however, the journal would give rise to a lamentable suspicion, whose after-effects resounded far afield.

It was a friend, who until then had delighted me with favors and true evidence of inner support, who in a local journal which soon thereafter went under expressed the accusation against me that I was intending by means of an article in journal to topple Spontini, and to become General Music Director in his place. This accusation against me, how strange! — against me, who before and after had tirelessly and steadfastly work for the understanding of Spontini — as I had achieved for myself, and preserve until today! And I, who after his departure from here was the only who was engaged in maintaining his honorable reputation from of misjudgment in the public eye!

My personal disposition would not allow me to reply in any way to such an unworthy and absurd accusation. In vain the publisher of the journal pushed me to break my silence. Soon, however, I learned that Spontini also had in no way remained unaffected by this accusation. Until then he had, when a new opera was staged, sent the score for the work to my residence. Now, just when his *Alcindor*[4] was being given, and I asked in writing for the score, he replied: for the moment he could not spare it, but it was available at his house for me to examine at any convenient hour. I understood, declined the offer, and certain of my memories after hearing the dress rehearsal and the first performance, I gave in my entirely positive report 20 to 30 musical examples. With this I thought the matter was closed.

That was a mistake. The publisher incessantly assailed me to publish a definite explanation, if it were only to calm his friend and mine, as he put it. This I could not understand; it disgusted me to have to still defend character and intellect. The only thing, which I could decide on, was a legal complaint against the accuser. He was, it could not be otherwise, found guilty. He still had the legal means of a further defense available, which at any rate could have led to a mitigation of the situation. He chose this.

Thus he approached me on the street on one dark evening with the words: "Dear friend, you won't do this to me!" He mentioned his family, the danger to his official position. — I replied, that I felt very bad about it, but that according to my juridical understanding did not see what more I could do for him, after the verdict had been issued. He replied that if I did not want to continue the matter against him further, then it would be possible for him to avert the consequences. This I promised to do, and willingly, even though not understanding the situation. For it already really upset me that I had had to go to such ends against a former friend.

Thus, with my silent acceptance the consequences of the verdict were avoided; — in which way is something I prefer not to go into; even the indication of the court involved may be omitted.

The matter was thus (except for my definitive separation from a former friend) resolved without repercussions.

Or rather, so it seemed.

Several years thereafter a certain G. Schilling,[5] supported by a recommendation from the University Music Director Naue in Halle, had won for me a position as collaborator on the *Universallexicon der Tonkunst*. He himself had published a harmony method under the pseudonym of Polyphonomos and had been severely criticized, exactly at the same time that my composition method had been very

---

[4] This work, written to celebrate a Prussian royal marriage, was premiered in May 1825; Weber had contemplated an opera on the same subject.
[5] Gustav Schilling, 1803-1881, whose early career was as a preacher, published from 1834 a multiple-volume musical dictionary that employed some of the leading names of German musical life; after accruing unsustainable debts, he eventually fled to America, where he died.

warmly welcomed. Swiftly he imagined (completely without foundation) that all the unfavorable reviews were either written by me, or at least at my instigation. To fight me off he, rather than contradicting the criticisms, began a repetition of the story of the conspiracy against Spontini, and similar ravings. I said nothing. Later I learned what Goethe had said, when, being told by Zacharias Werner, very upset, about a hateful criticism that he had received, but that he wished to reply to properly. "I", the Prince of Poets noted mildly, "would keep silent". He managed to calm down Werner, and to convince him. "Your excellency is right! I will never reply. They would have to say that I had stolen a silver spoon. Even then I would keep silent!" the poet replied mildly.

Soon I received a letter from Robert Schumann, who was editing the *Neue Zeitschrift für Musik*[6] at the time, and had just given his musico-fraternal support with an evaluation of my first Psalm. He offered me his journal if I wanted to reply to that diatribe. If I should find that unpleasant, as he expected, then he was ready to take up the pen on my behalf. I thanked him cordially for his sentiments, but bade him not to become involved in a matter that was as unworthy of his pen as it was of mine. The honorable Schilling had to get by without a reply.

So that the old saying "*calumniare audacter! semper aliquid haeret*" (slander boldly – something always sticks) would be entirely valid, after a long stretch of years there was a second echo of that lost war-cry. This time it was Dr. Fink,[7] former country parson, now editor of the *Leipziger Musik-Zeitung*. Our views and paths ran generally quite separately, but how my *Musiklehre*[8] was being published by Breitkopf and Härtel at the very same moment where his *Musikalische Grammatik*, a book of a similar nature was supposed to be published, and as I believe, precisely at the same company. At the same time, however, an article had appeared from the pen of a still-living Kapellmeister at one of the first court theaters (at the time a contributor to my journal), which compared my journal with the one from Leipzig, not to the benefit of the latter. For my part I had only much later learned about the essay and its author, but Fink considered that he was entitled to ascribe it, without further ado, to me, and to take his revenge for it, in which he engaged in the same old childish behavior. Naturally I did not think of responding.

[6] Schumann launched the journal in 1834, and resigned the editorship in 1843. The journal still exists.
[7] Gottfried Wilhelm Fink, 1783-1846, was also active as a composer and theologian.
[8] *Allgemeine Musiklehre*, *Leipzig*, 1841, a general textbook on music theory for a wide audience. Not to be confused with his more profound four-volume study *Die Lehre von der Musikalischen Komposition*, Leipzig, 1837-1847. Both these works, which were seen at the time, and since, as Marx's most prominent contributions to German musical life, are not extensively mentioned in these memoirs.

At that time I had a friendly relationship with General von Decker.[9] He was very active as a military writer and teacher, and also, if I am not mistaken, in making improvements to artillery, and widely known in the area of belles lettres through stories and dramas which appeared under the name of "Adalbert vom Thale". He had already at his previous garrison at Königsberg been a lively supporter of my composition method, and had even illustrated the section on keys, chords, in a very sensible way, which looked like the *Citadelle Vauban*,[10] and which he published through Mittler[11] in Berlin. Upon his relocation to Berlin this connection led to a personal association. Scarcely had Decker learned of Fink's omission, he hurried to me.

"Listen to this, friend!" were his first words, "the d—mned punk can't get away with this!"

I thanked him for his support, but calmly explained, that I would never respond to this sort of thing.

"No, that's not possible, it must go entirely differently". In short, he was of the opinion that I had to duel with Fink, indeed, he offered me financial support in the case of a questionable outcome, and said, in the days of the old lord, Frederick William III, the thing would already have been taken care of. In vain I reminded him of the personal connections of the old Fink, and the likelihood of meeting, not him, but the police upon the dueling ground. He had an answer ready for everything, and told me, in order to convince me, of a similar case from his own life.

"When my book on tactics had appeared, an infamous reviewer had behaved just so. Naturally I immediately sent him my card. Now, we were standing there with the pistols on the dueling line, and were ready to start. Then he lowered his pistol, walked up to me, and said: "Sir… I beg you to consider that I am the father of eight children." "Ha! You should have thought of that earlier" said I, and shot him down!"

My excellent, hot-blooded old friend! That was not my way! The student Marx could have, but the Marx who had just recognized his calling, he could not. He had a higher duty, and that you, dear hothead, were not mistaken about that, makes me happy, and I still thank you for it today. — In general this fiery and powder-seeking warrior was the mildest and greatest friend of men. But that

---

[9] Karl von Decker, 1784-1844, a distinguished military man and specialist in formulating notions of guerrilla and partisan warfare after his experiences fighting Napoleon, was also a literary figure, publishing comic plays and a literary supplement to the army periodical.

[10] A star-shaped fortification in Brittany, constructed under Louis XIV.

[11] E.S. Mittler, founded in 1789 in Berlin by Wilhelm Johann Heinrich Dieterici, and which took the name of his son-in-law, Ernst Siegfried Mittler.

is indeed the frightful consequence of the spirit of caste, which the privileged duty to kill in duels ensnares the most clear-sighted and mildest with shackles that they can scarcely release nor destroy. The noblest peoples, the most given to battle, the Greeks and Romans, knew nothing about the private duel. Their lives belonged to the state and to humanity.

I may not leave this surprising matter without giving justice to those who incited it, and to myself.

Regarding myself I must say that I did wrong with regard to Spontini's suspicion by going to court against a man, who had been my friend. Certainly, he had been first to injure the commitment of friends by that public accusation, but the injustice committed by one is for the other no sufficient grounds for ruthlessness. This must be even more true for me since the accusation at the beginning had awakened neither anger nor anxiety.

But as for the other, whose name I do not like to reveal even now, it would do an injustice, if one were to accuse him of intentional and conscious untruth. He was a man of the best character, with excellent spiritual qualities. But he had accustomed himself to let his passion follow the indications of his fantasy without conscious examination – a direction, that hindered him from allowing his excellent gifts to reach their full value.

In this regard a boundless, indeed entirely unstoppable and reckless enthusiasm for Spontini appeared, that even had the peculiar result that he composed much and often – without ever, not even for four measures, being able to free himself from Spontini's manner, no matter how much his ambition generally drove him to seek individuality. He was captured by my essays on Spontini, when he found them favorable, more than was Spontini himself. Nevertheless no new opera appeared without his having striven to cause me to have a good opinion of it. This was always oppressive, since it was my manner and duty to assure the independence of my judgment. This happened most sharply when the performance of Alcindor was approaching. My defense against meddling may have seemed to him to be resistance against his opinion, even against the thing itself. From there to seeking me as an enemy of Spontini, a conspirator, was only a step for his stimulated fantasy. At any rate, a little more patience on my part regarding the unquestionably annoying attempts of the enthusiast would have given no room to his apprehensions, and thus would have throttled the entire batrachomyomachia in its cradle. In this regard, the duty which I had taken on with the founding of the journal was unrelenting seriousness.

Nikolai Koshelev, The Music Lesson (1865)

CHAPTER 2

EXIT FROM A LEGAL CAREER

Alluring and often inspiring, life had shaped itself around me, as we have seen up to this point. However, it was not allure, but rather the ever more strongly rooted conviction that one cannot unify two paths leading in opposite directions from each other, and that what I had ever more clearly recognized as my real calling could only be achieved in the midst of artistic and literary life, which finally convinced me to first take an indefinite leave from the Kammergericht,[1] and finally to resign. The sort of employment that the usual legal career brought with it, and into which E.T.A. Hoffmann had wanted to direct me, had appeared unacceptable to me already in Naumburg. There was still a single direction, which would have put me on a secure economic basis, and would have left me leisure for my work; that was the career of an auditor, and certainly in Berlin. Twice, one after another, such positions opened up. The General Auditor at the time, President von Braunschweig, both times recognized that my application had a good foundation; but both times there were other candidates whom there was reason to prefer for Berlin. But no injustice would be done to me in this case; and so in the first case, an equal position in Erfurt or Magdeburg, in the other, a position as Garrison-Auditor in Stralsund, the latter offered in connection with a position as notary. President von Braunschweig estimated the total income of the position in Stralsund at more than 2,000 thaler. I thanked him – and now accepted my dismissal. For one entirely without means, and who in addition had to support his parents, the decision was far from easy. But to hold a hybrid position indefinitely without substantial effect on my vocation was evidently unfeasible. And how would it have been possible to have made my plans a reality in Stralsund or some other provincial town without a university, without a library, and without an opera!

With my exit, was the time and work that I had invested in my legal career fruitless, entirely lost? — Not at all. Once more I realized, that everything that happens to us, redounds to our own best interests, as long as it is not the result of our own guilt, and when we with unbending will strive through all barriers to the goal that has been set for us, as our conscience and yearning has created it. I was, given my situation and my development, without plan or goal, that I through no fault of my own had received, very much inclined to the fantastic,

[1] The Oberlandesgericht for the state of Berlin.

and averse to strongly held aspirations. What I had received at the gymnasium and the university in terms of training in strict thinking and action had not been sufficient to draw me toward stricter direction and order. Thus, Roman law now came with its iron consequences, and then the practice of the law, in which each deviation was a wrong, a breaking of the law. This double schooling was what I needed to give me strength and the bearing that I needed for my activities. I quit.

And besides, I had already found my inheritance in my musical activities; I had begun to give piano and voice lessons.

I was particularly lucky in this.

I was not a distinguished singer, and had also never trained great singers, nor developed great voices. Only later did I realize that the latter can absolutely not be achieved in the form of private instruction with two, at the most three lessons each week, but rather requires ceaseless training. But I strove to lead each student into a circle of accomplishment for which he had grown according to the capacities of his voice. In this regard I viewed empowering the voice, and developing mind and spirit to be my real task. Here I was certainly not alone. That métier of the voice-builder, who demands exclusively mechanical exercises for two, four or more years, in order to (according to the sublime expression of one among them) build the "Instrument", and then to once again rekindle the long-extinct sparks with indications over every note – strong! hesitating! pushed! melting! sublime! - was at the time not yet in fashion. Under the influence of the composers who had just passed way, or were still living among us, instruction could take place in none other than an artistic way. Thus we teachers prepared whole series of students who all were trained for artistic gifts, and each was maintained according to their spiritual and vocal characteristics, not, as was often the case later, mesmerized according to an invariable formula into a dreary uniformity of voice and understanding. Thus I certainly trained two women singers, who were capable and worthy of singing Handel und Gluck; but also others, who did not progress beyond simple songs.

Even the latter sometimes had its difficulties. In the case of my first vocal student I soon realized that she had no idea at all what she was singing about. I thus required here to tell me the content of the poem each time before hand. We then came around to some setting of the *König von Thule*. In the course of the discussion I came then to the final strophe:

> "Die Augen gingen ihm über, Trank nie einen Tropfen mehr," [His eyes followed it down, and he never more drank another drop] and asked her about its meaning. An ashamed "Ach!" and another "Ach!" came from her anxious breast. Finally, upon my friendly request, the dear child stammered, "He was drunk!" She was just eighteen years old.

As a piano teacher I had at least ten to twenty teachers by my side who far exceeded me in virtuosity, and of whom a portion played annually in public concerts. Nevertheless, fortune smiled on me, so much so that I could be quite satisfied. It was, perhaps, my striving to introduce my students to the mind and spirit of the composer that produced this success. In this area as well a very different spirit was evident in comparison to that of today. Beethoven was probably right concerning his contemptuous anger against piano teachers, whom he viewed in toto as his enemies. He used this word for those players and teachers for whom the piano and technical fluency were paramount, and who for this unthinkingly sacrificed time and nervous energy, mind and true artistic training of those entrusted to them. In those days we did not expect to train everyone who touched the piano into a wonder-virtuoso. For my part, I had established my goal: to make each disciple familiar with the literature of his instrument, independent of that which was necessary for the technical training in terms of finger exercises, and a few etudes, chosen with great consideration, for a very particular purpose, or according to the occasional necessities of the student. Those who did not quit too early, had to become familiar with the works of Beethoven and Bach (Handel's compositions for the keyboard were still remote from me at the time), Haydn and Mozart, and have become acquainted with at least the more important of the works of Dussek, Louis Ferdinand.[2] as well as Moscheles et al. ; — naturally practical performance went hand in hand with theoretical explanation. The material that I later published as a selection from Bach, as well as the explanations regarding it, and to the *Chromatic Fantasy*,[3] has its origins in this period. In this area as well I was certainly not alone among my colleagues. The effort to lead the student to the best, rather than to the most difficult, was quite general.

A third branch of teaching was offered me from the outside; important things would be connected to this. Ludwig Berger,[4] the leading piano teacher in Berlin, widely beloved through his spirited piano compositions and soulful lieder, sent me a number of his women students for instruction in "figured bass". We still believed at that time that this would lead to a deeper understanding of music. Thus I gave one of these ladies after another the conventional instruction in figured bass.

Once a Miss Romberg appeared, once again sent by Berger, and asked for the beloved figured bass instruction. She was one of those notable beauties,

---

[2] Louis Ferdinand, 1772-1806, a prince of Prussia and nephew of Frederick the Great, was a gifted composer whose works, now obscure, were much in vogue at that time and in that place.
[3] Marx published an edition of Bach's *Well-Tempered Clavier* in 1838, and selections of his keyboard works in1844 and 1853.
[4] Ludwig Berger, 1777-1839, counted Mendelssohn and Adolf von Henselt among his pupils.

whose intellectual content does not seem to match one's awareness of her external charms. I then gave her the thin soup of chords and inversions and the mysteries of figures. When however, she at the end of the first month pressed a roll of hard thalers into my hand, I thought I would have to sink into the earth; I was entirely overcome by the feeling of being a thief caught in the act. And was I to give this trusting maiden, noble in appearance and in effort a stone rather than intellectual bread! What did she want, then? She sought insight into the inward life in our art. She wanted to see, if not perhaps to lay her hand on, how the flighty tonal element settled firmly in the human spirit. Did she get that from the dusty junk of figured bass? Had it encouraged me, or, instead, confused and lamed me?

It cost me difficult night of battling and struggling, and then I saw things more clearly. The ways of life, the melodies of one or more voices, which full of blessed peace are companions to each other, or, in the discord of all earthly exist contend and struggle against each other – what I myself had seen and thought as my own leader in the dance of tones: that, that could be of use to her! That was what I had to give her, or flee like a thief before her noble, questioning glance!

The night decided the matter. It brought the seed of the composition method. Perhaps many clever readers later had an inkling in looking through that book that it was not cold understanding, but hot feeling, and a certain indescribable glimmering of beauty, eternally one, which had awakened it. Any sort of personal inclination of a passionate nature was entirely not the case.

The work had still to wait for many years. First I tested my new process with a few students, and then the system was completed in the classrooms of the university. For the time being what was demanded of me in my compositional career was more important. It is self-evident that I never stopped composing. The most important undertaking in this area was the composition of *Psalm 137*[5] for chorus and orchestra. This poem, in which the embers of implacable revenge flamed up, as only the oriental and tortured Hebrew can foster, so enflamed me, that I was able to feel raised up close to the poet. But the artistic creation did not correspond to my spiritual excitement. I myself recognized this, and the work was not made public. A symphony met the same fate.

The most important broadening of my training in composition took place over a long time, almost unawares, in the area of instrumentation. I had heard much, and often fought about Spontini, and had acquired many scores. Among these, the symphonies by Haydn first caused me to reflect. Strange! This old

---

[5] Beginning, "By the waters of Babylon…" This work was not published, but details of its music, based on a copy held by Therese Marx, are given in Hirschberg's article on Marx's compositions.

man with his little orchestra knew how to make such bright colors, to paint with such character, created with his two little trumpets such a roisterous noise, that Spontini's great sound-stage with its twenty-four trumpets could not claim to be more powerful. How did that happen? — He understood, this was my first answer, the art of the painter, how to share out the light, to give the full light at the most important points – and from there down - perhaps not to fall into Rembrandtian darkness, but rather in an attractive terracing to carry the play of light and colors down into dimness.

But such observations, skimming over the surface, cannot satisfy the musician, or he who wants to become one. How did he do it? — That is the question, which the musician must ask himself in relation to each masterwork, and which I posed to myself continually, with great seriousness.

Above all the scores and the little that was then available in terms of theoretical introduction that could be drawn upon for advice. However, all this only led to imitation of the available compositions. I was driven by a fiery desire to go more deeply into the basics; the sound and manner of each instrument, and then the blending of two or more into a new body of sound – that required investigation. At that time you would find me at every parade of the watch and every garden concert. Whether my dear colleagues played a simple waltz or a splendid overture, was all one to me; indeed, I scarcely paid any attention to the content, and perhaps did not always know whether I was listening to this or that key, major or minor. My entire attention was directed first at this instrument, and then at that instrument, and only on that; I perceived nothing else but its sounds, how it was in the low range, the high range, in the middle, how far its power of sound extended, which musical figures stood out, and exactly how they worked on this instrument. Then I stretched my imagination in order to guess how the sound of linked instruments might be shaped, and tested my supposition as soon as I was actually confronted with this sound combination.

Often I asked one or another of the musicians about his instrument and its ways. I always received the most freely offered information. Indeed, often these busy men came to me, to the unknown young man, the horn players, laden with their crooks (valve horns did not yet exist) and played the answers tirelessly for my ceaseless questions. There was no question of profit; such an offer would have wounded them. They came, in genuine musical brotherhood, to repay my devotion to their instrument with their devotion to my efforts. The fruit of this mutual interaction can be found in my compositions and in my teaching on instrumentation.

Now, however, my teaching position would provide me my first opportunity to really demonstrate what I had learned and thought out.

At the house of Geheimrat Naumann they were to celebrate their silver anniversary. The man who would later be their son-in-law, and also president of the Kammergericht, Bonseri, arranged the festivities, among which a pantomime/dramatic presentation could not be lacking. I, as a friend of Bonseri, and a teacher at the house, undertook to provide the music, and arranged a set of orchestral pieces, preceded by an overture. The limitations of the orchestra that I had at my disposal were rather odd. The orchestra only had room for two violins, viola, violoncello and double bass, one flute, one clarinet, one bassoon and two horns. But since it could not be otherwise, I was in good spirits. I remember, that my two little horns through unusual position and voice leading had to behave quite like trombones in a festive moment. The composition was soon ready, but I was overcome by an anxiety about whether everything that I had planned out would really have the right effect. Along with my ambition I was worried about whether the party would be a success, and not long before I had received a rather threatening report from Löwe. He had become music director in Stettin,[6] had performed a cantata with orchestral accompaniment to mark his taking on the post, and wrote to me with unchanged childlike simplicity: "Well, you see, Marxchen, that was a quite a damn thing. Where I had imagined I would make a big effect, there was nothing; and where I had not planned anything at all, then it sounded quite charming and beautiful." I took this very heavily. So, if I had erred in both directions – and nothing could be done – I had no better idea, than to go with my musically literate friend G. Nikolai along with some music paper to the rehearsal, so that perhaps some revision by his and my hand could quickly be done. But no fixing was needed; everything sounded exactly as I had imagined, and my concern gave way to greater confidence.

---

[6] Löwe became musical director in Stettin in February 1821.

CHAPTER 3

FIRST STEPS INTO PUBLIC LIFE

I had already learned in Berlin that it was difficult, if not impossible, to find a reception as a young composer with a grand opera. An opera by Hummel, who was highly regard as pianist and composer, and held an appointment at that time as Kapellmeister in Weimar (I believe the work was called *Mathilde*[1]) was accepted for performance by the direction of the theater in Berlin, and waited then seven or nine years for its production. How long would I have had to wait as an unknown newcomer, had I achieved a place on the waiting list. At any rate, I was lacking poem and poet for the serious, tragic opera for which I felt that I was uniquely suited; but the urge to work was always present.

A random impulse was decisive.

One morning I felt unwell, wanted to rest, and went to my nearby friend Sietze, — he might send me some sort of easy book. I received a volume from Goethe. Lying on the sofa, leafing through it, I came upon the *Singspiel Ierb und Bätelb*, which I, by chance, did not yet know. Without particular commitment I began to read. Then, for the little poem:

> Gehe!
>
> Verschmähe . . .

I came upon the mood and melody in a moment, unintentionally, and almost unconsciously. I took a sheet of music paper, and wrote down the tune. Immediately illness and everything else was forgotten. When Sietze came a few hours later to look after me, I had already composed the first five songs. He applauded them, and soon I no longer needed his encouragement – the whole *Singspiel* was completed in a couple of weeks, including the overture – only as a sketch, but with a definite idea of the instrumentation.

Earlier and later undertaking had never come to fruition without my having let them first mature within me for a long time. This time everything appeared spontaneously and without previous decision, I scarcely knew how. Now for the first time, with incentive from friends and experts in music, I decided to present the work for public performance. The score of the songs, and finally the overture, soon lay before me complete.

---

[1] Hummel's Mathilde von Guise, premiered Vienna, 1810, was the most successful of his fifteen operas.

131

I can certainly say that I was filled with Goethe's poetry, and each moment intended for composition by the poet had penetrated deeply into my heart. But I was unaware of one thing, until it was too late. These songs of the great poet, so inward, so true in character – are unusable for composition; they are too short to give the musician space for deeper, or only specific effect; and once again they are too full of character and too deep for one to fleetingly deal with them in the manner of a vaudeville or *Liederspiel.*[2] Reichardt tried his hand at the latter, and the worthy, marvelous old man was permitted, in his style from the time before Mozart, in which Liederspiel and operetta were not at all treated with seriousness and depth, but rather as a sort of "game of the Muses." Mozart pointed us down different paths. Thus I could do naught else, than give these inward moments, which the poet let gleam fleetingly like the first rays of the new sun, inwardness and complete depth. But the contradiction between the winged words and their melody remains and must have been felt from the theater all the way here.

Added to this — was a sin on my part, an offense against that which I considered to be true and right. Influenced by my musical friend Nikolai, who was a lively supporter of my composition, I allowed myself to be swayed to add here and there something that would give the woman singers the opportunity to show off a little coloratura. Without this, he thought, I would find no singers who would be interested. Thus my score went to the music director and was accepted. Now I would learn that it is easier to write a first opera, than to bring it to performance.[3]

After the opera was accepted, Kapellmeister Seidel visited me. As a member of the direction, which had accepted the work, he pointed out to me a series of places, whose instrumentation he thought seemed unfeasible. I had to commit in writing to bear the costs of the copying if the instrumentation should not be retained. The entirely benevolent man was particularly irritated by the accompaniment of the first song: "Sing, Bird, Sing...", in which I had put the flutes in the second octave and the violins in the third octave. The instrumentation proved to be entirely according to my intentions, and even though often deviating from the usual, was still artistic.

After this I visited the General Intendant, Count Brühl. He received me amicably, but explained to me, that he could do nothing for my *Singspiel*, but would do everything possible against its performance. Certainly, he had not the slightest objection against me or my composition, but his eternal friend

---

[2] A light theatrical genre of the early nineteenth century. Reichardt contributed an article on the *Liederspiel* to the *AMZ*, vol. 43, p. 801.
[3] The music for this work has been lost, and nothing is known beyond the account given here.

Reichardt was known to have set the same poem to music, the setting of which was the property of the Theater; he could not be happy to see another setting take its place. I reminded him in all modesty that Reichardt's *Singspiel* had already disappeared from the theaters for quite a number of years. "I will see that it is produced immediately" was his quick reply. This took place, but was not at all appealing, and, after the single performance, had to be put aside forever. Now it was my composition's turn – that is, after many delays.

The evening of the performance arrived, and I found myself behind the scenes. That the composition could have no decisive success, I had already realized, since the inappropriateness of the poem for musical treatment had become evident, and my sin against my own convictions had clouded my serene sense. But fear or concerns were far from me; I hoped to learn something, at any rate.

Now I would learn that I had already made enough enemies, and certainly through my sincerity in the musical journal, which will be discussed soon below. Before the performance one of our leading singers, Mad. Seidler, appeared to ask me: "Well, is your heart not beating yet?" Surprised, I asked "why?", and with her little feet she pantomimed a beating heart so maliciously, and with so much charm in her almost Hellenic little face, that I felt nothing but surprise and pleasure. I had always admired the entirely beautiful woman with the silver voice and gave her unfailingly bell-like purity of sound and coloratura due recognition in my reporting, but also expressed my honest conviction that she did not penetrate with complete devotion and passion into the sense of larger sections. This could not be forgiven me.

This time it was different. No sign of displeasure was heard, and well more than half of the musical numbers were met with lively applause. It is certainly true that to a great extent this was due to the achievements of the performers, the glowing Schulz, the noblest of tenors, Bader, the witty acting and singing of Blume.[4]

This may have been unexpected to one and all; one had to help out. At the second performance, after a rather long day, the overture, with its long-held chord for tuning by the wind instruments alone, which opens and introduces the work, began without its bass and fundamental tone – someone had hidden the keys for the bassoon chest. In a scene, where Bäteli's singing to the open window of her cottage is supposed to resound outside, the window was nailed shut; for quite a while, until the singer had come around the cottage onto the stage, one heard nothing but the rolling accompaniment figure of the violins

---

[4] Heinrich Blume, 1788-1856, a tenor best-known for the title role in *Don Giovanni*.

for quite a number of measures. Enough about these pranks. The Singspiel was taken off the boards; the overture was performed a few more times in public, without my participation.

Count Brühl now showed me his friendly willingness to assist me when opportunity appeared; and soon I thought to have found such an opportunity. Evidently in the wake of those participations by Hendel-Schütz in the Copenhagen ballets, I had created the plan for a ballet, and already begun the composition on my own.

My subject matter was Achilles on Skyros.

At the rise of the curtain one saw a bright area, which was sinking behind the sea. Deidamia with her companions was making a merry round dance, among them Achilles at the border between the age of boy and youth in maiden's clothing, with a bright headdress looped through his short curls. One of the maidens suddenly points to the sea; all look that way, and foreign ships appear; the song of the sails (represented by horns and bassoons) sounds over the softly rocking waves. — This movement continued to ring in me, and gave the first motive for the song of the waves in the first finale of *Mose*. In the ballet now Odysseus and his crew come ashore. The maidens, shyly, have fled, and taken Achilles, who is reluctant, away with them. Then from the land the king appears in robes of peace; from the ships, after Odysseus' nod, is brought costly women's jewelry of all kinds with elaborate garments, and everything that might be attractive to a maiden. Deidamia and the maidens dare to first timidly, and then more boldly, admire the costly gifts, and stretch their hands with longing toward this and that. Deidamia first dares to grasp a flowing purple robe, and her serving girls hurry to adorn the princely child in a noble fashion. But as the noble purple is unfolded, a gleaming sword in a scabbard glittering with noble gems is visible. Achilles sees it, rushes for it, swings it around his head in the heroic style. Quickly Odysseus's men bring the brightly polished shield of steel. Achilles looks into it, rips the womanly decoration of the bright band from his head, for which only the helm with the high plume is befitting, and all the Hellenes surround him, jubilant and paying him homage. He, from whom alone Ilium's fall and the salvation of the Hellenes can be expected, is recognized. On the endless waves of the green sea approaches Thetis, borne on the waves, the sorely grieved mother, with a great following of Nereids. In vain is her warning, her weeping: may he remain with Deidamia in the peaceful circles of the maidens; there outside, with fame, waits an early grave. The beloved approaches with her companions, the old Prince stretches out his hand to the youth, the Hellenes, undecided, waver. Then Zeus rolls thunder from afar, on lighter clouds Pallas Athene can be seen, brandishing weapons. Hermes, the messenger, points to where the Gods will complete the destiny of the heroic youth. The Hellenes, now already celebrating their future certain victory, lead their hero to the ships.

These were the outlines of my ballet. Foolish enthusiasm! Had I not just seen the performance of *Kia-King*,[5] with its hordes of grotesque Chinese, who, wobbling, or with leaps back and forth, threw themselves around, and finally performed the Lantern Dance with paper lanterns in a thousand colors, to the never-ending jubilation of the crowd eager for spectacle? Count Brühl was very interested in my suggestions, but directed me (entirely correctly) because of the further details to the ballet-master, who went by the name of Laucheri,[6] if I am not mistaken. The latter listened to me in a friendly way, and then told me two of his suggestions (in the taste of *Kia-King*), which would go on stage first, and from which I could remove what would later be used in the Ballet. I was enlightened and desisted.

On another side a new stage opened for my activity. Willibald Alexis had written a prize-novel of 60 or 70 lines and had used it for a melodrama[7] for the newly created Königstädter Theater. The subject was the love of a young French officer for a noble Polish woman, which had caught fire in Warsaw during the passage of the grand army to Russia, and found its tragic ending with the retreat of the army. If I am not mistaken, the mortally wounded warrior died at the feet of his beloved. The novel in general was full of talent and gripping; I could not so easily judge the melodrama, and believed that I could tell in advance that it would make as little a claim on the stage as did all works of this type. But the poet, a friend of mine, and compliant with my plans, offered me the chance to set it, and I was certainly not in a position to turn down a chance for exercise my craft.

The pair's love was the main content for the stage; the backdrop was provided by the immense procession of the army and its downfall. This was what I chose as the main task for the music; especially the overture and the entr'acte had to depict these moments. The composition did not seem to displease; the melodrama disappeared, as I had foreseen, after a few performances.

---

[5] A ballet of 1824 to a score by Adalbert Gyrowetz.
[6] A certain Laucher (perhaps Karl, the brother of a prominent singer, Antonia Laucher) was a dancer and ballet-master during this period, although the general ballet was under the direction of Michel François Hoguet.
[7] *Die Rache Wartet*, melodrama in three acts, composed 1828. Hirschberg notes that he could not find a copy of the printed edition of the novel in his article "Der Tondichter Adolph Bernhard Marx".

The last dramatic undertaking was a *Festspiel* for the wedding of the Prince of Prussia at the time, ===== *Greeting*[8]. I had used the characters from the well-known magical fairy tale for a country scene; my proposal won over the old poet Fouqué, who ever after called me his "dear comrade-in-arms". At least he had been a real comrade-in-arms in the wars of liberation – even if I was not yet old enough to be his comrade. Our work was performed on the festival day, and had the usual success of such gifts.

[8] A type of cantata for soloist and choir, whose music has been lost.

CHAPTER 4

BEGINNING A CAREER AS A WRITER

During the first few weeks of my stay in Berlin I had, busy with my cases for the Kammergericht, suddenly sunk into a near-collapse. Excitement and stress had overcome me. The first who by chance entered my apartment, was Nikolai. Through him the report with my files arrived at the Kammergericht.

Soon a carriage rolled up to my house and someone that I did not know, whose every trait emanated benevolence and support, entered. It was the Criminal Director, Hitzig[1]. He was, he said, also employed at the Kammergericht, had heard about my accident, and offered me, who perhaps had no connections in the city yet, advice and support; his wallet was open for me. My illness, I was certain, was already on the mend; I also did not need his support, but I was touched by his noble and humane friendliness, and it filled me with joy and inner thankfulness.

In the meantime E.T.A. Hoffmann had died. His stories were then the source of general amazement in Germany, as they would later give the major impetus to the burgeoning of the romantic school in France. Hoffmann became familiar in France long before Goethe and Schiller did. And he was not only a poet, but also a composer, had provided several dramas with music, and his *Undine* had been a great success a short time before at the Berliner Theater.[2] As if that were not enough, he showed himself to be a talented and spirited draftsman of portraits and caricatures; although it could not be denied that his portraits, for example several drawings of Blücher, wandered entirely unrecognizably to the other branch of his art. In addition he was an excellent jurist; his reports were often heard in session with amazement, although at the same time case files with the most amusingly grotesque caricatures were circulating amongst the lawyers, in which one thought one could recognize one or another colleague. Now, after an eventful life, he had become council for the Kammergericht. Not stylists, but probably Prussian jurists would have been able to identify his position through his style: for his stories, no matter how full of wit and fantasy they are, bear the mark of the way of writing of the former jurist, including

[1] Julius Eduard Hitzig, 1780-1849, was a civil servant, lawyer and literary figure; together with Willibald Alexis, he published *Der Neue Pitaval, a long-running periodical dedicated to publicising criminal cases..
[2] This Singspiel had been premiered in Berlin in 1816.

their unhelpful concision and the conventional usages of the profession, which are unmistakable.

I do notknow whether I became aware of it at the time; but this man, striving in so many directions, could have been an enticing or cautionary example for my own striving and living. His achievements, which I along with everyone else gazed upon with amazement, could have aroused emulation, although I was never receptive to such influences, and instead constantly followed my inmost impulses. However, at the same time it could not remain hidden that even the rich talents of this many-sided man were not sufficient to satisfy in such various directions. Finally, such excessive and varied activity led to the need for constant stimulation and overstimulation, and eventually to a painful death. Now he was delivered from all anxiety and pain, and Hitzig, his friend, took on the task of putting his literary and musical legacy in order.

Eager to show my gratitude for the excellent man who had been so benevolent to me, I offered him my assistance for the musical part. What was my duty towards him became beneficial for me. Hitzig turned over Hoffmann's musical works that had been left behind, and asked me to provide a profile of Hoffmann as a musician to the biography that he himself was writing. This was the first more substantial essay of mine that came to public notice.[3]

At the same time the writings from Hoffmann's legacy gave an unexpected insight into his musical education.

That he had not received a basic musical education, I had already surmised from his story about "Ritter Gluck". He counted as brilliant liberation from school rules that Gluck writes the part of the orchestra in octaves in the overture to Iphigenia in Aulis, which is well known to be something that does not at all fall into the prohibition on parallel octaves. Now I had written evidence in my hands that Hoffmann himself felt the need to complete his education in composition. He had imitated Mozart's Requiem movement for movement, and with an almost slavish devotion; I no longer remember to which text. Ah! I myself had already done the same thing in Halle. Since Marpurg had left me unadvised with respect to fugal writing, I had then tried to imitate first one fugue and another from the Well Tempered Clavier, but always giving up, when I felt all too clearly the oppression of that artistic emotion and freedom, and soon realized, that each fugue of the Master went its own way according to the law of its individual content.

---

[3] This was Marx's *Zur Beurtheilung Hoffmann's als Musiker, published in Hitzig's *Aus Hoffmann's Leben und Nachlaß, Berlin, 1823.

Thus the deathbed had led me into Hoffmann's confidences, after life, although my recommendation, and his benevolence, had failed me.

With similar lack of intentionality I began, in the course of my juridical career, my first great undertaking in the field of literature: the founding and direction of the Berliner Allgemeine Musikalische Zeitung. This was occasioned by the following.

I had attended a performance of Gluck's Armida with Nikolai; in the famous slumber scene I had poked him and whispered: "Listen to how enticing the sounds of the fifths! They lull one irresistibly to sleep!" — these are the same fifths that I would discuss later in my composition method; even for most non-musicians it is known that series of fifths were considered unacceptable for a long time. — Nikolai replied: the movement is enticing and drips slumber into your ear; but fifths have nothing to do with it. I had to stick with my opinion.

The following morning my compassionate friend came to see me very early. "Dear friend, the claim you made yesterday cost me a sleepless night; how can you claim that such a master writes forbidden fifths?" I replied that there was no claim involved, and that I even did not consider it to be the case that parallel fifths were inadmissible in all circumstances.

Now it was completely impossible to drop the subject; he almost dragged me by force to Breite Strasse, where A. M. Schlesinger had his music business at the time. There the tussle would be decided. We went into the old gentleman's office and Nikolai asked him for the score to Armida. It was presented to us, and while I looked Schlesinger pulled my friend to the side to ask him who I was and what we really wanted. Nikolai told him, just as I called out: "Here it is! There you have fifths, between violin and flute! Nikolai showed his amazement in a stormy way, as was his nature, and we left.

A few hours later Nikolai came to my place, very heated, walked a few times through my chamber without greeting or conversation a few times, and then asked me, impetuously: "Do you want to start a musical journal?"

I was literally overcome by the question; Nikolai continued, without waiting for an answer, by explaining: Schlesinger had told him, that he had had the intention for a long time to found a musical journal, that he thought that he had found in me the right person for the undertaking, and was ready on the spot if I wanted to go in on the venture. This old Mr. Schlesinger was an unusual man; he was what few people are, a character out of cast iron. One could not say that he had an academic or even artistic training; but he possessed a certain divination that substituted for judgment based on facts, and told him that something could be made out of this thing or this man, — and this was in no way only having to do with monetary advantage, but also with respect to the intellectual content and on the results which might grow from it for his firm, so highly dear to him. This last he called "the honor of the House", and he was ready to make considerable sacrifice for this if necessary. But he certainly understood the value of academic training as well. His three sons were destined for their father's business (the eldest was the most highly regarded music publisher in Paris), but had to make their way through a complete school and university career before they joined the company; this was their father's will for them before they got started under their own steam. The founder of the house had started very small, without a fortune, and from this small beginning had worked his way up to great wealth and fame.

And in my case he was not entirely wrong. Experience, insight into the needs of a periodical, reputation, connections – I was lacking all of these; the most important for quick worldly success — the pliability of the journalist as well. What I did have instead was a fiery eagerness for the subject matter and conscientiousness. I accepted and treated my editorial office like a public service, which I had learned to do as a jurist. The main condition for me was unrestricted freedom in the editorial office; often enough the articles by the publisher himself were entirely condemned.

My first business began. I needed to recruit collaborators. Already convinced at the time that only musicians had complete judgment regarding music, naturally if he really is a creative artist —and the other conditions for judgment are present, my invitations went out not only to writers but also to musicians, to Hummel, Spohr, Spontini, Weber and others. There were about seventy letters to be written; that one could use printed forms for this was something that I did not know, and also would not have liked.

Now an earlier school companion of mine was living in Berlin, later a country parson. Full of learned knowledge, but entirely unfamiliar with the ways of the world and completely awkward, in opening his way with people and their often so self-minded pressures, he had sunk into deep poverty in the great and cold city. So I found him, and hoped to connect his judgment with mine. I drew him toward me and hoped that he would write part of the letters for me.

I soon had to see that his letter writing was not working. In order to keep him busy, I gave him my long paper scissors, and asked him to cut envelopes, for at that time (as far as I knew) there were still none to be bought. In one window sat I, busily engaged in letter writing, and in the other, with my back to him, sat he. Then I heard him quietly laughing to himself several times; finally I asked him why. First I got an embarrassed "well, then!" for an answer. Finally he blurted out: "Well, then, I was thinking to myself of how it would be, if I sneaked up behind you and stuck the scissors in your neck." The unfortunate man had an attack of insanity. Remembering, that the insane fear blows more than death (I do not know, where I learned that) I went up to him very close and said with a strong look and tone: "And I was just thinking how it would be if I gave you a terrible boxing in the ears." The poor man bent over his work, silent and shy, and I continued with mine. We had not done anything to each other, and to my knowledge no other sign of insanity ever appeared.

The invitations were sent out. Many responses came back with all sorts of replies. From a renowned opera composer and virtuoso I received approximately the answer that follows: "I was very happy to receive your invitation; musical criticism must under such direction [do not forget, that I was entirely unknown at the time] move to a new height. Certainly you will powerfully oppose such opera composers who, without consideration of the dram see the only salvation of the Opera in twisted and convoluted vocal tissue and weak melodies...."

From a colleague of the first I received, almost on the same day, the reply: "I was very happy to receive your invitation; musical criticism must under such direction glimpse a new future. Certainly you will powerfully oppose such opera composers, who under the pretense of writing dramatically, shove the laws of music away from themselves, and wish to make their hack tunes valid as song...."

Now! The matter is told, the initiated will guess the writers; and they may also be named for those further away – they are called - Weber and Spohr. The little compliment to me, the hint that at any rate contained their sincere opinion, these were, if one wants to judge severely, little weaknesses, which, next to their great merit have as little importance as the famed "freckles"[4] on Beethoven's face.

I have already mentioned with what seriousness and conscientiousness I took over the editorship. The publication would not be my journal, would not belong to this party or that, but I gave it the mission: to become a place where all could speak; everyone would have free speech regarding the matters of art, and his convictions. I had high hopes for letting the musician express himself regarding our common interest, rather than, as before, handing this over to foreigners, and declaring himself unsatisfied in this respect, while they contribute to the school of inadequacy. How far the majority of musicians were removed from the experience of this duty, and from the capacity for this, was something I did not yet know then, but probably my impartiality would give me the opportunity to find out.

I had stated that the journal would stay open for every refutation, and would honor this, like every other commitment. Now I had, whether rightly or not,

---

[4] TM: Marx clearly uses the conventional German term for freckles here, *Sommersprosse*; the fact that he puts them in quotes evidently is telling the reader that he knows they are acne scars, but is avoiding saying so directly.

allowed myself to be seen as polemical against Zelter, the director at the time of the Singakademie founded by Fasch. This was the first time that there was public opposition to Zelter in Berlin. Once again I expressed my willingness to give space to any response limited to the matter. And immediately I received a response, sharp and not free from personalities, but what did that have to do with me? The writing was printed.

Another time, not I, but one of my co-workers, Kapellmeister Dorn[5] or Director Löwe, had not found a piano composition to be as valuable as it may have seemed to the friends of the composer. One of these, the valued pianist and composer Arnold,[6] later music director in Münster I believe, visited me, and began to talk with me under the assumption that I was the writer. I remarked to him, that he was free, like anyone, to contradict the erroneous review. "Yes," he remarked, "someone who had your style! I would like to write as well". I observed that this widespread distinction between style and content was something that I had never understood; he was indeed a musician and should only give words from his profession that would work well for him. And since he maintained his opinion, I offered him my assistance; if he would share his opinion with me in a simple and uncomplicated way, I would present it as clearly and eloquently as I could. At the same time I let him know that I was not the writer of the review, and so that it was not necessary for me to write against myself. But the pleasure of contradiction had disappeared for my visitor. In replacement for so many things where I was lacking, I had come upon an extraordinarily favorable time with my undertaking.

The only thing that can provide a periodical with strong and fruitful soil is a time in which new appearances and thoughts grow verdantly. That was such a time.

I have already noted the highpoint that the Berlin opera had reached at the time, and the man who stood at its peak: Spontini. Next to him appeared K. M. Weber. His Freischütz had made its way through all of Germany prior to the appearance of the journal, and had, supported by the charming gypsy opera Preciosa, made the composer the darling of Germany. The Berliners especially, in whose midst Freischütz had first appeared, and had won entirely unbounded enthusiastic support, such as the cool, more skeptical than enthusiastic capital had rarely expressed – the Berliners continued with their preference for Weber – or as an enthusiastic Madame Geheimrat loved to say "for my dear little Weber".

Now Weber's Euryanthe arrived in Berlin from Vienna. In Vienna it had not done particularly well; people had changed the name *Euryanthe into Ennuyante.

[5] Heinrich Ludwig Egmont Dorn, 1804-1892, best known in the period as a conductor.
[6] Carl Arnold, 1794-1873, was better known in Norway, where he arrived as a political refugee in 1847.

Here I would learn for the second time after Spontini about the lack of independence of the Berliners. That *Euryanthe* came from "their Weber", was not important. Vienna had made up its mind about it, and the Berliners, who otherwise liked to be in contradiction to Vienna, made their judgment: the opera could not put down roots, indeed, one could practically declare it a failure.

That was a serious injustice. *Euryanthe* may not have been popular with the people like *Freischütz*, it even had undeniable great faults, which the libretto lay at the base of. But, along with this it had extraordinary charm, and in particular a characteristic flavor and local color for the Middle Ages, with its knights, castle maidens and castle spirits, something that had never been such a success until then or today for any opera composer. This the quieter and more reflective Berliners should have been better able to realize than the Viennese, more given to life's pleasures and enthusiasm.

Spontini reacted in a strange way, but one entirely in accordance with his character. He had nothing against it, and had done everything for the opera that was part of his position, although Weber was his only close rival in the musical drama, and he could daily observe the predilection incited by partisan spirit of the Germans for Weber.

Now the day of the performance was approaching. The orchestral rehearsals had begun. Spontini appeared at my house one morning and put the overture before me in the piano arrangement. "Play it!" I played it until the march-like movement. Here, he grabbed my hand and asked me: "Now, what do you say?" I did not understand what he was driving at. Finally, extremely impatient, he burst out: "But this is my overture for *Olimpie*!" I, who had never put much stock in so-called reminiscences, which are usually imaginary or unintentional, sought in vain to mollify him. He believed that he had been robbed! Overthrown! And my prediction that the opera would not be a success, fell on deaf ears. Unfortunately, it would be confirmed. Later, long thereafter, I took the time to compare both related movements with a third related movement, the main movement from the finale of Beethoven's symphony in C minor, in order to demonstrate their relationship and dissimilarity, which so often are at play in music. That this opera had been a predecessor and model for Meyerbeer's depiction of character and instrumentation in his final opera, as well as for Wagner's bent for the medieval, certainly does point to the seeds of life that appeared in Weber's creation.

And the concerts of the time also provided rich material for the journal. Excellent and beloved singers gave concerts every year; foreign virtuosi lined up in great numbers. Among them I first name Hummel as a performer, as well as a highly respected composer for the piano. As can scarcely avoid being the case for virtuosi, his manner of composition for the piano was the immediately applicable expression of his manner of playing. The latter had been known to me for a long time. I had had the opportunity to get to know the man and his playing already in Halle, publicly and in intimate circles. Now he was in Berlin.

An external view of his person and activity at the instrument seemed quite individual; from his build to his spiritual creations he was, the entire man, of a piece. Short, and stockily built, his hands and fingers were not at all well-suited for playing the piano, namely for wide positions and spans, for wide-ranging transitions. Added to this was his obstinate refusal to use the assistance of the pedal; he preferred to give up the unification that it provides, rather than sacrifice the least amount of cleanness and clarity. Now, it was astounding with what industriousness, infallibility and niceness these little fingers worked. One could not expect spiritual elevation, the storm of passion, or even physical power and fullness from him. But whatever complete study, linked with the most extreme delicacy, could provide, that he had – and that is already something. In Halle I had heard him improvise five or six evenings in a row, and he never failed to introduce a broadly worked-out fugal movement with a tranquil theme and rolling counter theme. If you know Hummel's composition, will be aware of the concordance of these with his playing and personality.

Closely related to him, Kalkbrenner[7] came next to us. His skill, particularly in octave passages in both hands, was perhaps so much superior, or appeared to be so much more brilliant, as the progress in piano playing made in the span of time from one to the other, and perhaps Kalkbrenner's hands were more favorably built than those of his immediate predecessor. Only in terms of artistic education may Hummel have prevailed, at least in as much as it was a question of free improvisation. However, during a visit that Kalkbrenner made to me, he sat down at the piano, and indulged in broad, very well-managed effusions, one close after the other; and a fugue or fugato movement was not lacking either.

I was amazed, was very pleased, and begged the artist's pardon for the injustice that I had – luckily not in public – done him in my opinion. But I loudly expressed my surprise regarding what he had just undertaken, and how he was able to connect one movement to the next securely. "Where", I said, "do you get all of it from?" and he replied, with the modesty of the true artist, something like "Ideas…excitement….inspiration".[8]

Unfortunately a package of music had just arrived from my publisher, which also included Kalkbrenner's *"Effusio musica"*.[9] Ah! I had just heard the effusion.

---

[7] Friedrich Kalkbrenner, 1785-1849, was a prolific composer but better known as a piano virtuoso, perhaps the greatest before Liszt.
[8] Marx might be being satirical here: Kalkbrenner was notorious among contemporaries for his high opinion of his own gifts.
[9] Kalkbrenner's *Grande Fantaisie* Op. 68, a highly dramatic work popular as a virtuoso showpiece.

My preference, however, was for the subtle, soulfully playing Moscheles.[10]

I still recall a visit that I paid him with one of my friends at that time, Felix Mendelssohn. We found him with his young and beautiful wife at the *Brandenburger Gasthof, and he played us one of his masterful etudes. "That is excellent! You played that beautifully!" cried Mendelssohn. "What!" the young, beautiful wife pouted, "Doesn't my husband play everything beautifully?" We were both charmed by the partisan spirit of the newlyweds.

During these concerts I also became closer to the great Milder. I had gotten to know her in Gluck and Spontini. No surprise that I wanted to hear her sing something that I had composed. She was amenable, and I was burning to write a scene for her in her own sphere, for I regarded her too highly for a simple song. Zenobia, the unhappy queen of the Palmyrene Empire, in the moment where she learns of the defeat of her army, and the band of victorious Romans storms its way to the Queen – this is what I chose for my task. My friend Sietze provided me with the words, the composition was soon completed, and I brought it to the great singer.[11]

Now, you must know what a strange personality she was. He had spent her youth in Vienna, and had there laid the foundations for her fame. For the Berliners she appeared more matronly, still with a youthful, uninjured voice, and with respect to her important charms, preserved her powerful natures until past the midpoint of her life. She was tall and full, and in addition, extremely peaceful, and indeed slow and indolent in her movements. "I am not talking," heard many who visited her on the day of a performance. She then sat in an armchair or rested without moving on the comfortably curved sofa; the visitor could stay a while and entertain her, but could not expect the least word in reply. It might have been different at an earlier date. When young women from the theater, with girlish chatter, praised their admirers, she could listen for a long time without speaking. Finally, however, she would exclaim: "Be quiet you geese! What do you know about admirers? I was loved by Napoleon." Of course, there was no way that the young women could respond to that. This was how she was at home or behind the scenes at the theater; as soon as she went on stage, she was a sublime priestess.

So I brought her my scene, happy and full of expectation. It opened with a grand recitative, then, in E-flat major, the chorus of Romans stormed in, then the modulation moved to the bright gold of E major for the adagio of the Queen, and the allegro combined the solo voice with the chorus of men's voices. The thing could have been marvelous.

---

[10] Ignaz Moscheles, 1794-1870, was a successful virtuoso and close friend of Mendelssohn.
[11] The score of this work has been lost.

"I won't sing this aria!" after a moment's examination came the decision, slowly, syllable by syllable.

To my sad question the singer replied: "The aria begins with E, and my most beautiful tones are B-flat or B natural. And then also for the aria I would have to make a face like this" – and her face took on for a moment the most sublimely tragic expression – "and that won't work in concert."

I was mortified – and charmed by her expression.

Later, when Rossini was introduced to Berlin by Sontag,[12] my Zenobia sang an entire act of the *Thieving Magpie* in one of her concerts. She was lacking the necessary coloratura, but she also did not need the tragic mask.

Along with this soprano the image of another appeared on our horizon. This was la Catalani. If one might compare the German, so still, so large and solemn, to the Moon, as it with its full radiance passed through the still and starry heavens over our adoring German forbears, then the Italian was comparable to the powerful Sun of her fatherland, as it charmingly pour its abundance of light and warmth over those chosen lands and the green-gold sea.

Angelica Catalani[13] had sung publicly for the first time at age eleven in a church in Venice, and an Austrian infantry regiment had to turn out to hold the people, driven to insanity, from storming the church. From then on she became the idol of Italy, Portugal, and the entire South.

I had seen and heard her for the first time during my time in Halle; at the time she had permitted a Captain Valabreque to call himself her husband; she herself, with princely wealth, and celebrated like a princess, remained Angelica Catalani. Along with many others I also hastened to Leipzig. Peter Winter, the renowned composer, had come from Munich; and others from near and far. It was a very unusual drama. After the Overture to Figaro, masterfully played by the Leipzigers under their Matthäi,[14] she entered the orchestra, elegantly led by one of the matadors of the rich commercial city. A broad diadem of large diamonds, which sparkled marvelously over her dark wavy hair, crowned her royal head, a similar belt surrounded her noble body.

No queen would have rejected the jewelry; she had earned it. Having arrived at the spot where she was to sing, she noted that they had forgotten to put down a carpet. With a discreet motion she let her Indian shawl glide to the floor, and walked onto it.

---

[12] Henriette Sontag, 1806-1854, a leading German soprano who pursued a notably international career.
[13] Angelica Catalani, 1780-1849, one of the most celebrated sopranos of the first half of the century.
[14] Heinrich August Matthäi, 1781-1836, concertmaster in Leipzig.

And then the bell-like tones of a voice the likes of which no one had heard before or since vibrated over the breathlessly attentive throng. She began an aria from *Figaro*; her choice and conception could not be criticized. Then she sang a worthless aria by a certain Portogallo,[15] and trivial variations. But all of this was irrelevant. She, she alone was music today; the Leipzigers, accustomed to the classics, the musically educated visitors were entirely in agreement about this. Her voice at the same time so incredibly powerful, and so sweet and tender – the warmth and power of her personality, which only held the masks of Mozart or Portogallo playfully in her hands, completely aware, that her countenance and the warmth of her fantasy streamed over everything that might come between her and her astounded listeners – this it was, to which we all gave our devotion, from which we all received priceless treasures.

But along with her natural gifts, I should not forget the artistic training of her voice. This as well was individually shaped. That which a few years later would make Sontag famous, this *mezza voce*, in which the voice reduced to the quietest and yet brightest bell-like vibrating ring, this, before the little Sontag with her little voice, the mighty Catalani possessed in wonderful perfection. In this mezza voce she ran up the scale from g' to g", approximately in the speed of the sixteenth notes of a moderato. "Any singer can do that!" I hear everyone cry. Yes, but la Catalani hit every pitch, precisely distinguished, four times in succession. Thus flutters the newly emerged butterfly on little feet as quick as thought, unfolding its folded wings in shimmers, over the flower to its goblet.

Had Catalani been trained to understand our music in its depth: then in her, and only in her would have Gluck's *Armida* found its soul and body. And we would have all thronged to this *Armida*, the awe-inspiring princess and enchantress, as in those days crusaders and Saracens were drawn to the original.

Thus she appeared before the Parisians, who are known to be easily perturbed by any error on the stage, and moved to an orgy of mockery. In a performance of *Semiramis* she was supposed to follow her son into the grave of the father and there to knock him down. La Catalani entered the scene with the greatest passion, dagger held aloft, but by mistake, on the wrong side. The packed house stared at her, breathless, captured and captivated by her tragic performance, without noticing the error.

I found her once again in Berlin. In the overcrowded opera house she entered with the majesty of a priestess, turned to Frederick William III, half hidden in his box, and began to sing the "*Heil Dir im Siegerkranz*".[16] The entire orchestra, the entire theater chorus, and the thousands of listeners, rising

---

[15] Marcos Portugal, 1762-1830, a composer who, among other works, produced a version of the *Marriage of Figaro*.

[16] The Prussian national anthem. The melody is that of "God Save the King."

to their feet, played and sang the melody in unison with her voice. Over all voice soared her voice, untouched and undisturbed in the simple melody and the coloratura of the following variations, as the blue heavens arch over the earth.

CHAPTER 5

NICOLA PAGANINI.

Suddenly a new light appeared like a comet on the richly-starry sky of those days. In 1829 Paganini arrived in Berlin.

Earlier I had heard Spohr with his spouse[1], the notable harpist, on a tour through Thuringia in Merseburg. His broad stroke, his soft and yet piercing cantilena, his entirely noble, if also unison and always elegiac manner, enjoyed support and indeed amazement everywhere. Many other virtuosos, of the violin, or of other instruments, had passed through. Now the Italian virtuoso had arrived, and a tremendous clamor, which also had its peculiar side, had preceded him[2]. Once again the rare occasion had occurred–a fiddler had set people to talking, as they had only been accustomed to do in the dark and distant past. He must have been a freed galley slave, sentenced for political subversion. Out of pity he was allowed to keep his instrument. Because, however, with its help he had stirred up his fellow prisoners, inciting their feelings about their crimes and punishment, all but the lowest strings of the instrument had been cut off. People pointed to the odd, wobbling way he walked, with feet slightly pointed outwards: that was the result of the long years he had worn chains. Others whispered about a crime in hot Italy: he had found an unutterably beloved maiden in the arms of another, and killed her on the spot. Now he was wandering in foreign lands, without peace in the cold and foggy lands of the North.

Was there some basis to the rumors?—Probably only in the excited fantasies of the people. But they were there, though one did not know where from. And they were believed–not with that veracity that required by the researcher or judge, but with that credulous and macabre devotion, with which we see the poet and the poetical folk shine the light on the truth amidst its fairy-tale trappings.

Now he had arrived!

The opera house was full to bursting; everyone was waiting expectantly. Some sort of overture was played. Inaudible steps, unseen, like an apparition, and he had arrived at his place, and his fiddle was already sounding, speaking

---

[1] Louis Spohr was married to Dorette Scheidler, 1787-1834, a pianist and harp virtuoso.
[2] Although Niccolò Paganini's reputation had been high for a long time, his true international fame began only in 1828, at the age of forty, when he began to tour more extensively outside Italy, especially in the Germanic lands.

to the crowd, which still breathlessly stared at the deathly-pale man with deep-sunken eyes, glittering like black diamonds in the bluish white, with the over-boldly drawn Roman nose, with the high-vaulted brow, which appeared amidst the black, wildly disheveled locks of his hair.

Soon after this first view I met the strange man together with the Mendelssohns at the family table. He was quiet and very friendly; nothing would have caused a stranger to have fantastic or even weird impressions. And yet the first impression remained. The man seemed to be a magician, and worked magic, not only on me, on this or that person, but on everyone.

Now he stood there, and immediately (I am following here, in part, the drawings, which I at the time jotted down in my journal) began the ritornello, in which he led the orchestra with a few musical sparks–and blitzed through, without completing a phrase, indeed without resolving a dissonance that he might have struck; and now the most melting and bold cantabile, as it had never before been conceived of on the violin, progressing insouciantly, unconsciously over any difficulty, in which the most audacious thunderbolts of a scornfully destructive humor were thrown; until his eyes ignited with a deeper, blacker glow, and the tones rolled forth more cuttingly and crashingly–so that one thought that he was striking the instrument as if it were the deranged pain of love of that miserable youth who tenderly sees the image of the faithless and murdered beloved, grimly smashes it, and once again forms it amidst tears. Than a stamped foot- and the orchestra storms in and resounds with the thunder of the exceptional enthusiasm, which the artist barely acknowledges, or answers with a glance looking deeply downwards, or with a smile wandering all around, with which his mouth opens strangely, and brightly shows his row of teeth; seeming to say: thus must you rejoice with me, whoever I may be, whatever mood my sorrows may feed me, whatever burdens my feet are bearing, and may have lamed my youthfully merry and bold stride. Before one can think this, he disappears from view; and whoever has captured his image in eye and spirit, cannot understand why they still make music by Mozart and Mercadante, until he comes once more.

Then he unrolled a painting full of pleasure for us: what a painting! Thus, perhaps, a disguised Moor sang of the destroyed grove of Granada, the marvels of the Alhambra, still enticing though in ruins, in which his people, his house, his mother and his beloved, his tender sisters were slaughtered, so that he now entirely orphaned travels the world, and wanders over the hot sand of the desert, and risks death and life for his return, and mishandles the old, merry zither, and torments pleasure with these tones, and thus in pain passes away before the lost paradise.

There was something unusual about this man. What one could take in and be amazed by externally about his playing–these playing-figures seeming impossible for all others, this mixture of stroked and plucked tones (*coll'arco* and *pizzicato*) in a course rolling rapidly forward, the octave leaps on the one hand (the lower octaves as lightning-quick, barely perceptible grace notes), all this was only the means, and in itself meant nothing at all for the man: the inner poetry of his fantasy completing its creations before our eyes: that was what took the listeners captive, and then carried them away to strange visions.

In one of these strange compositions a little bell that is struck mixes its bright vibrations with the melody of the fiddle[3]. Our brave and honorable Möser[4], himself a distinguished violinist, took over the little bell. And how he stood there, close by the foreigner, involuntarily bending backwards, as he sent his sounds to the violinist and spoke in alternation with those from the latter's instrument: it was as if a spirit under compulsion spoke from within the little bell and awoke the magic formulas which slumbered in the instrument. —

And once again, when this violin resounded on its own, and sighed sadly, as if in the sweet necessity of love, or alternating with this murmured hasty sounds, like a busy old woman confused between laughing and crying, messages and consolation, vows of love and scornful betrayal; that was not violin-playing, not music, but magic–thus music, but not the usual sort.

A spirit, consecrated in its origin, exalted in its vision, captivated within a degenerate virtuoso in the service of the moment.

This was the first time that I happened to see a demonic nature in the area of my art.

I have just called Paganini a demonic nature, and in the course of my communications I will use this expression once more about another. It is well-known that this expression does not belong to me, but is used much more often, and should firstly probably denote an especially power. But then it would be nothing but a variation of the words talent, gift, genius, enthusiasm, which we so frequently use loosely, even in scholarly works. This sort of arbitrariness and lack of definition has never appeared acceptable to me; you will please allow me a few lines in order to fleetingly indicate the meaning that I find in the word.

---

[3] Presumably his *La Campanella*, the rondo extracted from his second violin concerto, often performed as a solo piece, and later used as the basis of one of Franz Liszt's *Paganini Studies*.
[4] Carl Möser, 1774-1851, best known as a concert organizer and for his string quartet performances, which concentrated on the 'classic' repertoire of Haydn, Mozart and Beethoven.

The artist can take two positions. Either he devotes himself with self-denial entirely and unconditionally to the idea that moves him; his personality is given in service to the idea as bearer and as the organ, through which it enters reality. Or he has forced the impulse that provided him with the idea into the service of his personality, in order through that idea to make the inclination, the propensity of his subjective nature valid, and to let it have its way. In the first case, thus, the idea is determinant. The idea, however–each idea is an immediate expression of the all-powerful world-reason, and indivisible from it, and one. In the second case the personal and thus the limited is preponderant and conditional, if at the same time perhaps brightly illuminated by the eternal or absolute, and holding to it, and exalting it.

Thus I would call a Paganini, or the great Devrient, demonic; also Napoleon I, who with his immeasurable gift only had as a final goal himself or his dynasty; and I would also call Lord Bryon demonic, who in his poetic retelling of *Faust* (*Manfred*) only used the forhim unattainable ideas of his great predecessor in order to assert the brilliance of his fantasy and the wealth of the views that he brought home from his travels.

For a Goethe, for a Beethoven the label of demonic would not be employed. They and their peers are not, like the gloriously radiant Lucifer of myth, fallen spirits, in order to be valid in themselves; they are true messengers, imparting the ideas revealed to them.

Let no one, through the term "demonic" and "Demon", be led to that one-sided interpretation which denotes the devilish, the evil spirit. The Greeks already, and before them, the Persians, recognized good and evil demons (Agathodaimons and Kakodaimons); Socrates ascribed himself to a demon, and probably did not mean to indicate any "evil spirit".

Chapter 6

The *Musikalische Zeitung* and its End

How favorable the time was for the enterprise to which I had been called–I must put it that way, since the impulse for the decision had come from outside–is something that I could call a number of witnesses to testify to. The task of doing justice to so many artists and performances, and to make one's best effort to educate the public about them, was no small one: at the same time it was the strongest incentive for the undertaking. Of all those named up until this point, there was no question that Spontini stood out, not only because of his artistic significance, but also because it was importance to arrive at a proper evaluation amidst the back and forth of partisan bickering. Next to him Beethoven was in the foreground. Just as he, as the last of the great composers, stood far beyond all contemporaries in terms of purity and majesty of artistry, to that same degree the times, and in particular, Berlin, were far from being able to properly value both him and his ideas. Publicly, up to that point only E.T.A. Hoffmann and A. Wendt[1] had done so with expression and clear insight. To communicate regarding Beethoven was an important task for the journal.

In this connection something peculiar came to light. Looking around for items for criticism, I happened upon the Scottish songs. The publisher gave them to me. I was astounded at the wealth to be found in these three small volumes, and was tireless in referring to them repeatedly. Bewildered, the publisher asked me whether I was serious that the songs really were valuable? I emphatically attested to this, and the surprise of the old gentleman veered toward the most vehement aggravation, for up to that point there had been so little demand for the item, which he had paid dearly for, that the publisher had had the plates melted down. Thank God, that has changed.

With equal vigor I spoke in favor of the first volumes of ballades and songs by Löwe. I had recommended the composer, who had remained unknown until then, to Schlesinger, and thus provided him an entry in the world, often so difficult to achieve. This happened, however, because of my deepest conviction of the worth of those composition, and even today I continue to hold the same opinion, mine, indeed, that many of these songs, and particularly the *Erlkönig*,

---

[1] Amadeus Wendt, 1783-1836, a Leipzig-based philosopher and critic who published even-handed and intellectually adventurous assessments of Beethoven's music.

which so far exceed those by Schubert in terms of artistic worth and originality, have yet gradually surpassed by the latter in popularity. For the public does not decide based on the inner worth of the work of art, but rather on how close it comes to their sympathies and their ability to comprehend.

Of greater importance was the impulse that was given to the publication of the major works of J.S. Bach by the journal, and the relation to Schlesinger which it provided me.

Johann Sebastian Bach had had that strange destiny, to have been admired by his contemporaries as a great keyboardist and organist, and by his contemporaries and successors as the most artistically rich of composers, or rather of contrapuntists, while the core of his life, his sacred compositions, were avoided as formless, and one even heard them labeled as unchurchly by men of note (F. Rochlitz[2]). The latter was the necessary consequence of the weakening of churchly and religious feeling, that had made itself evident since his time, while he, a spiritual and Bible-faithful man, through and through, entirely filled with faith and zeal, followed the Evangelists devotedly and without conditions—most closely, the zealous Matthew—in order through his own language, that of music, to pour the "Good News" down to the listening people.

I got to know the few things published so far from the sacred compositions of Bach: a few of the eight-voice motets, the *Magnificat*; I was amazed and astonished, but they could not entirely satisfy my soul; Handel still stood as the unreachable, the only, for sacred music.

Now, in talking with Mendelssohn, the conversation frequently came around to Handel, and Mendelssohn put this name next to Bach's as one of the "greats". He had come into the possession of a copy of the *Matthew Passion* through his teacher Zelter. Destiny often follows strange paths! Zelter had many years earlier gotten the score of the immortal work from a cheese-dealer as waste paper. He had then thought of performing the work, or a part of the work. But he had seen the work, at least in part, as unenjoyable, and the recitatives and choral parts, which at times, in the sense of Gothic architecture—petered out in strange undulations and *fioriture*, he had recomposed, more or less in the style of Graun[3]. I myself had the parts in my hand. It was only through the desire of Mendelssohn's grandmother to given her grandson an unknown musical work

---

[2] Friedrich Rochlitz, 1769-1842, aesthetician, writer and long-time editor of the *Allgemeine Musikalische Zeitung*—a publication, not to be confused with Marx's journal, that began in 1798 and continued until 1882. Rochlitz, a particular enthusiast for Mozart, was instrumental in raising Bach's profile at the beginning of the nineteenth century, but in the process tended to depreciate certain aspects of his art.

[3] Carl Heinrich Graun, 1705-1759, a contemporary of Bach's who concentrated on the Italian opera.

that had led to the finding of the real score, bringing it to Mendelssohn. He it was who had the good fortune and merit to be the first to perform the work in Berlin. Zelter, with his academy, and the extensive connections of his father's family provided him the necessary means to do so.

Long before the performance I was so entirely filled with the work that day and night I could not get it out of my thoughts. Here, here was fulfilled what for the longest time I had viewed as ideal for composition, and especially for church music: a spirit entirely penetrated by the holiness of the task, entirely and devotedly given to the truth and grandeur of those wonderful traditions, a language, that was not satisfied with simply putting sound to the words, but which gave interpretation and fulfillment through emphasis and shape–an immersion in those processes, which they partially presented to our eyes in perfected drama, as if it happened now.

Naturally, I spoke everywhere and to everyone who would listen about my new spiritual experience that I had had, not with any special purpose, but because I could not do otherwise. And so old Schlesinger heard of the work. He asked about the publisher. It had never been published. He asked whether this music was really so incredible, and whether I had it. I could answer yes to both questions. "So I will publish it!" he shouted, and printing of the score and the piano reduction was agreed upon. This was not the case in the opinion of the friends of the house–they believed that the enterprise should be abandoned. A midday meal was arranged at the publisher's, and the question put to me in a very formal way: whether I really through that "something could be done" with the work. The guests were respected musicians, and everyone was excited to hear the answer. I explained, very peacefully in the general silence: I did not know whether something could be done with the music, and I had never claimed this; I only knew, that the work represented the highest level of sacred music. "And I will publish it!" shouted the old gentleman with his voice like a lion's, and pounded on the table, "and even if it should cost me three thousand thalers! I am doing it for the honor of my house."

The *Passion* appeared, and material compensation was not lacking for the entrepreneur.

I will pass over the other editions (Bach's High Mass, two volumes of church cantatas, etc.) that followed the *Passion*.

Now, however, it seemed advisable for me to resign from the journal. What I had been able to at it and with it had essentially been done. The danger present in the fragmented activity, which every periodical demands, of finally ending in distraction and aphorisms, had gradually become clear to me. My other motivation was my appointment to the university. Along with my own labors and my activity at the university there could be no time left for the journal.

Finally an event occurred which showed with all the light of day the point to which musical life, at least public musical life, had sunk, and how fruitless any resistance on the part of individuals against the *zeitgeist* must remain.

Several attempts had already been made at the Royal Theater to present the operas of Rossini, Auber and their companions. On the part of the direction enough had been done, but in vain; the operas found no response on the part of the public, which was accustomed to more dignified fare.

Now the Königstädter Theater was founded. It was the first to be permitted in addition to the Royal Theater. I myself was a member of the commission which, under the direction of Count Redern, was to decide any possible disputes regarding repertoire to appear at the new theater.

A significant portion of the new repertoire was the Italian opera and French operettas, with the best choice of personnel for this purpose.

The most artistically significant personality in the new troupe was the bass Spitzeder[4], an exceptionally talented young man. His incomparable voice, his eloquent expression, whether singing or speaking, his training in acting, his perfect comedy, never sinking to the common–all of this was in service of the task at hand. What he was supposed to be, he was completely, and he would do everything in order to see that this was the case. Thus he was, without intending it, on the stage, before the eyes of the audience, the living principle of performance; every member of the company, without exception, was under his influence, and was moved by his electricity. In those finales by Rossini, in which some meaningless phrase is repeated over and over, first by one or two instruments, and then with one or two voices added, and then reinforced by more and more entering parts, until finally the charivari of the entire orchestra and chorus with trombones, piccolos, bass drum and triangle worthily crowned the whole–in these movements Spitzeder was perhaps the first to enter, and carried the growing weight with his resounding bass voice. Once everyone had entered, he stopped for a moment, and then started in once more such all-ruling power–and sounding so fine and light, that often his fellow singers in the Bacchanalian merriment were pulled in and were swaying in their roles. Sontag then usually burst out laughing, which put an end to her singing for the nonce. Yes, sometimes she could do so little on such occasions, that she in view of the whole audience she would sit down on the floor. Spitzeder, but without denying the seriousness of his aging *buffo* role for a second, would look about in amazement, and then start in again, undisturbed. I saw him make a completely imperceptible transition from speech to song, and vice

---

[4] Josef Spitzeder, 1796-1832, was appointed to the Königstadt Theater in 1823.

versa–an art, which is all that make mixed operettas both understandable and artistically bearable–such I have seen from no other singer.

But it was not him, but rather Henriette Sontag who was the favorite of the public.

What made her their darling? Her voice? It always sounded well, although always covered, neither very strong, nor very extensive: you could not call the voice anything but small.

Her skill?—She was certainly not superior to the singers of the time at the Royal Theater. But only Sontag had a fine, ear-tickling *mezza voce*. Before her, the great Catalani had it, after her, Jenny Lind, and many others did; with her it sounded new and–it was enough for her to be a great singer.

But her personality came to the aid of her singing. Her form was not in any way distinguished, neither were her face and eyes, but her mouth had a sweet little smile, and she was not stingy with it; and in her eyes there was a half-innocent and half-mischievous expression, which did not fail to produce ecstasy in the young guard and the old guard, as the two crowds of her devotees were known, who offered her hearts and poems, and Indian shawls and Epernay champagne, respectively.

Thus, it was no surprise that under her aegis, the weakest of operas - Rossini's *Turco in Italia*, Auber's *Le Maçon*, produced unending sensation. I do not deny that I sat listening to the singer in such operas. But I never visited her, no matter how charmingly she invited me (the Editor!).

Thus, through her were Italian operas and French operettas domesticated in Berlin. The deeper meaning of this event was presented by my late friend, Professor Eduard Gans[5], in my journal with a masterful hand. His words will be welcome here:

Mademoiselle Sontag. A Characteristic Description.

Were the appearance of Mademoiselle Sontag purely musical, thus the author of the present essay would not have ventured to lay down his opinions in relation to her; only the relation in which she stands to all the general thoughts of the time and with the present-day presentations of art can entitle him to do so.

In fact it can scarcely be denied that the artistic life of Mademoiselle Sontag, the ovations, which she received in Germany, France and England, the great importance, which was linked with her appearance, let alone her performance, are something so extraordinary, that an actress

[5] Eduard Gans, 1797-1839, a Hegelian legal theorist.

probably never enjoyed such an influence on the attention and the conversation of her time. In many countries she replaced public life and caused the present to at least not seem without interest; in others she knew how to claim a place for herself alongside the most important events. Along with these facts there is also the not less important fact that it is not the power and majesty of a powerful personality, but grace and loveliness, which celebrates this victory, so that a closer investigation of this phenomenon for an assessment of the period will likely not be without its usefulness.

For our time a life, which leaves behind it, as the great and exalted do in art, movements and vibrations, no longer seems to be acceptable. Its heroes are heroes of moderation, peace-loving warriors, their vision can be imposed on no one, and one must, no matter how distant they may stand, be able to see in them equals. Love, as much as one would like, but no respect, because this is related to fear. In art the high, grandiose figures, that one may view, are no more, for no listener recognizes himself in them, and they offer the mirror comfortably to none, so that each may see his own personality reflected therein. Since then, however, art should no longer elevate, and through broader channels lead to satisfaction, but rather, ex officio, is and remains satisfaction, since it has come to serve, and in its servitude, in spite of the fact that it is art, must once again, in order to please itself, rely on art; the magnificent and shocking figures are only bothersome Catos[6], who should be rejected as superfluous, or at the most are considered to be colorful. Our time has even found an excellent word for labeling the elevated, which it can no longer bear, with a reproach. Our time calls it one-sided, and correctly so. Every greatness is one-sided, precisely since it differentiates itself from the others, since it stands out and is noticeable. What our time praises as many-sidedness, is this flexibility which makes art and the public one, and which eliminates spiritually and physically in every moment an elevation that separates the performance from the performers. In the theater the public wants to see a broadened salon; no greater traits of character, for these disturb the equality, which is generally necessary in society; nothing shocking, for one does not go into society to return home having been assaulted; the crowns that the public hands out, should be kisses, and amazement should be expressed in embraces.

To this direction corresponds the union of multiple talents, of which certainly not all can make the claim to being outstandingly significant, for that in itself would already be a basic defect, that one could not forgive, but, like a mosaic, they should mutually support each other, and thus form a pleasing whole. In looking at each talent of this mosaic anyone from the public must be able to say, look, you can go this far with your natural talent, and with redoubled effort; that which an individual presents, must at least be presented to the collective in public. One must be able to say, she has a much more beautiful voice, but she is lacking in corporeal charm, this one is much more beautiful, but she cannot sing, this one combines both, but she does not understand how to imitate.

[6] Cato the Elder was known for combatting degenerate Hellenistic influences on Republican Rome.

Mlle. Sontag now seems to me to be the individual for this direction; hence the impression that she makes far beyond her artistic appearance. Without a voice that shatters and leaves behind long-lasting impressions, her voice is nevertheless sufficiently strong and significant to attract in this way to captivate, without being one of those imposing beauties, that arouse astonishment, she is much more a pleasing appearance, who certainly would make no impression, but on the stage, where she stands, leaves behind an entirely different impression. In this way–versatile–she is lucky that often one talent combines with the other, in order to enhance it, without reducing the total through comparison with the other. If one is talking about the singer, then the auxiliaries are brought to bear that she receives from the actress, so that the various talents from a sort of federated state, for whom the various parts must mutually support each other in case of need. Added to this is the German individuality. To comprehend everything and make it one's own, this eternal damnation of translation, where we have the advantage of learning much that we did not think of for ourselves. Miss Sontag is in this sense a translating-talent of the first magnitude, and I would be very surprised, if she were to be so lucky outside Germany in this respect. The German woman, who in spite of her generally retained peculiarity of moving like an Italian, who knows how to express Rossini, Mozart, Weber and Spohr with equal talent, who substitutes volubility and learned strength for liveliness and inborn power; who knows how to deal with a lack of luxuriance through economy, who above all this still knows how to add the art of a German mind and a German eye, must be a very individual appearance for foreign lands up until now accustomed to Italian or French one-sidedness. We have found that Mlle. Sontag with her current appearances has won to the deepest part of the being. How one may do this seems inexplicable to begin with. But for Mlle. Sontag this expression is correct. She has also made the deep, like a foreign composer, her own; indeed, perhaps, has attempted to study her own unhappiness and her own experience with the most tireless effort. Along with all these talents, which certainly must be acknowledged, there is also her great comprehensibility. Mlle. Sontag is a clearly written book, into which for the sake of completeness a few mystical chapters are incorporated, which alongside the openheartedness of the rest of the content add, further, the charm of the mysterious.

For this reason the fame of Mlle. Sontag also made its way beyond the sphere of the musical world. She is thus not only an individual, but rather an event; she is essentially eclectic, since eclecticism is generally the taste of the time.

The way in which she was the expression and symbol of the entire period, celebrated enthusiastically everywhere at the time, has been conveyed sufficiently by the brilliant speaker above Let us put this very important consideration aside for now, and ask: was she an artist in the highest sense of the word?

I must answer "no".

The roles, which she chose at the Königstadt, and in which she found satisfaction and fame, are not at all suited to provide access to true artistry. For they are neither characters nor performances to move the soul in a high or passionate way. Once, at her instigation, Mozart's *Cosi Fan Tutte* was given; it was however, an attempt to put this opera, so rich in charming music, but unfeasible in the theater, on the stage. Miss Sontag took the leading role, but became ever colder as scene followed scene (she can blame the ineffectiveness of the work), and finally she could so little hide her dissatisfaction that she sat down at a table, and sang the rest of her part that way, like a badly-behaved child reciting his lesson. Later she appeared in the more dramatic Mozart operas, but was far behind the demands of these. Yes, even in the lesser operettas there is certainly evidence that she in those roles was only looking for and found herself. In one such she appeared as the wife of a desperately poor shoemaker, given to drink, who was beaten by her husband. For the part she had chosen to wear a silk or *Atlasrobe* with a *Tändelschürzchen*, all according to the latest Parisian style! And when finally the opportunity to wed a diplomat appeared, her artistic career was left behind with the daintiest little step[7].

I did not leave my seven years of activity so lightly and with such grace. I could not look back without satisfaction upon that which I had desired and the achievements of my comrades and myself. At the beginning I found it strange to realize how long the resentment of those who had felt that they were injured by the sincerity of the journal continued to resound;—and how quickly everything that I had done, just as sincerely, to the benefit or furthering of this one or that one, was forgotten. I had to learn, that gratitude is like winning the lottery, something that one may not count on. And that is good! So much the more it honors the giver, and gives pleasure to the receiver.

Among the irritated was also the worthy Friedrich Schneider[8], the composer of *Das Weltgericht* and other oratorios. The journal had never spoken about him. But he was unsettled by the frequent remarks regarding Sebastian Bach's works, particularly regarding his *Passion*, with which I sought to open a path for the publication and performance of the work; indeed, in this he believed that thus he was suffering an indirect attack against his own works. For a long time I had the name of "the Bachian" in the circle of his students—somewhat in the way that once upon a time in any unsettled head was called a "Catilinarian", and in Paris at the time of the great Revolution one heard *Catilina ante portas* at every moment. Later Schneider was very friendly to me. During a visit in Dessau

---

[7] Sontag had secretly married Count Carlo Rossi, Sardinian ambassador to The Hague, while performing in London in 1827. The revelation of this marriage some three years later persuaded her to retire from the stage.

[8] Friedrich Schneider, 1786-1853, composed sixteen oratorios, as well as sundry other compositions and arrangements; his *Das Weltgericht* of 1820, based on a vision of the Last Judgement, was enormously popular in Germany.

he conducted for me alone with a quickly assembled orchestra Beethoven's C-minor symphony and a second C-minor symphony of his own composition in a masterful way, then led me to the church and improvised for me, almost entirely in a figural and fugal style, with complete mastery of the development and playing for an hour. It was remarkable to observe that the fugal movements that he improvised where by far more artful and energetic in terms of shape than any in this style that were contained in his oratorios. In this works he wanted to be as comprehensible and popular as possible, and put fetters on himself, while improvisation he let himself go without care. A strange error by many artists! They consider it a point of honor, or decency, to include fugal movements in their works; but then they then lower these movements, and deprive them of power, through a fear of not communicating.

One thing I had not managed, because it was unattainable: to attract musicians in great numbers to collaborate on the journal, to awaken them to writing about their work, to thus make them appealing. Gluck did it in his time, Reichardt as well, K. M. Weber and Robert Schumann, and after them Wagner, Liszt, Berlioz and others as well. Among creative musicians I was joined by Löwe, the witty H[einrich] Dorn and a few others. My dream of a common hall for lectures was never realized. Thus the *zeitgeist*, whose signature was so brilliantly drawn by Gans, along with new and higher duties decided the fate of the journal.

Since I have discussed one of those who felt offended, let me name another, who benefited from the journal. This was the renowned Bernhard Logier[9] — really the first methodical thinker in the field of music.

Logier was from Hanover, and felt moved in his youth to emigrate to England. Entirely without means, he joined the musical band of a regiment garrisoned in Dublin, then managed a post as an organist, and gave piano lessons as well, in order to earn his living. Soon he did not have enough time for both occupations. His daughter had to temporarily substitute for him as organist, but her young hands and fingers were too weak. Then he invented the *chiroplast*, which, with its metal strips gripping between the fingers bring them into the correct position and strengthens their attitude. A second machine, the *manuductor*, holds the arm at the right height over the keys.

Soon this tireless worker recognized the importance of harmonic knowledge for piano playing (at that time we were still in the middle of figured bass). Now he developed his system of harmony and piano study. It was extraordinarily sensible

[9] Johann Bernhard Logier, 1777-1846, a composer and teacher best known for inventing a number of pedagogical methods and technologies.

and entirely fulfilled the goal of its author. Logier was renowned, and perhaps the more renowned, the less one really paid attention to his system. Spohr, among others, provided a public test, in which three or four students went to the board and provided a given bass with harmony—one in the first measure, the second and third at the same time in later measures—which was entirely correct and connected—an amazing result, that, above all, proved that the procedure had remained incomprehensible to him.

Now Logier, summoned by the ministry, had arrived in Berlin to introduce his teaching method here. He met a great reception.

I was among the friends of the house as well. He asked me to do the translation of his method from English into German, and I had to admit that I did not understand English at all; "That doesn't matter!" exclaimed the strangely energetic man. "You will soon; in the case of necessity Lichtenstein (the zoologist) will advise you." I accepted and completed the work without needing advice. The system is available to the public in the German edition.

At that time a shameful injustice that befell the excellent man forced him to leave Berlin and his creative work in that city, which had not yet put down strong roots, hastily and forever[10].

In this situation he turned to me. "Take my place, represent my system!" he said. "You know it, and I will show you the practical side. I will give you all the apparatus (a grand piano, three or six square pianos, etc.). I believe that I can guarantee that you will be named professor."

I thanked him cordially and declined. No matter how ingenious I found the system, I could still not accept its basis and represent it, since it was built around a mechanization of music, a direction that had been suggested to Logier in a mechanized England, and might be applicable there. The title however, which he suggested for me, had no meaning for me. Already in my youth I had read with amusement that Unger in his *Arzt* had called the crabs that in large shells have very little meat "titular" crabs. All external honors and decorations had never had any meaning for me. A man gives himself his honor, as great or as little as it may be.

[10] It is not clear precisely what injustice Marx is referring to, although Logier's system, while initially successful around Europe and evidently remunerative, was subject to constant opposition.

Chapter 7

The Mendelssohn house.

Along with the journal, and all the activities and work that I have related up until this point, I had not, as is self-evident, stopped working on the completion of my artistic education. For, in spite of my experience in Halle, I was repeatedly driven to the conviction that no one, no matter how talented he might be, and who is able to be so certain and sure about the level of his own talent?–can have sufficient performance in music, without training his gift.

Driven by this conviction, I had turned to Zelter not long after my move; I had been recommended to him from Halle, and met a friendly reception. I did not find his compositions (lieder and ballades) to be very weighty; and even less, what he had produced as a writer: the biography of Fasch[1], well-written but lacking in content. Now, however, Zelter's fame and reputation in Berlin, where he led Fasch's Singakademie, the oldest and largest that there was, was so important, that it gave me the idea that the reason for this had to be found in his teaching ability. I thus informed him of my concerns, told him what I had learned in Halle, and how much I had already composed, but also expressed my conviction that neither inclination nor talent for creative activity could be enough were it not assisted by thorough training.

"That is true, that is excellent!" was more or less his answer. "Yes, the young men come and think that with their little bit of natural ability…yes, it can even be with considerable natural ability … that they can do everything! But *prosit*…"

That pleased me, and happily I took a piece of music paper; I was to work through it and then come back.

Then I sat at home, for it was a sheet with figured basses, of which I had already prepared quite a number in Halle. I quickly worked through the one I had just received and brought it to my teacher. He looked through it, and gave me a second page to work on, without expressing anything substantive.

Now I thought that in such a way nothing decisive could be expected. Thus, I intentionally let some mistakes get into the second sheet, as well as couple of spots, which might raise questions, undone. Zelter corrected the mistakes

---

[1] Zelter's biography of Carl Friedrich Christian Fasch, 1736-1800, a composer in the service of Frederick the Great, was published a year after Fasch's death.

and was about to fill in the gaps in the places left empty–everything just like the first time, without further explanation. Here I plucked up my courage and said: I left these and the other places empty, because I did not know, whether one completion or the other was to be preferred. "Yes", came the answer, "that must give one a natural feeling". I had had enough. It was well known that, one should not rely on one's natural feeling, but should call on the teacher for help. But the teaching had now to call on natural feeling for help. My instruction was now at an end.

Had Zelter failed, then? No! not according to the thinking of the time; for the entire old school never and nowhere would admit consideration of the basis of things and of the bases for teaching methods and systems. What it was able to offer was technical training, of the sort that boys can take in with pleasure and success. I had outgrown this sort of teaching, but at the same time I could observe its applicability for earlier years, and for Zelter's fruitful activity, and certainly for his later-to-become-famous student, Felix Mendelssohn. In general I would find much to experience and much to observe with the latter.

Mendelssohn was, when I first met him, at the boundary between boyhood and youth, and had already made a reputation that went far beyond the city with his masterly playing and composition. I had occasionally noticed him in concerts, and enjoyed his fresh, first excited, then dreamy countenance; it bloomed so healthily and so warmly from the fullness of the wavy hair flowing down from his head. Several times it was suggested to me by someone or otherthat I should have myself invited to the Sunday musical performances at his house. I had always declined, partly because I did not enjoy visiting at the houses of people that I did not know, and partly because my position as editor made such rapprochement even more problematic. Finally, however, it came to that. Whether and through whom I had myself introduced, whether Felix or his father had first spoken to me somewhere, I can no longer say. At any rate, Felix came to visit me either immediately before or immediately afterwards; for I took the opportunity to play for him my *Psalm 137*, which I had just completed, and in which I had even dared a fugue on the words "May I forget thee, Jerusalem", a form that was not yet any further elucidated than had been possible through Marpurg's teaching and the riddling example of the *Well-Tempered Clavier* of Bach.

Felix looked through the score, first with an astonished expression, then shaking his head; finally he could not hold it in: "That–that doesn't work! That is not right! That (pointing to the fugue) is not music at all!"

I was delighted. I could not be hurt; for I knew well that along with my hot desire and possible talent the third factor was lacking: musical training. But I was delighted, for here I found openness! And this seemed to me to be the basic condition for any human relationship.

Now I was, thus, in one of those Sunday concerts, for which Felix had written a string of symphonies in three or four movements, the first movement a fugue, or a fugato, the entire thing for strings alone; instead of the winds the harpsichord came in, played by Felix, mostly or continuously accompanying in the manner of a figured bass.

Truly, there was no reply that I could give, but rather a conscientious seriousness as I, in response to Felix's question how I had liked it, expressed my amazement at his skill in composition, but then added, there was nothing in it, I had found no content which corresponded to the proficiency of the composition.

So we stood facing each other, I knowing, he with a sense, that the other could certainly be right, both certainly convinced that every word was meant honorably. This was the foundation stone of a friendship that growing quickly to be strong would provide us a mutuality and strength that is rarely to be found among brothers. Who could have had an inkling (probably not I), that it would come to an end, and certainly without an external reason, in complete, deadly cold alienation.

Next I won the attention of a well-ordered and wisely directed family, and learned, what an immeasurable advantage birth into such a family provides, especially when old reputation (Moses Mendelssohn![2]), wealth and widespread connections come along with it. Poor me! I came from indigence and helplessness! Destiny had put me at the crossroads of a hundred paths for life, and had said to the stranger to life, ignorant of all of these paths: Go you! Choose, which you may. Here I was faced by another, for whom each step was advised and watched over by an insightful fatherly eye. From time to time, and still rather late, Felix complained to me: once again his father was doubtful about his vocation, unsatisfied with the artist's career, whose success always remains uncertain; again, and once again, he suggests that he should become a merchant, or choose some other more certain road. I smiled at this, and reassured him, while I pointed out how wise his father was in always pushing him to self-examination.

When, later, I said in writing and verbally to my students, a hundred times: the only ones who should become musicians are those who cannot do anything

---

[2] The eminent philosopher and critic, 1729-1786, was the grandfather of Fanny, Felix, Rebekka and Paul Mendelssohn; their father was Abraham, the second of Moses' three sons.

else, this conviction, to which I still hold firmly, may have its roots in those conversations with Felix. Another word from my father had a strange ring for me long after, before I recognized the deep life experience which underlay it. In a somewhat later time, when his father was convinced of my faithful support of Felix, he said several times to me: he did not believe that his son had the highest gift (he meant genius) for music; but that his life could take a happier form. Indeed, happiness in life and genius, how rarely are they compatible, how rarely are they lastingly connected!—Was Schiller happy? Have we forgotten, that on his deathbed he pushed away his most beloved little daughter with his countenance looking away, because grief ate his heart? Was Goethe, who we think was the happiest of man, truly happy? He wanted to be the dramatist of his nation–did he become it?—And you, most exalted! Who raised your blessed instrumental world up to the realm of the conscious spirit, Beethoven! Last of our masters: who can read your life without tears?—No, happiness in life and genius, they are rarely, if ever, unified, they seem to avoid each other, and fly from each other. And for this reason the chosen one - many are called, and few are chosen! is given the bliss of those moments, in which his eye is valiant enough to view the immortal faces, which the glow of his spiritual power, melting everything together in a single moment, first calls into existence, - an entirely different glow, than the heat of hard work, however praiseworthy and rewarding it may be as well.

Probably he had seen and understood it correctly, the insightful son of Moses Mendelssohn. And he was certainly competent to speak about music. The course of his life had prepared him for that. When, in younger years, he had lived for quite a while in Paris, he had seen the incessant productions of the operas of Gluck, which at that time still stood in high repute among the French, and were performed according to the not yet faded traditions from Gluck's time. At that time, he was also witness to the first performance of Cherubini's *Les Deux Journées ou Le Porteur d'Eau* and would repeatedly talk about it with pleasure. Until that point Cherubini had had not great success in Paris. Then came *Les Deux Journées* with its echoes of the ideas of the Revolution. The reception was unheard of, truly frightening, the crowd incited to mania. While the performance was still going on Mendelssohn looked for the composer behind the scenes, and found him feverishly excited, walking around: *"Ah! Ça frappe, ça frappe!»* he kept repeating with a very hoarse voice. Auber, his student, had no reputation at the time, and was not even respected by his teacher. Who would have imagined that the highly celebrated master would (in his *Abencérages*³) come to be an imitator of his student!

Next to the father stood the sharply intelligent, and perhaps less cordial mother. In her traditions or echoes of Kirnberger⁴ lived on; through Kirnberger she had become familiar with Seb. Bach, and had established the continual playing of the *Well-Tempered Clavier* in her house. It was very interesting that the great fondness of the father for Gluck had so little influence in his family. Gluck was well-regarded by everyone, but not really loved and continually kept in mind. This was only the case for Mozart and Bach, and already much less the case for Handel. Completing the family circle were the daughters and Paul, the youngest son in a related cast of mind, in a pure continuous line. The oldest daughter, Fanny, stood next to Felix and participated very closely in his musical studies. At the piano she was weaker than he was in skill and power, but often outshone him in tenderness and intelligent conception, particularly for Beethoven. Several of her songs, for example the duet and some songs of Suleika, were included in the first song collections of her brother under his name. Another is known to have been published later.—The younger sister, Rebekka, intellectually less prominent than Fanny, was really the secret darling of everyone, particularly of her brother. The impression she made was comparable to that which a half-veiled maiden makes; one senses richer, tenderer charms, the less clearly one sees. —Paul was still very young, modestly diffident. When Felix played, which almost always took place without music, then the boy, with glowing face and short black curls crept now and then quietly up after the conclusion, tapped his brother on the shoulder, and said softly: "oh Felix! In measure …. you played f; it is supposed to be f-sharp."— He also, I believe, had an inclination and confidence in my regard. Once he sought me out, and asked, naturally with the foreknowledge and permission of his father, my advice: whether he should join his father's business, or become a bookdealer; the latter he was ready to do, if he was intending, with his means and serious effort, to accomplish something salutary for his intellectual interests. I could not speak on behalf of the latter career, but only agree with the father's choice. Later he became one of the most respected of bankers.

³ Cherubini's *Les Abencérages*, premiered in 1813, was a departure from his usual, rather terse style, and incorporated much use of the chorus and dance numbers; this was a precursor of the lavish *grand opéra* later associated with Daniel Auber, Fromental Halévy, Giacomo Meyerbeer and others.
⁴ Johann Kirnberger, 1721-83, was a pupil of Bach's. He helped crystallise Bach's techniques, especially in the treatment of harmony and counterpoint, into methods and precepts that had a powerful effect over German music into the early nineteenth century.

Next Wilhelm Hensel[5] joined the family, at the time professor and court painter, the later spouse of Fanny. He had already earned a reputation through the masterly copy of the Transfiguration, which now is part of the collection in the Raphael Gallery in Potsdam, and through his own works done in Italy, but in Berlin he could not so fully assert this, as he should have deserved. In the case of this man, who has always been a faithful friend to me, I could observe, that for the artist the favor of luck can easily be a fatal gift. His father, a country parson, had, after the battle at Jena, given service during the flight of the queen. This, and Hensel's charming talent, had led to his favorable acceptance in court circles and his trip to Italy. At court festivities he had been helpful with respect to ideal costumes and *tableaux vivants*, and had taken the opportunity to make portraits of the "Beauties" of the court with a fine and flattering lead pencil. Later as well he had continually practice the art of his pencil. Particularly the characterful head of his Fanny, now with the attributes of a vine-crowned bacchante, now as one of the "Daughters of Zion", who with their infants in their arms turned away from the abomination on Golgotha, now in other character-pictures. But exactly his close connections with the court, his activities, full of praise, during its festivities, his continuing use of the fine and smooth pencil had taken him away from serious and powerful truthfulness, without which the fully satisfactory cannot be achieved in any art.

I became fully convinced of this with his painting preserved in the Garnisonkirche in Berlin in a highly unfavorable setting. The subject is Christ led by the high priests to judgment before Pontius Pilate. The topic seems to me to be one of the greatest that can be presented to the painter. The man sent from God—let us say instead, the Genius, - from the Law, which in the light of new ideas feels itself hollow and unsustainable in spite of the power, which existence, because it exists, provides—led before the secular authorities, so that it can judge the spirit that is foreign and incomprehensible to them. I held this for a task, which extends from that ancient event until our battling age, and beyond into the future. I was a contemporary witness for the origin and execution of this work. Now I had to be amazed at the power of vision and brush with which Hensel in one shot (alla prima) brought his models (mostly Polish Jews, including important female heads of the Jewish community) onto the canvas; and then again I had to notice with deep dismay, how these powerful figures were moderated and formally melded together in being carried over onto the great canvas. The artist began, and the court painter completed it.

---

[5] Wilhelm Hensel, 1794-1861, was best known as a portraitist, and became court painter in Berlin in 1828.

So it seemed to me at the time. Now, or rather for a long time already, I have had a different view, which at the time could never have come to maturity for me, nor generally could have purely emerged from the wavering outlines of the transformation of the time, frame of mind and way of looking at things that was just beginning.

Was it really the court painter who was lacking here? Was it not the immediate expression of the direction of the time, which guided by ideals that asked for unfettered truth, and if necessary, merciless directness, led to the conventional views of "society", a society which, in the mirror of art, only sought to view the flattering representation of its own comfortable life, instead of digging down to the deep kernel of life. —Perhaps it was already the subject (with regard to the choice of which I had not remained unpartisan) that was the first push towards the new direction of the time. To our mutual friend, Felix, the image had always been unpleasant.

Whatever the judgment regarding the work may now be, the Berliners, the majority of them neither with a gift for nor training in art, knew no boundaries, once cold and vile criticism, which has so often shown itself to be at home in Berlin, had entered. No picture by Hensel was properly valued. I felt especially sad about a little picture–a half-naked Italian shepherd boy sits on an ancient marble sarcophagus, and has decorated his hat with bright ribbons; the powerful colors of these correspond to the southern coloring of the boy and the landscape, and are balanced by the yellowish marble, turned brown in spots. Overly quick with words like "bright" we had broken his staff.

Around the family there was a rich circle of male friends of the son and female friends of the daughters. Towering over these young people were the old familiar friends of the house, Alexander von Humboldt, Varnhagen von Ense[6], Professor Gans, and the clever brother of the master of the house, Joseph, who participated happily in the games of the young people and often lamented when the "foolish business" was disturbed by rehearsals and preparations.

Here it was that I for the first time found myself facing the important figure of Alexander von Humboldt. I already know, to the extent that this is possible for a layman in the area of the natural sciences, the achievements of that man, towering over all, who simply through the way in which he created and worked occupied a truly royal position. For since through his journeys, his fame, and his connections in all realms (particularly Russia as well) he was familiar

---

[6] Karl August Varnhagen von Ense, 1785-1858, followed a diplomatic career until 1819, after which he devoted himself to literary enterprises, especially biography.

and influential, he had the opportunity to promote younger scholars in their investigations and to support further journeys. So a circle–I might say, a court, but a highly active one–of younger important intellectuals had formed around him, which received influences and often direction from him, but then with their researches and their collaboration once more repaid the help received with rich and spiritual interest. Among their number I will only mention the witty Dove[7], who since then, despite the warning rejection of Scripture, has taught us "whence the wind comes, and to where it travels". At that time Humboldt was engaged in sending his associates, among them Lejeune Dirichlet[8], out over the whole earth to make magnetic observations which later became famous. Natural science needed such a man as a center point which received nourishment for intellectual life from all directions, and which sent it out once again like new life in all directions.

Now, then I would get to this man, unique of his kind, face to face. The room was rather full when he quietly entered, and his slim and not large figure slid through the groups in order to take a place in a corner. Immediately the middle point of the space seemed to have changed; everyone turned in his direction, and formed concentric circles around him. He, however, turned first to this one, and then to that one, and I easily realized, that he shared with each a piece of information from that person's own field, giving the philologist an indication from his older brother Wilhelm's immortal works on the Kavi language[9] , and to the businessman news regarding the economic situation in South America. He turned to me as well with a couple of remarks on the history of Italian and Spanish music, the complete veracity of which I could not vouch for, but even less wished to cast doubt on with a simple grimace. He seemed to be not displeased with the fact that I noted the confluence of the Spanish and Netherlandish with the Italians in the papal chapel–"as you yourself have observed in Rome", and suggested that German music from Luther to Bach as an important contrast (naturally questionable) to consider.

Amidst the younger and older friends of the household, but more of a companion to the former than the latter, stood Ludwig Robert[10], the poet, with his beautiful wife. They were living in the Mendelssohn house at the time, if I am not mistaken; I had only met them here.

---

[7] Heinrich Wilhelm Dove, 1803-1879, director of the Prussian Meteorological Institute.

[8] Peter Gustav Lejeune Dirichlet, 1805-1859, was most active as a pure mathematician, making substantial progress in number theory. In 1828, he worked as part of a team organised by Humboldt to measure and map the geomagnetic shape and potential of the Earth.

[9] Wilhelm von Humboldt's last work, on the Kawi language of Indonesia, was instrumental in creating the modern understanding of language as structured around a set of rules, rather than as sounds corresponding to meanings..

[10] Ernst Friedrich Ludwig Robert, 1778-1832, was the brother-in-law of Varnhagen von Ense.

This was an unusual and interesting couple, each of them in their own way.

He, beloved as a pleasing poet, looked on favorably as an easily excited and stimulating participant in company, would, precisely around this time, through a sort of chivalrous deed, make a name for himself, in releasing the city and liberating it from a shameful and truly deleterious devotion to a strange personality and the tribute it exacted.

Around that time, that is, M.G. Saphir[11] had settled here, and at the same had founded two journals, which in terms of shamelessness and disregard of every barrier of journalistic ethics went far beyond anything which Berlin had ever experience. If other journalists occasionally and exceptionally strayed into personal details with regard to the matters about which they were writing, with Saphir the situation was turned entirely on its head; for him the matter about which he was writing was entirely the meaningless subsidiary subject, and the personality involved, was the main thing, or indeed the whole. This personality was not only overwhelmed with merciless bitterness, but also with every kind of injustice imaginable and cheap insult, which found its unique content in a Judaizing play with words, something in which Saphir was inexhaustible and which are the greatest source of his most understandable wit. But not only the great houses, but also the stock market and the other circles of society provided a rich contingent for the readers of this journalism. Indeed, the philosopher Hegel, then held in the highest regard, was one of the most enthusiastic readers and admirers of M.G. Saphir; he called him "a phenomenon"–naturally, in those moments where he was less focused on his "Phenomenology of Spirit". There seemed to be no weapons to use against this phenomenon, for any retort, apart from the fact that it would not have been at all easy to equal him in wit and injustice, only further immortalized the scandal, and gave him the opportunity, to add new dirt to the old. True, he was banned from public locations (once even with acts of physical violence); but he always found another open door through which he could once again slide in, in this area being similar to Ajax, whom Homer is well-known to have compared to the always-returning fly.

At one point seven, let us call them seven literati, headed by Willibald Alexis had joined in order to enact a sort of declaration against Saphir, which would give it greater weight than an expression of any of them individually. The names of the associated writers were worthy enough of attention; and they were right in speaking the truth without reservations against the shameless interloper, but what they could easily have foreseen, happened. The phenomenon was happy

[11] Moritz Gottlieb Saphir, 1795-1858, a highly acerbic satirical writer and critic from Austria who sought refuge in 1825 in Berlin, where he remained for the next four years.

to have the excuse for a new and larger scandal. Indeed, he presented himself as the one who was being persecuted, and them as the conspirators - and found not a little support from those who had already recognized the impropriety of his demeanor. Berlin seemed unalterably to be his domain.

This is when Ludwig Robert appeared as a true knight as champion of the defenseless city. He wrote his *Jocko*. Jocko is a man-sized ape, who, directed by his evil lord, appears in human clothing as a "Lion of the Salons", and becomes welcome in the finest company. The history of the ape is known from the stories of E.T.A. Hoffmann and W. Hauff. Robert created a melodrama from this, and when finally its hero, Jocko, appeared on the stage, the house resounded with loud laughter and jubilant shouts: "Saphir! Saphir!" The ape was wearing a mask that was the spitting image of the unfortunate journalist, and conversely the face of the journalist was the speaking mask for an ape. Saphir had to leave Berlin[12]. Later, with more harmless wit and enjoyable sentimentality, he found a place in Vienna as a humorist, and was greeted by not a few as a successor of Jean Paul.

This was Robert's deed. His far greater service however, at least for the young people at the Mendelssohn house, was his beautiful wife[13]. She was truly beautiful, although so calm, that it made her seem like a pictorial work, that just now had been touched by the animating beam. Thus we often saw her in the circle of the other women, not participating, with motionless features and eyes, which, though awake, seemed to be slumbering. Then, however, any celebrity would appear, perhaps even a charming woman. Then, as if convulsed by an electric spark, the fair figure straightened up, and gained, apparently unawares and unintentionally, a painterly expression, her features filled with energy, and became characterful, her eyes glinted in the new light. Woe to the beauty who had entered! She was outshone by one who in desire for and certainty of victory was unable to bear any competition by her side. Such moments were really the attractive thing about her, since they were the constant content of her existence. I never came closer to her, for she seemed to be lacking that which to my mind gives beauty its power: spiritual motion, which shimmers through the physical form. At least, I never perceived this about her; she was a virtuoso of beauty. Felix seemed to have seen and felt otherwise. "But Mielchen!"—I heard once from the lips of the poet, when the beautiful woman gave herself perhaps all too compliantly to the admiring gaze of an onlooker.

---

[12] Saphir did not leave Berlin as a result of his lampooning in *Jocko*, but because his aggressive literary tactics finally alienated the king, who had been an admirer of his prose; his residence permit was revoked in 1829.
[13] Robert's wife was Friederike Braun, known as Friederike Primavesi since her earlier forced marriage, arranged by her father for business reasons, to an Italian bookdealer.

One poet calls to the other–Ludwig Robert, the divine Gamin, the naughty schoolboy of the graces, Heinrich Heine. His travel pictures, his book of lieder had brought him boundless favor at that time. While young women enthused about his lieder, and composers competed to tear the quills from their hands to newly compose them once again, more mature men noted that the facile poet had succeeded in moving his people back to a proper and just view of a great historical personage, from an only too-well-founded bitterness. Napoleon, completely hated to death by the Germans, and justly so, was still the object of their curses and revulsion. Then Heine led the figure of the hero, carefree and harmless, upward from the darkness of hatred. And the German followed the passing heroic image, forgot their hate, and once more learned to view him fairly, while the English sent forth the greatest reporter of those days, Walter Scott, to insult the foreign enemy, and the French, over and over again, became intoxicated by the sound of his name. With Heine as well I found myself together, and we often wandered homewards, first I to his residence, then, in return, he accompanying me to mine. I still have a vivid image of the young, fine, and indeed elegantly built man in my memory, the way he once, at Mendelssohn's, leaned from one side of the table to the other with an inimitable grace of fatigue and exhaustion, to where Rebekka, the youngest daughter of the house, sat, and spoke to her (who was very enthusiastic about his poetry), in a broad and not at all secretive tone: "I could love you!" Rebekka turned away; I do not know whether it was to hide her smile or her maidenly anger. Her determination is well known to have later led her to Lejeune Dirichlet[14].

In looking at the entire circle one could perceive how beneficial for the future of the young composer the rich society meeting in his father's house was. Here each resounding song, each masterly performed new piano work gained a public that was inclined toward it in advance; it was here where the performance of the Bach *Passion* was prepared, here, finally, where distant connections were established, which would be highly advantageous for the young musician. For the rich and well-regarded house hospitably and benevolently took in every significant musician visiting Berlin, and had the opportunity to support him in his Berlin undertakings.

Thus the ground was prepared from which Felix was launched; one may also add the influence of Louis Berger as his piano teacher, and that of Zelter, whose instruction had begun early enough so that the student did not miss what the old teaching method could not provide.

---

[14] They married in 1832.

All that taken together was promising and auspicious enough. But each situation, in which we humans find ourselves, has its entirely unavoidable conditions and consequences. The provision of the means for education, the earliest successes and regard, along with the circle of active and partially intellectual friends, the presence of a crowd of attractive girls–this provided an incessant refreshing bath, stimulating and strengthening the power of the nerves on the young man, already so fresh by nature; quickness and merriness were the fundamental tone of his being. This was at one and the same time happiness and a pledge of further happiness. It was expressed in him in a particular musical trait. When he performed one of his compositions for the second or third time, one could observe, that he accelerated the tempo each time–and quite considerably; given his eminent technical skill it could not be the case that he played slower the first time out of lack of technique. Fanny was often despairing because of this in no way always appropriate increase in the tempo; but it was the unavoidable expression of increasing excitement and impatience.

Far more serious, but just as comprehensible was the influence that the joyful environment and the surroundings, and the constant interaction with the young female friends of his sisters played on him. In the broad park of the house Felix, the intellectual Klingemann[15] and myself founded a garden newspaper. The capital for this was in a wooden table with a sliding drawer, which sat day and night in one of the broad shady corridors. Anything that anyone had to contribute would slide in here. Drawings, tender poems, witty letters, all possible sorts of things were found there in order for everyone to enjoy them, and to reveal the more hidden meanings to the beauties to whom they paid special homage. More than once I climbed up to the roof of a neighboring building with Felix, in order to let costly peaches or ripe bunches of grapes slide through the open window onto the night table of a young lady with a Polish name.

Was it then any wonder, could it have been any other way, that the tender homage he awoke and received from so many caused that faint reverberation to be heard in this compositions which we later liked to call either sweet, or courtly, or tender, and has as a consequence that "Song without Words" which from that time onward crept through the whole life of the composer?–At that time, with the others, I took pure pleasure in this, and I was permitted this. For only insistence in this sphere of the small and soft sweet things, the return to the easily comprehensible motives of the barcarolle, or devotional forms in the manner of chorales, and finally the inclusion of all the weaker and smaller

---

[15] Karl Klingemann, 1798-1862, was the diplomatic representative for Hanover in Berlin [15] at this time.

talents in this form, more playing with the intellectual than filled with the spirit, made evident the true meaning of this direction.

Another trait, also the necessary product of those happy circumstances, had already secretly entered my soul, before I understood its scope. It was expressed only in a single word, but words are the expression, or rather the betrayers of what takes place in the soul and must be expressed, or wishes to hide from others, even from the speaker himself. "That gives me no pleasure!" I so often had to hear, when the conversation came around to this or that in music, painting, and so forth; and that certainly rang out the most, when the deepest, most serious, when the soul in its greatest power came to be expressed. I remember the fateful phrase being used against Dante, against Michelangelo, and even against Beethoven's compositions, and precisely against the deepest, namely, the Ninth Symphony. And strangely! as much as I was amazed by and loved his playing, his performances of Beethoven rarely satisfied me. This led on several occasions to arguments, particularly with regard to the great B-flat sonata[16]. But this led nowhere. My playing was not strong enough, and I was not yet fully aware enough that, for the discussion to have borne fruit.

---

[16] Number 29, op. 106, the *Hammerklavier*.

Jakob Ludwig Felix Mendelssohn Bartholdy, 3 February 1809 – 4 November 1847

CHAPTER 8

FELIX MENDELSSOHN

Undisturbed by such considerations our bond became so strong and close, that rarely would a day pass on which we did not mutually exchange visits and notes. Of course, the content of these was curious, brightly woven from particular expressions and allusion that only we understood, from musical movements and wild pictures; for Felix also had diligently practiced drawing, and particularly in the area of landscape, as I had in capturing human form. Soon we discovered that the art that we really had in common was not music, but drawing. For music imperiously puts an end to all conversation beside her; drawing, however, especially when a pair of faithful friends are peacefully sitting next to each other, draws forth even more lively conversation, and if momentarily the conversation should flag, then a look at the other's work, or a call for help from one or the other will always renew it.

But our mutual conversation easily took on peculiar forms, particularly when it turned to matters, for example instrumentation, which from a strict point of view are inaccessible. I still recall, the sort of astonished glances back and forth that Droysen produced, when he, during a visit to my room had to listen to me saying to Felix: here pure purple must be used; here the horns dampen the splendor of the trumpets; and Felix replied: no! no! that is too much screaming, I want violet.

And yet this relationship had to end. —

Or rather, the basic difference in our characters, way of looking at things, and musical directions finally, in spite of everything, finally become increasingly clear to our feelings and our awareness. Did he move away from me? Or I from him? - the latter would have been entirely unfeasible, even had it been within my nature. For I had taken his side too frequently and too definitely, and spoken out about him in my journal. The former – at the time, I saw the matter thus, and the feeling of simply being abandoned by him was for me a corrosive drink of vermouth, that long years later still had a bitter aftertaste. Now I think that I can see more clearly. The external separation was simply nothing but the necessary consequence of the inner separation, which both of us had avoided looking at for such a long time.

Finally it had to come out.

I had finally achieved the means and leisure to move forward in carrying out my old favorite plan, *Mose*. It was clear to me that it could not be a double opera, as I had imagined in my early youth, but that it had to take the outward form of an oratorio and that the Bible had to provide the text for it. My erudition in the Bible meant that the preparation of the text did not seem too difficult. I had quite often spoken to friends about my plan; now, that it would become a serious matter – ah, it had always been serious for me, but my circumstances always got frustratingly in the way – Felix was the next with whom I shared. A few days later he came to me to tell me that he also wanted to write an oratorio, and take his text from the Bible.

"That's wonderful!" I replied. "I had been worried that looking around for texts could influence the freshness of the composition, but now we are both safe. You can put together my text for me, I will put together yours for you, and we both will come fresh to work."

He happily agreed. Now I asked about his subject. "I had thought about writing on Paul."

I was concerned. Paul, the teacher, the wise man – I was tempted to say: the Protestant, the rationalist. Forgive me the inappropriate expressions; I can find nothing better to express my view of the exalted, profound matter, should I imagine it as the subject of musical treatment. The thinker, the painter, perhaps the poet – these can build their work around Paul; but the musicians, whose creativity belongs first and foremost to the sphere of the inner life, the sphere of feeling?

My awareness of the unviability of the artistic decision was too clear for me to dare to immediately express my thoughts. For such a decision is not at all (as those looking from outside often think) a matter of free choice. It is the product of an entire way of thinking, of outlook, and disposition, which draws the artist directly to this matter, and no other; within him speaks the necessary mutual connection between the artist and his subject, like a magnetic connection, that draws one to the other. Thus, once the spirit of the artist has chosen his direction, rarely is it altered or assisted; the entire development of the spirit must have prepared it. In spite of this, commanded by my secure conviction, I tried first of all to bring external thoughts to awareness only through questions. Paul, I offered for consideration, is a figure without a definite beginning or end. He is a teacher and martyr, but not the first one; Stephen, unquestionably, precedes him as martyr. His end, according to the legend, comes by the sword in distant Rome. The high point, however, for his life for artistic representation can only be the appearance of Christ. This is a task for painter and poet, but what can the musician do with the words: "It will be hard for you to kick against the pricks"? How can he bring into sight the exalted state of the Holy One, who speaks them – and the alarm of the one to whom they are directed?

I mentioned this and other matters. I even suggested another subject, Peter, the Prince of the Apostles, of whom Christ said: he is the rock on whom I will build my church – Peter, who before our eyes staggers and fall, and then is uplifted as holy hero – Peter, finally, who after the conception of the Mother church continues to work in it and in the vicars of Christ, who gives the Church of Christ its first secure form. Even if we Protestants do not hold to the interpretation of the Vicariate of Christ (the artist as such is at any rate neither Protestant nor Catholic), yet the figure of the founder remains a highly exalted one.

I publicly relate my view of that time, which I continue to hold, unaltered, entirely unconcerned by the fact that *Paulus* was composed and found extraordinary recognition.[1] An artwork has such manifold content, and there are so many reasons for success, that the latter provides no elucidation regarding the former, but rather is only to be created through penetrating consideration.

My suggestions were not listened to – and I wrote the text to *Paulus* as well as I was able.

After some time Felix asked me whether I would not like to include chorales? "What? Chorales in the time of Paul? And among the circumstances which shaped the course of his life?" I did not understand it, and stepped back. The text, as it would be composed thereafter, was put together by Superintendent Schubring[2] in Dessau and the insightful theater-director Eduard Devrient, friend of the composer, the two of which were staying in Berlin at the time.

I had shared the idea and plan for *Mose* with Felix. Not long thereafter he brought me the libretto, titled "Moses, an Oratorio, composed by A.B. Marx." I have preserved it as a memento; it bears at the end the date of August 21, 1832, and the signature F.M.B.

I only include the beginning and end here for the purposes of evaluation:

Moses.

First Part.

Overture.

---

[1] The work was premiered in 1836.
[2] Julius Schubring, 1806-1889, a priest, made the acquaintance of Mendelssohn while training in Berlin in 1825-1830.

And the Egyptians forced the Children of Israel to serve with rigor. And they made their lives bitter with heavy work in the fields and with all kinds of heavy labor, which they laid upon them with rigor.

A Voice.

Oh Lord, behold and see, how I am become miserable.

Chorus.

Behold ye and see, if there be any sorrow like unto my sorrow. How sad I am!

A Voice.

God, hear my cry in my complaint. Guard my life against the fearsome sorrow.

Chorus.

Pursue them with wrath; consume them from underneath the heavens.

A Voice.

Ah, that help might come over Israel, and that God might redeem his captive people.

Conclusion of the text.

Chorus.

Halleluja! Thank the Lord, for he is good. Then there arose thunder and lightning, and a thick could upon the mountain, and the sound of a very strong trumpet, and the entire people was frightened, and Mount Sinai smoked and quaked greatly, and the sound of the trumpet became ever louder. Moses spoke, and God answered him loudly:

"I am the Lord your Good, who brought you out of Egypt, out of the house of slavery. You shall have no other gods beside me. You shall make yourself no graven images. You shall not take the name of the Lord in vain. Remember the Sabbath, and keep it holy. You shall honor your father and your mother. You shall not kill, you shall not commit adultery, you shall not steal, you shall not bear false witness. You shall not covet."

Chorus.

This is love for God, that we keep his commandments, Amen!

CHAPTER 9

TRAVEL AND RECREATION

Before I go more deeply into the course of this matter, which caused so much heavy heartache for me at that time, I will turn, to catch some breath, back to an earlier experience, that provided me some beneficial refreshment then.

Already before 1830 my economic situation had become more comfortable. Instruction in music, the journal, many editions of writings (*The Art of Singing, On Painting in Music*, participation in *Caecilia* etc.[1]) and musical works (Chorale- and Organ Book, Lieder, Choruses etc.) had prepared me for a larger journey. Alone, on foot, carefree and merry, as those who go on foot are, I wandered through the comfortable hills and dells of Thuringia toward the south. In a village south of Coburg I was to take a guide, as I had been advised, who would take me on footpaths through the wood to the most attractive point, the Kloster Banz[2]. I entered the village in the early morning. It was Sunday, and a secret stillness, like the peace of God, lay over the sunny meadow; from near and far one could hear church bells ringing. But all the doors were closed, with not a soul to be seen; it was the hour of the early service. Not without embarrassment, I looked around; I saw the head of a blond boy, which leaned out of the window of a little house, and as soon as I saw him, drew back as fast as lightning. This was a wink for me; I went into the entryway, knocked on the door of the room, and went in, since I had heard nothing. No one but a quiet old man was in the room, but was not working with farm or housework, but rather with metalwork for pipes. Upon my question, looking for a guide, he answered unfavorably that I would have to look elsewhere. In the meantime I had noticed a piano next to the window. With the words, ah, there's an instrument, I went up and tried it, not without pleasure with respect to how it played and its sound. The old man had walked up, nodded his head with a smile, and said: I built that for my Heinrich, the schoolmaster let me have the soundboard! I looked with amazement at the old man, who in addition to his hammering on pipes had made a piano correctly. But he added, apologetically, "This is really not my métier, but I have made more than one clarinet, which sounds quite nice in Kirchmett and wherever else the young folk

---

[1] *Die Kunst des Gesanges*, op.cit.; Über *Malerei in der Tonkunst*, Berlin, 1828. *Caecilia* was a music journal published out of Mainz by the musicologist Gottfried Weber: Marx had contributed from the first issue, which appeared in 1824.
[2] A Benedictine monastery, in Bad Staffelstein, Germany.

are making music. Then he handed me such an instrument, which I for obvious reasons was unable to try out. And so I had arrived in a true music workshop. Even before this I had entered such a location of rural skill. In Dessau I had found the son of a local who had begun to be a passionate bird-hunter. If he had knocked down a beautifully feathered creature (his father had made him a fine rifle for this purpose), he wanted to preserve it as well. The animals were skinned and stuffed, and in such a talented way that they would earn their place in any museum. Many of them were sold, and the best he would not part with. And then he had the notion to draw them and paint them, and further to the bold decision to engrave the pictures, and color the prints. Then he sold them in collections. Unfortunately I have forgotten the names of both villages; but at least the young bird-expert was widely renowned in his day.

Long since the blond boy had made his way in and looked me perkily in the eye, since once his grandfather and uncle had noticed that I was "in the business", they were transformed. "And my Heinrich will lead you to the cloister, he knows the ropes; just three weeks ago he took a painter from .... Dings there, and the painter painted half the forest, he was so happy." At his first words Heinrich had clapped his hands, had jumped away, and came marching right back. Now we went up and down hill. As soon as I had become more familiar with the boy, who probably was about fourteen, he was inexhaustible in his happy loquacity. First he showed me a mighty oak which "just last year" had been split by lightning; then he motioned me to be silent, with his index finger pressed to his lips, and pointed into the valley, where a slim mother deer was leading her baby deer to feed. Then she held her head up high, seemed to notice something different, perhaps ourselves, and then the shy animal fled, her knees sharply bent, along with her young one. But the boy was inexhaustible in describing "the beautiful music" that they had at the cloister. Boys and young men came from all the villages and the Cantor put them in the organ choir for music for the mass, which they sang in unison. Others played clarinets or violins, and whatever else there was, and it was all very beautiful. It was not long until the Kloster Banz appeared before our eyes, formerly a cloister, then a princely residence, brightly upon its hill. We hurried to arrive at the stately terrace, which opened so invitingly. And then we could look far, far out over the morning meadowland, as it was laid out with its pastures and bushes in the mild sunlight, richly sprinkled with villages, here and there interrupted by small towns, and crossed by the young river Main, which snakes through the countryside like a sky-blue ribbon of silk. It was not a "beautiful view" or a "beautiful vicinity", as the painters say, for it was lacking in a "point" at which the whole culminated and was drawn together. But it was a view, bright, wide – almost boundless, blissful, and peaceful, as if the dear Good himself had laid out the table for his earthly children for their refreshing gathering together. "How lovely is it when brethren dwell together in unity!" – but the most blessed of men said "I am not come to bring peace, but the sword." Man is safe, and the artist is the one who is called and faithful, who carries peace in his soul, and preaches a firm heart the hardest, when the voice of his artistic conscience thus dictates.

Solemnity and secrecy surrounded us in the quiet church. On its walls gleamed white marble and gold, witness to former episcopal majesty. When I wanted to try out the choir of the respectable organ, my hands quickly retreated, for completely different sounds came out than I had expected. The manual apparently began with great F, G, A, B natural; among these lower keys, lay the upper keys F#, G#, A#, but they played neither these notes, nor the C, D, E, which should have been beneath. Naturally I had to play the wrong notes; it was the first organ of this kind; I have never seen a second such.

And so noontime had arrived. With my Heinrich I joined a procession of other guests from the region, for whom the castellan or administrator had prepared a table, naturally for a fee. When I tried to enter, the host grasped me softly by the arm and pointed out for me: over there it is set for the honorees. I declined, finding it more appealing to stay among the people with my Heinrich. While we were eating at the long table, the door opened once more, and a strange man walked in. He seemed tall, but walked all bent over, as if he wanted to kneel down with each step. He was dressed in an entirely worn-out hunting jacket, whose colors, green with crimson borders, could scarcely still be distinguished. With a broad and somewhat uncertain stride he slid from guest to guest, and offered each one his hand. On his ravaged face, as it seemed, one could see a mixture of begging for help and curses flow by. I looked for a gift to give him; and then my neighbor grasped my arm and whispered to me: don't give him anything! He cursed anyone who did him a favor. Upon my amazed query I was told: he had been with Napoleon in Russia; and was supposed to have eaten the flesh of a child there, --- or perhaps it was the tortures of the frightful retreat that were enough, he had come back weird in the head, and now dragged out the rest of his life, all the year long floating about and begging.

A scarcely still glimmering firebrand, cast all the way from Moscow to this paradise!

The journey continued to Munich, the first point of arrival on the journey. At that time King Ludwig still ruled in the old Monk-City, and soon the new city began to spread out next to the old streets and buildings. With what lack of insight and gratitude did public voices and the attitude of his own people (at least in part) speak out against this king! People never get tired of holding against him his poems, his participial[3] amateurishness, his weakness for a dancer swirled up high by love for dancing and wantonness. The fact that he planted his capital and his country far and wide with marvelous buildings, that he elevated his Munich to a rich treasure-chamber for the visual arts, that he recognized the most talented painters in the twilight of their earliest positions, before they had had the opportunity to achieve fame and high importance, and commissioned them to produce rich and grand works, and thereby created a new period for German art – that, I think, would have been enough, and more than enough, to cause someone to forget these trivialities. And that, finally, he preferred to put down his scepter, rather than live at odds with his people, or reign further against his own convictions, is something, if one of these amateurishnesses may have contributed to it, that seems honorable.

Now I was in his city, on the left, belonging to the fifteenth and sixteenth centuries, on the right, to the nineteenth; there were spots where twenty paces led from the Middle Ages to the greatest modernity. The Glyptothek already stood with the immortal sculptures of the children of Niobe with the sleeping faun who is just about to wake up (his marble breast is already rising). The Pinakothek was built, but the collection not installed. The spaces over the arcades in the picture gallery were still empty. That was my first visit.

I entered this series of halls the width of churches – there were nine. Later at table I told my neighbor, a Bavarian that I had just come from the nine halls of the marvelous gallery. "I think you meant to say eight". I was amazed, and a little ashamed to have so grossly miscounted. The next day I counted again, and there were nine halls, but whenever I said this, I was contradicted. Finally I solved the riddle. The first hall, which contained the less valuable pictures, nevertheless still significant enough to adorn other museums, the Müncheners simply refused to count. And they were right to be proud, since what was in the other halls was simply priceless. Among others, I counted, if I remember correctly, eighty-eight Rubens, all belonging to the first rank among his fabulously numerous works. Outstanding for me was a *Decius Mus*, in the moment where he offers his death for his Rome.[4] He stands before the *flamen dialis*[5], who lifts his hand in priestly consecration over the head of the leader of the troops, an elderly, dignified figure. To the side a warrior holds, with intense effort, the war-horse, which, spooked by unseen horrors, wants to break loose, and rears up. But all of this is subsidiary. He himself, consecrating himself irrevocably to death, he

---

[3] TM: *Partizipial* in the original German, which, as in English, refers exclusively to grammar and syntax. Perhaps Marx meant "participatory".
[4] The finished version of this painting, along with many others in the same series, is in the collection of the Princes of Liechtenstein.
[5] The *flamen dialis* was the high priest of Jupiter.

is the entire picture. He has pulled his warrior's mantle over his head, so that it blocks our view of his forehead and eyes. What else should they do? Thought has become the decision, the struggle against the human that inhabits each of us – fear of death and pain – which could be expressed in the eyes, they are already overcome. There he stands, from inside to outside transformed into brass by the inextinguishable glow of his heroic soul, like a pillar, upon which "eternal Rome" rests, strong and secure, he himself the picture of a thought which built and sustained Rome, and finally collapsed. But what renunciation and fidelity by the painter, who denies himself the expressive eye, and the brow, which the spirit itself chose for its residence, in order to give full expression to the thoughts of the event. Veiled, as the story goes, Decius falls, seeking death, into the troops of the enemy. This trait was faithfully and boldly represented by the artist. But the reward was in the deed. What remained visible from the face, the Roman nose, the pained mouth, closing in unchangeable firmness, and the figure, for which each member, each muscle conveys the spasmodic intensity – these would not have gained in expression, but lost, had brow and eyes remained visible; they would have only given the viewer new target points. The Munich picture is only a colored sketch, but the idea is solid and clearly legible.

It is not my intention to mention the best, as selective art connoisseurs say, or even much. I will not mention all those Raphaels and Titians, and the other great names in the realm of light and color. I would only like to remember one picture, by the Spanish Zurbaran. This is the returning home of the Virgin Mary from the Cross[6]. The tall figure wanders with hasty step, bent over, through the night; her robes of mourning are blown backward by her hurried motion; her countenance, turned downward – has a look ever had the color of life? And next to her is walking, just as quickly, the disciple "whom the Lord loved". He is clothed in a green tunic; the color, though it scarcely appears in the dark of night, works like a cry of mockery. He has turned his upper body toward the person walking next to him. With upraised arms and outspread hands he speaks to her; but his expression and gestures show – he is speaking words, and he himself does not know which. And she does not hear him. What was there then to speak of and to listen? So the two of them flee into the night, they know not where, they no longer have a purpose.

Each day I spent several hours in the gallery. I felt as if I had entered a new world, full of most various sublime and tender figures; like a silly boy I wandered, now shy, now exalted high above everything personal and mortal. What the great masters of the past, Raphael, Titian, Rubens — this long procession of priests of the truth had seen in their hours of worship, I could now see, follow

---

[6] No painting fitting this description is extant.

the trail, which their own hands, not those of imitators, had left behind. And when my soul had become inebriated from the never-ending fountain of the eternally beautiful, within me I could hear the inner voice repeating the old words "I will not let you go unless you bless me!" to the great masters. For I felt the importance of the place for me. The amateur will simply enjoy, take into himself, that which is given. He who wants to become truly at home in art, does not remain with the What; he asks after the how – how did the artist make it. And what we recognize in one art, comes to be present for us in every other one.

In these halls there were even my own connections to the life of the Müncheners, and certainly unsought for, and in an unusual way. It was rarely or never that I went through these halls, without finding there young artists, but also younger and older women, before a picture that they were copying. If I walked up, and they noticed, that I, in pure love of art was only looking at the original and the corresponding copy, I was so openly and amicably welcomed by the painter, and so soon engaged in conversation, which had nothing to do with my person, but rather with our mutual love for the matter, that one could scarcely imagine it in our colder and more brittle northern lands. Some of the young women painters regularly conversed pleasantly with me, without either finding it necessary to give our names.

One of these ladies, simply dressed, but evidently belong to the upper classes, seemed to be pleased by my unremitting zeal. She was working with a not particularly important work, which she, however, was completing with love and fine sense. When I expressed something similar, she replied, she only rarely and exceptionally tried her hand with the brush, for really her favorite activity was sculpture, and she only picked up the brush in order not to let her eyes become unaccustomed through cold marble with the color of life.

"What a lesson you provide for my artistic comrades, the musicians! Ah, if only they would learn from you, dear madam, or from Beethoven!"

She looked at me, surprised, and I added, by way of explanation: how could it be that this eternal lingering at the piano would not chill the pulse of life, if mind and hand were not from time to time to bathe in the stream of the orchestral world? She answered, hesitating: she was not at all musical, but she had a notion of the sense that met here in the two arts. If I wanted to see something of her métier (she smiled in pronouncing the word), then I would have to visit her at her residence. And since this lay outside the city, she suggested that she would have me picked up the following morning, when the gallery was closed.

On the following morning an elegant wagon appeared at my house, and a

liveried servant came up to my apartment with the announcement: Mad. ....
– only now did I learn that she was the spouse of a high court official – was
awaiting me in the wagon.

We traveled among low shrubs, over fields, over branches of a small river,
perhaps the Isar, to a tasteful country house. Her spouse received us, and we
viewed several works in marble on the ground floor, which I spoke about with
warmth, which I truly felt. Her spouse accompanied us, polite but mute; he
was, he said once in passing, entirely untrained in art, really perceiving little,
"but you must also come to my workshop, that I cannot omit." And thus he
led me upstairs to the flat roof, where a costly telescope and other astronomical
equipment were installed. His avocation, which he was very serious about, was
astronomy.

I would like to take this opportunity to share an observation, which I made
at that time and in my circle of vision, without being able to claim that it is
generally applicable and also for the present time. While the North strives for
a comprehensive education, and everyone, particularly our young ladies, seem
to have planned to learn and practice everything – singing, piano, embroidery,
drawing, two or three foreign languages, not to forget literary history, which due
to the insatiable need for conversation is presented at all girls' schools, I noted
in Munich that everyone, particularly the ladies, whom I had the opportunity
to observe, limited themselves to a single area of area, which, however, they
practiced with full pleasure and strength. One was only a singer, but she sang
excellently; another was a pianist; a third (Fräulein L .....) was not important in
either, but she created – without instruction – charming and naïve songs. The
painter did not slide from the pallet to the piano. Thus each remained true to
their inclination, and was as strong in it as nature permitted.

Banz Abbey, Kloster Banz, Germany

CHAPTER 10

THE WIDE WORLD.

When the foreigner looks out to the south from Munich on bright days, in the far distance silvery high plateaus shine toward his astonished eyes, seeming to float in the air without roots in the earth. Never has he seen anything like this in the north, nor in the mountain heights of Thuringia or of the more serious Black Forest, never has his untrained fantasy reflected something so great and quietly powerful. These are the glaciers and the snowy peaks of the Tyrol. Wonderful, beautiful, and powerful at the same time, are the glaciers and snowy peaks of the Tyrol. Wonderful, beautiful, and powerful, all together; Nature builds gradually, when one rises upward from the serene places of the golden Au, over the soft hills of Thuringia, to the bolder lines of the Odenwald, the darker riddles of the Black Forest, in which a strong race passes its life in a combination of strict and solitary work and fairy-tale like dreaming. From there the path then leads to the powerful foothills of Switzerland, which to the east bear the name of Tyrol. The commanding peaks of this entire massif, Switzerland with its crowning Mont Blanc, I would see only later.

This time those silvery heights winked, and drew me irresistibly toward them.

How might I wrap myself in silence here? may I be permitted only a few fleeting words of observation.

First, it was in the valleys that lead to Parthenkirchen that I would learn how deceptive, for those only used to the northern plains, all sense of perspective becomes in the clear mountain air of the South. What seemed a small hill, perhaps a half-hour distant, demanded, in gradually diminishing illusion, six hours of road, and grew to a mighty mountain massif, which seemed to push its way in amidst the still mightier walls of mountains on either side. High over the bottom of the valley, in which, passing by fields and meadows, the road led through handsome villages, a second row of villages looked down, arranged upon sizable peaks, with their cemeteries next to them. If the entire view was already full of pleasure and life, and so broadly spread out, that the eye could find no boundary upon which to rest from all the excitement, yet the cemeteries as well had their part to contribute to the fairy-tale-like scene. From hills, all covered with greenery, which closed in on themselves, blinked a bright mixture of steel-blue crosses, and golden garlands of flower, from here and there. They were made of metal, and the crystalline air took from them none of their gold and steel glitter. But they were so far in the distance that everything appeared to be at the scale of those tin toys which we had enjoyed playing with as children. One would have thought that they were cemeteries for elves, if elves could expect burial. Soon, as well, I would become aware that I was in the bosom of Catholic life. Soon I had thought to hear sounds as if of Gregorian chant or hymns; but then the deep still of the valley returned, only the harmonic noises of the herds, larger and duller. Bells from the unhurried cattle, brighter and livelier bells from the restless goats, leaping here and there, chimed in to make the quiet yet more blessed. In the meantime, the singing had come closer, sounded without ceasing – and now the singers appeared. It was a pilgrimage of a group of village communities, men, women and children, who moved past the happily tarrying wander along the valley, up and down over the heights, hence the apparently intermittent silences. How close to nature, and how refreshing such devotion! The wandering through the sunny valleys, with cool breezes coming down from the heights, so calmly and innocently pleasant! Here one, there another, mopping their blazing brows, taking a brief refreshing draught, whilst nodding familiarly to neighbor and to wife. We poor sons of men! No one wants to accept the other. Everyone falls prey to the seductions of eloquence and the thumbscrews of cool logic! Should not we rather think of the words "In my father's house are many mansions?"

Further along, in Innsbruck, before the imposing guesthouse a tall cross was erected, and in front of it the statue of the Archangel Michael, I believe, and the guesthouse was called, if I am not mistaken "*Zur Sonne*" [to the Sun]. And there a loud noise of people in prayer called me to the window; the whole front side of the large building was a single window. Below, on the broad street (or was it the "Ring", or the marketplace), a prayer leader was placed before the cross, who responded to the thick press of worshipers, who filled the room, in the manner of a litany.

It was in Innsbruck where I entered the first cloister, a Capuchin cloister. The porter showed me which way to go, and soon one of the brothers would lead me. And after a few steps my leader appeared, a slim, still very young monk, who, like all his brothers, had no other garment but a coarse brown robe, gathered at the waist with a rope, and sandals on his bare feet. His features, and even more his voice, conveyed complete self-mastery; gentleness and sadness came through, without disturbing the quiet and friendly smile. I later heard that my guide had renounced his vow; he was, they said of noble origin, and the pain of love had driven him to refuge in the cloister.

Our way led through a side-door into the refectory. In the corner opposite us I observed two of the bearded monks playing with cards with images of the saints; sheepish, they quickly sought to hide them when we entered, and looked at us with contrary and timid faces, as if they were boys caught in the act. It seemed like an unpleasant surprise for my guide; he immediately turned around with me going back to another door. Opened, it led into a completely dark chamber. When I, surprised by the darkness, pulled my foot back, my guide spoke with touching humility: have no fear, I am true, and there is no danger here. The chamber led to the cloister-church; Emperor Maximilian lived there when he was in Innsbruck for devotions.

My final path in the notable city led me to the Castle or Court-Garden. The lovely sunshine gilded bushes and flowers. Suddenly I was standing before a church; the area before the portal was made up of tall, slender wooden statues. As soon as I walked between them into the church, I found myself in deep half-night, entirely alone, behind a broad circle of dark brass figures of far more than human dimensions, which stood around a sarcophagus, of brass and dark like the figures; if I am not mistaken, it was the memorial of former lords of the Tyrol. The impression was very deep, almost frightening. Quietly I slipped past the wide circle. Suddenly, at the other end, powerful sunlight poured through the window of a side chapel that until now had been entirely hidden from me by the brass figures. The mass of light, dazzling at first for eyes accustomed to the darkness, and then mild once my eyes had become adjusted, fell upon an altar, richly decorated in the way that they love in the South, stretched out before it, kneeling, was a young blonde maiden, one of the charming blossoms which the mountain-land provides so many of. Kneeling was she, so entirely absorbed in fervent devotion, that she neither noticed my approach, not was able to know anything else about the outside world. I slipped quietly back. Probably the continuously open churches, the unabashed and undisturbed devotion of individuals for consecrated places a necessity and a blessing for the more excitable minds of the South. We, in the cooler North, with quieter minds and more conscious spirits, seek after that which strives to fly upward from the unfree soul – quiet and solitude; privacy seems a necessity for us. Yes! There are many mansions. . .

Back my path went to Munich. The city was at the highest level of excitement. On the street, on every corner, at the kiosk of Tambosi[1], who offered his costly ice, and everything else that was delightful, under the arcades, people of every condition stood and pressed in their hundreds, with from time to time one of the multitude climbing on a table, around a corner post, and read the news from the newspaper. For the reports of the July Revolution[2] had just reached Munich.

And, wandering from Munich to the Rhine, in Mainz I saw the first ship with the three-colored flag. Everywhere, whether in Mainz or in Munich, joyful excitement reigned.

---

[1] The coffeehouse of Luigi Tambosi, dating back to 1775, and still operating today.
[2] The French revolution of 1830, overthrowing Charles X, and replacing him with Louis-Philippe, head of the Orléans branch of the ruling family.

What did the Germans have to do with those events in Paris, what can the tricouleur have meant to them, which only a few years before had threatened them with or brought them disgraceful subjugation?

It was sympathy with a people, who had liberated themselves from these Bourbons, who were unable to understand the thinking of the time, and the dignity of the people.

Chapter 11

Mose

I had returned to Berlin from this first longer trip refreshed and enriched. This is the real benefit of maturity, that it makes people free from the narrowly-drawn boundaries within which one's life moves, and that which he sees and experiences in foreign parts, leads within him to ever-renewing fruits.

If only I could persuade everyone to practice for such a journey by drawing. Drawing means learning to see. Thousands, nay, millions learn to make music – and how few of these bring home fruit from this for their life! If only one could explain to everyone, and to their teachers, that the practice of music is unavailing to those who do not have an understanding and pleasure in music as well. In contrast simply everyone should learn to draw, so that his eyes will be opened and bright for all beauty and meaning which the world offers in visual forms. It really is entirely irrelevant whether someone achieves excellence or even only competence, but rather that he should have looked keenly and with love, because for him his vision has truly become his own, and cannot be lost for all time. From my trip I brought home not a few drawings, some of personalities, some of landscapes. They have all gone missing. But now, after so many years, I could produce series of view from Thuringia and Tyrol, and they would correspond to the forms they had at that date.

In Berlin I was free for the creativity that I had carried in my soul since the years of my youth, of which I had so often dreamed and spoken, and had always been repressed due to the adversity of my situation.

Now I had won my way through, and could begin. I already held in my hand the text that my comrade in art had put together for me.

As I read through it, and read it again, I felt like I had been struck by lightning. This, is this then *Mose!* About which you have dreamed so long and so innocently? and who knows whom you have talked to about it? And now you are facing it, cold, without feeling? With no pulse beating for it? No dawn of intuition?

I felt, with true alarm, that I could not compose the work. Had I lied, then? And if not, must I not appear as liar or deluded about everything that I had said regarding my plans? — This was the condition into which I was thrown by reading the text. Finally, though, I had to say to myself, that, what I had nurtured and reared so long within myself could not be a disappointment, that the text had to please, and the task stood there as firm as a rock.

Here it became clear to me that my friend and I had wandered down very separate paths. Certainly – there was no doubt about it from the beginning until now – he had worked for me in good faith and with firm conviction. He had produced the text as so many had done before us, and had been accepted without object by the greatest masters. The mixture of narration, lyrical effusion and dramatic moments, was a regular form for Handel and Bach; the favorite work for both of us, the *Matthew Passion*, had this same design. Mendelssohn thus was entirely free of the possibility of reproach. Why had I failed, or not been able to clearly outline for him the new form that I needed!

But this new form was not being sought by me; it had grown necessarily out of my entire way of thinking and spiritual direction.

Wherever I looked around me in the arts, everywhere I could see that for the masters as the basis of the writing and thinking one found the highest degree of veracity – in as much as everyone was given to look at the truth. I never, among the greatest, in the works of Homer, Aeschylus, Shakespeare, Raphael, Bach, Handel, Gluck, Beethoven – came upon consideration on the attraction of the so-called beautiful or graceful, never speculation regarding the new or original, inasmuch as it is new original, as a moving force; my marvelous Beethoven expressed that so naively and so appropriately. To follow in the paths of those great figures, even if from a distance, had been deeply ingrained in me as the first duty of an artist. However much might be lacking for me in terms of pure musical talent and in the arts of flattery and accommodation might be replaced by me with veracity and fidelity to circumstances. Gluck is the shining example of this for all who come after him.

Thus it was necessary to present Moses in full and living veracity. For this, however, music, which cannot narrate and cannot describe, knows only one form: the dramatic; this was, as I did not know at the outset, what was needed for Moses.

It is evident, that it was not possible to think of a scenic presentation of the drama of Moses. But to my spirit figure after figure appeared in fully living form, yes, in corporeal form – Moses, Miriam, and the rest. And also the people in their exodus, which according to the indication given by the poetic manner of the psalms, appeared in two caravan trains (strophe and antistrophe) moving alongside each other on both sides of their leader.

For all of this the Bible was a sufficient source. Now, however, we read in its depictions nothing about the Egyptians except for the hateful scorn of the priests against foreigners and idol-worshipers. That provided no perspective.

I acquired that in the Egyptian Museum. For weeks at a time I was a daily guest there. The rigid colossal statues only expressed the immutability of the Egyptian spirit and existence; in the bas-reliefs of the temple walls I saw the people, agile and supple as snakes, often gracefully posed, as one rarely finds in depictions of the Hellenes. For the Hellenes always strove for moderation, and only approached this Egyptian manner in a few Dionysian figures, while on the banks of the Nile slavery and the most extreme license alternated. At such moments that Bacchanalian vortex in which rage and lust flowed into each other was ignited. This what I thought I saw on the ancient stones, which perhaps even Moses himself gazed on. What Herodotus relates does not seem to contradict this.

How much I needed to see personally what was presented would only become evident later, and certainly in a way that may seem burlesque to those reading about it.

After the rapid completion of the first part I felt almost emptied out by the stormy work, entirely unable to move forward. This feeling pitched me into a depression that threatened to become a real illness. My Therese[1] persuaded me to take a walking tour in Kreuzberg[2].

Suddenly from one of the side streets on the right appeared one of those wandering foreigners, who thus seek their bread, with his camel.

I, who had always been a friend of strange animals, stepped unintentionally in front of the peculiar creation, and it looked at me so peacefully with its big, always tranquil, brown eyes, as if it were thinking and remembering—

The entire view of the desert unrolled before my spiritual eyes. I hurried home, to begin the second part of the oratorio, "In the Desert". Constantly seeking after the truth, Moses did not appear to me with the sort of abstract holiness or piety that listeners might have imagined in their devotions. Nothing of that sort, not a work of immediate devotion was my task, but rather a true depiction of those persons and events, as the Bible itself presents, which also is not continuously devotion and prayer. Thus, Moses was for me above all the leader of the people, but the leader sent by God. Thus necessarily the voice of God must speak, just as in the Bible; what it transmitted was the goal and pinnacle of the work. This voice had to give expression, in being true to the ancient scriptures, to all of the turnings of human thoughts and feelings, it need to have grandeur, mildness and consolation, it had to pour down the wrath of Jehovah. For exactly so, according to the witness of the Bible, did the God

[1] See chapter 12.
[2] Although very close to the centre of Berlin, Kreuzberg remained little inhabited and even rural until the second half of the nineteenth century.

of the chosen people appear in those times: he comforted and promised, he threatened and showed his wrath, he repented of punishment and forgave. But this was unshakably clear for me, that Moses could not exist in contrast to the later presentations of the Godhead, but only with respect to the ancient Jehovah, who had sent Moses, and to whom Moses led the people.

Two friends were by my side, and their thoughts were of the highest significance for me. Although I could not give up my conception of the voice of God for theirs, yet the latter still seemed important as a character trait for both.

The first was Felix Mendelssohn. When I told him that I was planning to use both choruses with the greatest possible separation and mixing of the choral voices for the voice of God, he shook his head and said: that won't work – no one will understand that. Use a bass! Just look at Raphael's Bible[3], where the old man with the long beard flies through the heavens, grasping Sun and Moon with both hands. I answered that the highest example in this direction had been given by Bach in the *Matthew Passion*: but that was God become man, who could do nothing else but speak with the voice of a man. It is something else again when Jehovah speaks to us; we perceive his speech from all of creation. All that has voice streams together so that we may hear it – he also did not accept my half-joking reference to the vision of Ezekiel.

The other was Spontini. My journal had been closed for a long time; there could be no misunderstanding of Spontini's actions, which only came from a benevolent feeling toward me. When I first shared my plan with Spontini, and we came to talking about my presentation of the voice of God, he said, with his Italian liveliness in his speech: the only right way is if you use *canto fermo*; he meant the ancient melodies of Gregorian chant. This was for me, entirely putting aside the content of the melodies, entirely unacceptable. My work could not and should not have anything to do with church worship. Only at two points during composition were there suggestions having to do with the soul; one during the ancient worship of God by the people in Egypt. Here, from my earliest boyhood the tune of the penitential song came back to me, which the Israelites in their "long night" would sing in recognition of all their sins and in prayer for a pardon from punishment. The second moment had to do with the address by Moses to the people leaving Egypt. Aaron gives priestly solemnity to the powerful words of the leader; to his words I gave the beginning of the chorale melody "Nun bitten wir den Heiligen Geist" ["Now we pray to the Holy Ghost"]. Whether someone would hear it made no difference to me; above all, I wanted to satisfy myself. This chorale incipit was the only slight indication

---

[3] Raphael's Bible is the collective name for the decorations produced by the artist for the papal palace in the Vatican. The images were frequently reproduced in book form.

of the later period of the Christian church. But the conclusion of the work contains as the climax of the whole the prophecy of the Messiah and the new covenant, as it is contained in the Old Testament. Spontini allowed my view to have validity; but he as well, as Mendelssohn had before him, declared he was against the choral form for the voice of God. *"Je prendrais* (he said) *une basse-taille* - two bassists, all the bassists, all the trombones – and the timpani must be thundering continually!" The excellent man had in mind the thunder of Sinai, the most powerful oracular voice that ever resounded from the stage. My soul had something else in mind.

With the composition begun (Mendelssohn had already left Berlin) it was once again Spontini, and only him, whose support and advice encouraged me.

The work intends to represent the slavery of the people in Egypt. Entirely filled with the event and my participation I had not been able to do enough. After a broad choral movement there was a recitative and aria, and then a chorus again. Spontini convinced me that with all this I had gotten no further than the first chorus had done, that I would become smaller rather than larger. I began anew, and now the shape appeared which the work would take on, and in which it later would appear in such a luxurious score and so forth from the great publishing house of Breitkopf und Härtel. I am not in a position to report everything that the seasoned master said to me. Once, when I was certainly recognizing the correctness of his judgment, but stubborn because of the love which every artist has for his image during its creation, I became visibly perturbed, and could scarcely come to a decision, he looked kindly and sympathetically at me, and said placing his hand on my arm: "Ah mon ami, j'ai tant pleuré!" If only I could have repaid him for this minute!

And his gentle tenderness of feeling would become evident to me. During a visit of his, due to the score, my young and pretty wife sang the aria of the Queen for him: "Du, den meine Seele liebt". In the first two measures I thought that I had seen a subtle smile on his lips; at the end of the aria he first praised the singing, and then the aria. Only later did I realize that those two bars bore an undeniable resemblance to *Alcindor.* Spontini had certainly recognized his motif, but was considerate enough not to disturb me by remarking on it, and nodded contentedly, when any resemblance disappeared with the turn toward C-minor in measures three and four.

CHAPTER 12

THERESE

I have already reported that, at that time, when so many things were pressing together, I received the most precious thing that a man can have the privilege of enjoying: a loving wife[1].

I had found her in Dessau. Dessau is a friendly garden spot, situated amidst broad meadows and a stately oak forest. At that time (1836) I had the same experience as did Saul, who went to find his father's asses, and found a kingdom. Since then it has probably happened for many people; I did not find a kingdom, but something more valuable. The view of the little provincial capital, where once the old Dessauer [2]brought his pharmacist's-daughter home, and later Basedow[3], Müller[4], and Schneider had worked, seemed quite individual to me. I was not very much aware of my, whether it was her fault or mine, they may well have dabbled, preached, cured, visited the Leipzig Fair. But when I walked through the sunlit Kavalierstrasse in the mornings, in order to see my young Therese, upon every ringing of the hour that resounded far through the stillness, ten house doors would open at once. From each of them a young and delicate man with a green and white hat came forth, then to disappear again into another door. These were the students of the old Schneider, who was the shepherd of Apollo's musical flocks here. The friendly young men walked from one beauty to another in order to share once more their musical wisdom, as fresh as it was when they received it.

But this young beauty was the warm center of the life of the small town. In the healthy quiet, amongst the scent of flowers and the breath of the majestic oaks, she had grown up; I had never seen so much charm and beauty in such a small space. The distractions and the unnerving din of the big cities, and the peacock pride of their feminine circles, were unknown here; what one wished to enjoy, one had to create for oneself; this is the secret blessing of small towns. Thus, the young daughters of Dessau – perhaps without exception – were

---

[1] Marx married Maria Theresa Cohn in 1838. Born in 1820, she was as much as twenty-five years his junior.

[2] A reference to Leopold I of Anhalt-Dessau, an early eighteenth-century prince who married a commoner.

[3] Johann Bernhard Basedow, 1724–1790, educational reformer, founded the Philanthropinum in Dessau, 1774

[4] Johann Ludwig Wilhelm Müller, 1794–1827, poet and translator, best known for the verses he provided for some of Schubert's finest lieder.

filled with the desire to spiritually broaden their circle of acquaintances, and to populate the quiet of their lives with figures of creative fantasy. The Ducal Library was open to them, and what it could not provide, was created by the individual fantasy of each soul open to stimulation. When I arrived, the dear children were still all excited by the words of a traveling actor; he had revealed in their circle, with the mysterious bearing of the true mystagogue: he had to listen to nature while she was at her toilette. That gave them something to think and to dream about. Out of this circle I had brought my Therese to Berlin.

What had attracted me to her?

She was very beautiful! But I had known and marveled at even greater beauties, most recently, in Berlin, Eugenie Hitzig, the daughter of that philanthropic criminalist, to whom I owed my entrance into my literary career, the sister of the architect who was later to be so well known, and at that time a wonderfully beautiful boy with an authentically Hellenic countenance[5].

It had not been beauty. She herself, Therese, must know this, since like many she had attracted this. This was something peculiar about her – that she, a passionate admirer of foreign beauty, was with respect to her own and its praises indifferent and cold. For me, however, what one calls beauty had only had value in so far as the inward spirit and character spoke in its shell. I thought that both shone through, and I had judged correctly.

When I, in Berlin, introduced my young wife to one or another among my friends, and she had to hear: He wrote this book, and that one, this book, it was almost too strange for the young being. "Does everyone here write books, then?" she asked, rather anxiously; the barely sixteen-year old woman, who did not like being behind in matters of the spirit, had only met one writer in Dessau, the worthy creator of "Norder's Reisen." He had enjoyed providing the ambitious girl with teaching and books; and even Mendelssohn's *Phaedo* had thus come into her hands[6]. That a certain Plato had also written a *Phaedo*, she did not know; but when I, in receiving by letter information about her strange reading, which I would not have imagined any young woman doing, allowed a certain doubt to be glimpsed in my answer, I received immediately such a fundamental instruction regarding *Phaedo* as no doctoral candidate in philosophy would have been ashamed to have written.

One should not think, for heaven's sake, of any hothouse culture or tendency to show off on the part of the young creature. During a preliminary

[5] This was Friedrich Hitzig, 1811-1881, designer of many of Berlin's most prominent public buildings.
[6] Moses Mendelssohn's *Phaedon* of 1767 was both a translation and an imitative updating of Plato's reflections on the death of Socrates.

visit that she made to an aunt in Berlin, I thought I would please and encourage her by taking her to our Museum. There I showed her picture after picture, by Correggio, Titian and God knows whom else. She patiently followed me, looked where I looked, and listened attentively to my deep and sensible presentations, but afterward I had to feel that I made no especial impression with my pictures and explanations. I thus left with my beauty. Suddenly, on the way back, she stood entranced before a shop window – "Ah, what a heavenly doll! A large doll in sky-blue silk clothing had erased all of my chatter – and that of Titian and Correggio.

In the meantime I had been named professor at the University of Berlin in 1830; in 1833 my naming to a second position, that of University Music Director, followed, which had earlier been held by Bernhard Klein[7], and most recently Zelter, still my professor during the first part of his term.

The position as professor, which Minister von Altenstein[8] had newly established for me, was probably the result of my earlier literary efforts. Soon, however, I would experience the first benefit of the university position, and the happiest effect of the position on those entrusted with it.

Until then I had still not made any public lectures (discounting a few dilettantish lectures on acoustics in Halle), and not once taught in school. Now, I would occupy a chair at the first German university, a weighty moment, even if I could hope to have more or less grown to the demands of my task. I thus worked conscientiously and carefully on my first lecture, and walked up the steps, with the lecture prepared. But I had not realized that my eyes were not keen enough to read what I had written. Impatiently, I put the little volume back in my pocket and continued to speak, extempore. I felt odd when twice in the course of the lecture erroneous information escaped my lips, and I was aware of the mistakes as I spoke. Here my experiences in the juridical examination came into play. I spoke further without mistakes, and made my corrections at the first good opportunity, when everything was already going more smoothly. From then on I have only lectured extempore, and have realized what a secure master of the material permits this free and new creation. Above I related, how the instruction of a young woman entrusted to me gave the first impulse toward the creation of my system of teaching and compositional method. Now I found myself facing youth with academic training, and certainly young people for whom for the most part the study of composition was not – or not yet – their life's vocation, not their "bread-study", as the unfortunate term goes, but the

---

[7] Bernhard Joseph Klein, 1793-1832, a composer specialising in oratorios.
[8] Karl vom Stein zum Altenstein, 1770-1840, the minister responsible for religion and education in Prussia from 1817 until 1838.

freely chosen subject of the desire for knowledge, that precisely in the nobler minds is impatient with limitations to the necessities of future employment, and instead lets the gaze fly free, in order to see and examine what is appropriate for it overall. Here it was appropriate to provide fruit for the nobly-yearning spirit of youth, the benefits of the consumption of which would remain, no matter what career path might be chosen in the future. Here it was completely unacceptable to set up abstract, half-true, half-false maxims and prohibitions as if they were like wooden barriers and railings. One must place oneself by the side of this youth in spirit, ask, look, doubt, boldly and securely move forward, place them and oneself before the only judge that everyone recognizes and must recognize: their own reason at work in each and all.

The first presentation of the compositional method, and its transformations in the sixth and seventh editions of the books, are to a great extent the fruit of my university activity. For I continued to build my material for – no! with my listeners out of the free spirit of the new.

I am happy to acknowledge that in doing so I was animated by a particularly uplifting feeling. I was appointed to the university through a purely ministerial decision, without the participation, indeed without the knowledge of the university. Now I stood in the circle of very highly deserving men. There was Ritter[9], who had brought geography from its prior status of chance and caprice into the power of reason and true science. Immediately before my nomination I had sat at his feet, and followed with the enchantment of a gourmand his light hand, as with brilliant traces it first laid out the basic lines of the construction of the high Alps, then, amidst the ancient worlds of granite, caused the smaller mountain masses and the river valleys to appear before our eyes in a new day of creation, and continued into the last little valley with its racing little river or stream – as I later hiked through Switzerland with Therese in our repeated wanderings, Ritter's declarations were our guide, and the construction of the granite masses and the Jura was for us readable text.

Along with Ritter there was the Brahminical-silent Bopp[10], who, for us Germans built with bold, secure wings the spiritual bridge to the ancient homeland of our people and our language by the holy streams of the Ganges.

Then there was Böckh[11], the Nestor of the philologists, who showed his disciples the broadened bounds of their discipline, and gave them the

[9] Karl Ritter, 1779-1859, whose principal contribution to geographical thought was his constant insistence on treating phenomena as part of a larger, organic whole.
[10] Franz Bopp, 1791-1867, a leading scholar of Sanskrit.
[11] August Böckh, 1785-1867, a classical philologist who produced an edition of the verses of Pindar.

confidence to see poetry, history, and archaeology as realms belonging to them to. His Pindar, his *Staatshaushalt der Athener*[12], along with Ritter's *Geography of Asia*, provided powerful support for my studies of history.

Who could name all the worthy names! It would be ungrateful of me should I think to neglect our astronomer, Encke[13], here. He had, for me, not at my request, but out of his own free will, assisting me and my weakness in larger calculation, himself worked out a calculation, which would be useful for my musicology.

I must give space for yet another name: Eduard Gans, the jurist. In his field he was happy to appear as the opponent of the renowned legal historian Savigny, he as student of Hegel, with the tools of philosophy against the investigator of the sources of Roman law—though he as well, the editor of Gaius and creator of general inheritance law, was familiar with source study. His brilliant activity at the University took place in his public lectures on history, especially that of the French Revolution. This immense event, without doubt the beginning point from which the most recent period of history has unfolded, was presented by Gans in a truly rousing manner. Only the very largest lecture room, the *Aula*, could reasonably accommodate the press of listeners; and yet it was necessary to read the course twice during the same semester in order to satisfy the demand. Among the listeners were rows of generals, high officers and *Geheimräthe* at the front. Even those who found the matter off-putting could not avoid hearing about it. The fact that Gans while lecturing had the example of his friends Guizot[14], Thiers[15] and other French before his eyes was evident in his predilection for brilliant antitheses. Nothing could be more resounding than when he, for example, in speaking of Queen Elizabeth would with pleasure utter sonorously "Elizabeth, this Virgin among Queens, and Queen among Virgins....!" to the air and the ears of his listeners.

Along with the feelings and drives of my own vocation it had become a spiritual necessity to feel that I could participate not unworthily in such circles. It is not the patent, but the products that give legitimacy. The first volumes of the writings mentioned above also belong to the commotion of that point in time in which I set up my household with Therese (those volumes paid for the construction), and wrote my *Mose*.

---

[12] A work of 1817 on the economy of the ancient Greeks.
[13] Johann Franz Encke, 1791-1865, notable for his work on the periodicity of comets.
[14] François Pierre Guillaume Guizot, 1787–1874, historian and statesman notable for his role in stabilizing government after the overthrow of Charles X.
[15] Adolphe Thiers, 1797-1877, another statesman in the administration of Louis-Philippe and thereafter, who also wrote a much-read ten-volume history of the French Revolution.

At that time, and at other times as well, I learned that one works hardest, when one in the press of work scarcely knows where to begin.

I learned as much three years later in taking over the direction of music. In his day Klein had written and performed various motets etc. for the academic choir, which were enthusiastically sung, and were well-fitted to use within the University. Zelter had contributed his *Liedertafelgesänge*, whose fresh if sometimes homespun humor was certainly appreciated by the younger singers. At the same time the choir had been reduced considerably in size; Zelter was in his last years of life, and had so many positions and responsibilities, that he could find little time for the academic chorus; and in addition the academy that he led provided better activities for the singers. This last advantage was something that I was lacking. In addition, it seemed to me that an exclusive preoccupation with lighter compositions was not befitting the worth and character of an academic choir. These songs by Zelter, Löwe and others were in no way excluded, but were not, in my opinion, to form the core of the activity, but rather should serve only as relaxation from things that were more difficult. I was of the opinion that one could only improve power and pleasure through higher and at the same time more difficult tasks. Because such compositions for male chorus were not available in the necessary quantity, thus I willingly and fully undertook their arrangement. The six-part hymns from Trautwein's, and the Festival Songs from Härtel's publishing houses are the fruits of this activity, chosen from among a much larger number.

Now I had already made that decision in the first summer semester of my music directorship. I wrote for the chorus, which for this occasion increased to a size of more than one hundred members, an oratorio, *Am Tage Johannis des Täufers*[16] for solo voices and choruses with accompaniment by organ and trombones, which was performed twice publicly in the church, and several times in smaller circles. When I was busy with this and with rehearsing for the approaching day of St. John the Baptist, I received an invitation from the rector to write a festival cantata (three movements) for the approaching jubilee of Hufeland[17], the medical doctor, and very soon thereafter the request to write the necessary music for the celebration of the third of August[18]. So three not inconsiderable compositions (the two festival pieces with orchestral accompaniment) appeared unexpectedly within a very short time from each other. I had not foreseen this, and could not change it; it had to go, and so it did.

---

[16] A short work of 1834 on the subject of John the Baptist, which is not extant.
[17] Christoph Wilhelm Friedrich Hufeland, 1762, 1836, the Prussian royal physician.
[18] The birthday of Frederick William III.

That was the great time for the academic chorus. With the reconstruction of the university building it unavoidably lost the necessary spaces for its large group, and the best choice of times.

In the midst of this bustle of events and activities I brought my Therese home. I had never felt tired in the midst of my labors. Now my life was renewed. When at that time my dear comrades from the university brought me a serenade, as they did annually for my birthday, those who had been sent were pleasantly surprised by the view of the young Mrs. Professor, with many *studiosus theologiae*[19] often visibly embarrassed by the invitation to sit down beside her. "This is a hairy story!" whispered, unseen, an honorable old boy to his neighbor on one such occasion. The fact that she actually asked, quite naively and amicably, one of the "highly honored gentlemen", who may have spoken a few words of Latin, "Do you also speak Latin?" was considered to be especially amusing.

The composition of *Mose* took place in the first period of our marriage. One piece of happiness did not disturb the other, but rather increased it. When I had sketched out some aria or chorus, then I called my rose to the piano, and she sang with her bright and lovely voice what I had barely sketched, at sight. She had learned little, but received much from nature. If it happened that she did not catch the sense of an aria, it would have been unbearable both for her and for me had I wanted to use the usual school-tyranny of "Piano! Forte! Forwards!" and the various other tender gestures. I sketched out the situation in a few words, and said to her: "So –Miriam raises her eyes and hands! — So — the elderly mother of the pharaoh shuffles under the burden of her years and care, and her old and weak voice finds its last power for its last warning." That was sufficient. She understood me, and performed wonderfully, when we two were alone, or when Spontini was with us. With strangers she was and remained maidenly and bashful.

But even given this maidenly shyness she could prove herself brave if the need arose. Once, towards evening, my door was pulled open with force, and in stormed a troop of students with the cry: "Herr Professor, the house is burning! We want to rescue you!" At the same time the other door opened, which led to my wife's room, and she came, pale, but calm, with our recently born little boy in her arms. She said to me, unruffled: "I have the child, take the score, the house is burning!" She did not think at all about the possessions that we had just acquired.

And her shyness with respect to strangers disappeared, when she needed to help out. The Archduke of Strelitz, who had learned about *Mose* from his

---

[19] In Latin in the original text - "scholars of theology".

chamberlain Oertzen[20], wanted to hear the work. The performance (which took place in May 1843) presented great difficulties for the young academy, whose highest achievement until then had been Graun's *Tod Jesu*. From time to time I received comforting news; between the lines, however, there seemed to be more to worry about. Because of the novelty of the work and its ideas it was necessary to introduce the performers above all to the meaning of the work; and that could only happen, if they heard it, overlooking any faults, once as a whole. For precisely the unity of the whole, the interconnection of all the individual details was, to my mind, the strength of the work. I was invited to come over, and direct the work. At the first gathering of the academy, I declared: we would like to sing the work straight through, without worrying about any mistakes. Since the solo passages had not yet been assigned and rehearsed, my Therese came up next to me, and sang, between the choruses, the solo parts assigned to her so brightly and courageously and expressively, that from that point on success was guaranteed.

[20] Numerous Oertzens served the archdukes of Mecklenburg-Strelitz; this was presumably Karl von Oertzen, 1816-1893, whose father, of the same name, had by then died.

CHAPTER 13

SUCCESSES

When I had completed the largest part of the composition, my longtime friend Mosevius[1], the founder and director of the Singakademie in Breslau, visited me. When he asked what I was occupied with, I named my oratorio, and played the part that was ready to him, at his request. He immediately announced that he had to be the first to perform the work. I was delighted about this. He reserved the right to direct it; it could not have been in better hands.

Soon the score went to Breslau and the rehearsing began.

Here I had the same experience that I have related above of the later performance in Strelitz. At the beginning I received news that obviously were concealing more than they revealed. My hopes sank. Then a short letter arrived from Mosevius, in which he begged my forgiveness; I did not know for what. Immediately thereafter a second, explanatory letter arrived. He had, wrote the excellent musician, begun to rehearse the work; but it wouldn't get started on the right foot, he himself had taken the wrong approach. Then he had decided on a final attempt, and to let the work be performed in its entirety. Now for the first time he had really comprehended it, and the performers as well had gone into it with understanding and pleasure. Soon thereafter I received the invitation to come to the dress rehearsal and performance. At the appointed time I was there.

I had, however, a curious feeling, when I entered the great hall of the former Jesuit College, which has now become the *Aula* of the University, and found the long arched space full of listeners up to the orchestra. It was in fact the custom that the students received free admission to the dress rehearsals; many others had arranged admission as well. The Singakademie, including the best singers of the seminar of Breslau, large at the time, with men's and boys' voice, and the instrumentalists behind them, were in place. With my wife I took my place in the twilight of the space for listeners on one of the benches placed there.

Excited to the greatest degree I awaited the opening, for I had sent off the score without having heard a single movement of the chorus, or a stroke of the instrumental music. The rehearsal began: chorus after chorus unfurled; I

---

[1] Johann Theodor Mosewius, 1788-1858, a singer and music director who was one of the first outside Berlin to imitate Mendelssohn's performance of the *St Matthew Passion*.

was pleased, but nothing surprised me. Thus, precisely thus, I had imagined it. And now the "Voice of God" began. Here–I simply relate what I experienced, what seized me, literally, an attack of fever. I had stood up, and had to cling to the back support of the bench in front of me, so as not to fall down. And the heavy bench trembled, or did it simply seem that way to me? beneath my hands. This—yes, I had planned it this way, but yet there was something that had come in, that I had not foreseen. Later (when Moses, with the words "Here I am" appears before God, and begins to speak to him) I imagined that I heard amidst the orchestral playing a chorus of men's voices, that was simply not present; the situation and the leading of the wind instruments had caused the illusion. But it was not simply a fantasy of the composer. At a later performance in Weimar various listeners had the same impression, without my saying a word to them beforehand about my "hearing-vision", forgive the expression!

One may be permitted space for a couple of lines on one more naïve moment from Breslau. When, in the second part, Pharaoh rejects the demand of the people to go out to their worship of God, then approves, frightened by the plague, and once more takes back his approval, the pressure of need and his hardened heart grows ever stronger. Finally, at Pharaoh's words "So go from me, and take care that you come no more before my faces, for on that same day you shall die!" suddenly a boy's voice was heard from the middle of the chorus calling powerfully "The bad boy!" The boy had become fully immersed in the reality of the story. He had had the same experience as I had had before.

The performance and success left nothing to be desired.

The third and most successful performance (after the one mentioned above in Strelitz) took place in October 1843 in Erfurt. There, without my participation, Music Director Golde[2], one of the most distinguished conductors, had decided to perform *Mose*. When I arrived in Erfurt on invitation, I found the work already entirely rehearsed; Golde not only had arrived at the meaning of the work for himself, but had also filled his collaborators with it as well. I certainly took over the direction, at his request, for the further rehearsals and the performance; but the credit for the success belonged to this both energetic and warmhearted man, and next to him to the loving participation of all those involved.

In this old city the deepest and most beautiful joys which a composer can receive from outside, were granted to me. Why has it not been granted me to repay this to my unforgettable Golde, to whom I owe this!

Erfurt, though so small in comparison to our empire-defying capital and commercial cities, was at that time a leading place for music. Three academies

---

[2] Joseph Golde, 1802-1886, a specialist in military music and director of the Soller singing society.

and five men's choral unions worked happily side-by-side–just think–in a city of 30,000 residents! This shows the widespread love for music in this Thuringian city: but at the same time it is an indicator of that tendency to cut ourselves off from each other, and to shut the others out, which is unfortunately characteristic of we Germans, and is instilled as the opposite side of the noblest drive to preserve oneself independently in our individualities. My first thought, in learning about the situation, was, to bring all the *Vereinen* together; probably it was not simply a matter of doing my music; I would have considered myself fortunate, if it had been the reason for a continuing union. But from all sides I had to hear: that was out of consideration, that was simply impossible; and besides the best members of the other *Vereine* had already joined Golde's *Verein* for *Mose*.

But I had to deal with a consequence of the split; during the preparations for *Mose* another *Verein* had prepared an oratorio for performance, new at the time, but which had already gained great recognition; mine was scheduled for performance on a Sunday evening, October 14, the other was performed four days earlier on a Wednesday. For this the Weimar orchestra and the court opera singers there were recruited, and the performance took place, as the newspaper declared beforehand, "at the enlightened church". The solo parts in *Mose* were in the hands of dilettantes, and the orchestra made up of friends of music and regimental musicians.

The news was not at all unpleasant or worrying for me; my conviction remained unshaken that the world had space for more than one, that it had room for both works; indeed, it was attractive for me to observe how *Mose* would tolerate the close comparison. With respect to the advantage of the performing groups, I did not recognize this without conditions. I knew that the friends of music in their naivety, far from performing with unrestricted perfection were much more open for advice and direction and much readier to accept a new idea than often musicians in the pride of their long-since achieved fame. This was evident at the rehearsals that I held with the solo singers and the chorus and orchestra. Everyone was unconditionally and inexhaustibly devoted to me and to the work, none of my words were ignored, none of my desires remained unfulfilled. For Miriam I had an established singer, for the young queen a young maiden, who underwent her first rehearsal in the most charming way. For Pharaoh (tenor) and a few minor parts I had a young man, with an excellent voice placement, but still entirely untrained. In the church at the dress rehearsal I had to make it clear to him how and where he had to direct his voice in order to fill the large space. I thereby experienced once more a demonstration of how much the will of man is capable, if necessity demands. In order to elicit the right performance from my young friend, I found it necessary to sing various passages for him. I must have succeed, for immediately the word spread that I possessed an excellent tenor voice; but I have never had such, but rather only a small bass voice, which would not have been capable, without pressing need, to have performed the same passages once again in a satisfactory way.

Now the day of the performance had arrived. When I arrived at a meeting of the board in the morning in a house opposite the Predigerkirche, where the performance was to take place in the evening, I was shown through the window whole processions of country folk in their dark Sunday finery, who were slowly heading to the church in a serious group. On Sunday evenings they perform Haydn symphonies; now they are coming, many from two or three miles away, in order to hear the new oratorio.

In the evening the performance took place. It went marvelously. The large church was full, and the response of the listeners was a final confirmation of my faith. When I returned to my apartment, the landlord received me, and led me, rather than to my room, under some pretext into a little hall, from which folding doors opened into a larger one, which we had used until now for rehearsals and practice. These doors were still closed, but the noise of many made its way into the smaller room, in which I had been left alone with my friend Sietze.

Now, the doors opened, and deputation after deputation came in—from the singers, from the orchestra, and from the Erfurt Academy, etc. to bring me good wishes and mementos of their appreciation, Golde's *Verein* honored me with a precious silver/gold baton, another *Verein* presented poetry, the charming singer of the Queen (Mlle. Ernestine Gassmann) as spokeswoman for the singers, the first of those to enter, presented me with a laurel wreath, which I have preserved as an eternal reminder of those presenting it.

Until this point I was filled with joy and thankfulness to all, but still tranquil; for my often-tested heart had already learned to stay firm where others overflow. Now, however, the delegation from the orchestra entered, led by the young and very tall leader of the violins. He began a speech, but overcome by inner emotion, had to break off; and now I began to feel most deeply, that I was not being offered the toll of respect, but sympathy and love.

The unforgettable moment—it was evening—would receive its surprising conclusion. There had already been a growing noise from the street. Then the landlord brought the news that below the doors had been opened by force, people had made their way in, and wanted to see me. So I went out onto the steps to speak to the densely packed crowd, and give them my most deeply felt thanks.

Franz Liszt in 1858 by Franz Hanfstaengl

CHAPTER 14

AUCH DIESES WORT HAT NICHT GELOGEN

Auch dieses Wort hat nicht gelogen. Wen Gott betrügt, der ist wohl betrogen.

Goethe[1].

Mose came to be performed in several more places, and finally also in Berlin. The Singakademie had provided the chorus, and its directors at that time, Rungenhagen[2] and Grell[3], provided me the most welcome assistance. King Frederick William IV had (if I am correctly informed, at the recommendation of Meyerbeer) authorized the Royal Chapel as the orchestra. In spite of this the performance was extremely deficient, and the success insignificant. The guilt was no one's, but rather the circumstances. For the jubilee of F. Schneider, according to the wishes of the Queen, one of his oratorios, one of the Greek tragedies (*Oedipus*, I believe[4]) was to be performed in Potsdam, while at the same time in Berlin an opera of Gluck was to be prepared. The orchestra traveled back and forth between Berlin and Potsdam almost every day, from one rehearsal to the other; at the same time the Singakademie had more than one commitment to deal with. And the solo singers also found themselves hindered and exhausted in the press of all these demands. And so a careful level of study, and sufficient rehearsals were not to be achieved; indeed, it even came to the point that not even a single complete dress rehearsal could be held.

My last joy in the work was something I had to thank Franz Liszt for, and once again, without my involvement. First I received a verbal greeting from him from Weimar, with the information that he wanted to perform *Mose* there. Uncertain whether this was a serious decision, I did not reply. Soon thereafter, however, the formal written request arrived.

I had met Franz Liszt in the unforgettable days, when he visited Berlin as a virtuoso, and in a series of concerts, which he could have easily multiplied by a factor of ten, put Berlin into an ecstasy, which, before or after, it had never seen

---

[1] This epigram of Goethe's, slightly misquoted (it should be 'Sogar dies Wort', not 'Auch dieses Wort'), translates as 'Even this may be believed: Whom God deceives, is well deceived.'
[2] Carl Friedrich Rungenhagen, 1778-1851.
[3] Eduard Grell, 1800-1886.
[4] Marx is perhaps confusing this with the first performance of Mendelssohn's *Oedipus in Kolonos*, which took place in Potsdam in December 1845; Schneider did not write an oratorio of this name.

the like of. At that time we had not made a closer acquaintance, but probably had spoken repeatedly, and I had heard him in all his concerts and in many private circles. The enthusiasm for him had left the entire city weak; not only his musical performance, but also his personality, and his, in the noblest sense of the word, knightly bearing had nourished the flames. More, among many great demonstrations of charity, the people had been moved that, in hearing the complaint of an old piano tuner, who put his instrument in order, and had complained that he had still not been able to afford a ticket to his concert, he had played for over an hour - for the tuner alone. A deputation of students had asked him for some complimentary tickets for their impecunious brethren, and he had instead invited all of the students to the hall, where he played for them for two hours. The young people – this appears so natural to anyone who hears him – unhitched the horses on his return home and drew his carriage in triumph from then on. When, at his concerts he took his place on the narrow space before the piano, while the entire remaining space, usually intended for orchestra and audience, was overfilled with listeners: then he was surrounded by a rich crowd of young ladies, all brilliantly attired. And now, if, perhaps he played his *Galop chromatique* or some other salon piece in a lively rhythm, it was a sight so amusing and refreshing, that he could have amused and rejuvenated a Timon[5], as, in listening to his powerful and yet spiritual accents, the young crowd flew upward rejoice from their seats, entirely surrendering unintentionally, indeed, against their wills, to the power of the rhythm. But it was not only this most nervously excitable crowd, all the listeners felt that they were irresistibly drawn to him, as in the folktale the crowd of children to the piper of Hamelin, who with his magic sounds enchanted them away from their safe homeland to the magic mountain, which opened before him, and closed again after the children. I could permit myself a judgment in such things; for I had heard him earlier, and along with him all the renowned pianists. The least was that he far surpassed them all in virtuoso power. I had never set much stock in that; the decisive thing was that his piano playing, even though the movement might have been one that was already written down, took on the shape and power of a poem that was just being born, and that was his playing, in fact. For what was already present in him was reborn and appeared new and as fresh was when it was made. One could see this as well in the play of expression of his noble and expressive face. Colder people may have now and then suspected intention and ostentatiousness; someone who knew how to look more deeply into a man, who through himself or another learned that the whole artist must follow the movements of his soul and give it expression, knew better.

---

[5] Timon of Athens was a proverbial misanthrope.

That was the most brilliant sight that his virtuoso career afforded me. Later, when I visited him in Weimar during the performance of *Mosè*[6], I gained a yet deeper view of his artistry. Here (and yet later during numerous visits to my residence in Berlin) I heard him either entirely alone with my wife, or in an intimate circle. And here it was, where the artist revealed himself to the artist in finer and more deeply felt compositions, for example, from his *Harmonies Réligieuses et Poétiques*[7] [sic] and his *Années de Pèlerinage*.

He played, I must say, not for us, he spoke to us, spirit to spirit, but with the words of a new language.

Now I accompanied him to the dress rehearsal for *Mose*. He directed.

The chorus (the Singakademie of Weimar) was really not up to its task on this occasion. Thus it was remarkable, in what a spirited – rather, an inspiring way Liszt transported the young people from the previous everyday world to the visions of the work. One example will suffice. My great predecessor in the subject, Handel, had presented the individual plagues: the river turned to blood, the plague of the countless locusts, flies, etc. in short choral movements, with that grandeur that only he can call upon. Completeness was not necessary for my vision; I only needed three of these colossal pictures. At the same time, however, the impossibility of including each epic moment lay in the entirely dramatic posture of the work. Everything had to move the dramatic action forward. Thus appeared for me the plague that transforms the river into blood. Pharaoh, as I saw the moment, reigns, surrounded by princes and warriors, in the royal hall, which opens to the holy river. This river is not like the other rivers of the earth; it is the holy river that nourishes the land and its people; dried up – corrupted, the desert will bury the land in the dead sand. Here now reigns the King, and, throng after throng, the horrified people storms up from the riverbank, voice upon voice calling, full of horror: the river has become blood. I could not paint the wonder, the horror; so the horror had to convey it.

The Weimar lambs, in their white and sky-blue outfits, behind them the young men, who pronounced the words so lamb-piously and patiently – what did they know about horror, and why should they care about the plagues of Egypt? – Then Liszt strode from his director's chair into the middle of the chorus, and from voice to voice, as one after another had to enter, he whispered to one after another "The river became blood!" with a such deep expression of horror, that one after the other, with their shy look at him, they uttered their word with horror, and the whole thing built and grew, as the moment demanded.

---

[6] This took place in June 1853.
[7] Recte: *Harmonies Poétiques et Réligieuses*.

Yes, Liszt was the second demonic figure that I had encountered in my area of music.

This performance in Weimar was the last in which I heard my *Mose*; in Berlin the picture was distorted, as when the wanderer sees his own countenance distorted in the unsteady stream. Other performances that took place in Prague, Elberfeld, etc. I did not attend. The work did not achieve the wide familiarity that would have been needed for it to put down lasting roots with the people.

This blow struck me harder than any other. I had seen my work as the foundation stone on which I could build further.

Above all, *Mose* was for me only the first part of a trilogy of oratorios; the second would have been *Elias*[8].

Elijah appeared to me as the middle moment between Moses and Christ. He appeared at the time when the people had sunk from its original power and has lost its unshakable belief and zeal for the service of Jehovah. Kings rule the people who themselves have fallen away from the old God and have turned to the foreign Baal. They draw the people after themselves into ruin. Elijah stands there in the complete power of prophecy. The miracle takes place at the sacrificial altars of Baal and Jehovah, and without mercy the prophet slays the idolatrous priests at their own altars. But the people are weak. He must flee into the desert, and laments to his God, that all his zeal has been for nothing.

Here I wanted now to give voice to the wonderful vision of the prophet: "And see, the Lord passed over, and a great, strong wind, that ripped the mountains, and broke the cliffs, before the Lord..." "Then comes the earthquake, and after it, the fire. But not in the wind of the storm, not in earthquake and flame, does the Lord appear. After the fire came a still, soft whispering." In the beautiful whispering the Lord is announced. I assume that it is here that the mild depiction of God in the time to come, in contrast to the old, came into view in the prophetic picture. The conclusion of the whole would be given by the assumption into heaven of the prophet, received by heavenly choirs.

I was not yet clear about the third oratorio. Prophet after prophet would announce the Messiah, in solo and choral song, and people after people – the Orient (from which the sterner figures of Egypt, of distant India, and Moorish lands, hovered, awaiting their Prester John), Hellas, Rome, Germany, join the global movement of the new belief. The poem for *Elias* I hoped to create from the Bible, and I was certain of its success. For what had the

---

[8] Mendelssohn's *Elijah*, which Marx significantly declines to mention here, was premiered in England in 1846, and in its German version two years later.

Scriptures not provided me for *Mose*! Not just every expression of devotion and grandeur, but also the most appropriate words for strife and pride, for luxury and voluptuousness and Bacchanalian frenzy.—The success of the first two would bring me the poet for the third.

All this, the career as a composer – it had to be abandoned. My duty to my family demanded it. I had to sacrifice myself. Of course, much was still composed, much was published as well, but the great undertakings, the oratorios and operas had to be renounced. Happily only for a few is it ordained to understand what this secret murder in one's own breast signifies.

True — there was still a way open. I could have made concessions to the power of comprehension of performers and contemporaries, particularly as they became after 1848.

But that was no way for me. To go down that road would have been easy, but to enter it would have been entirely impossible to my way of thinking and the strict and holy duty to truthfulness, that had always stood for me as an unbreakable law for the artist. Probably the difficulties posed by its polyphonic movements had already become evident to me during the composition of *Mose*. But its pervasive dramatic character required it. If only I had been able to think to make the accompaniments lighter for the   Frühlingsspiel[9] , which appeared later, as their role in proportion to the pictures which were unrolling permitted. And yet I certainly knew, how our pianists prefer to make things easy for themselves, when they are not concerned about putting their "bravura" on display.

No! to choose to retreat from the ideal pictures, which hover about me, and still today have lost none of their brilliance, or to betray them, and faithlessly to falsify them, was no choice at all for me.

That was how my feeling at the time, and it has remained thus until today, and will never change.

At that time I made the decision with bitter pains. Only later, and gradually, would that word of the poet become clear to me, which I have set at the beginning of this chapter. In retreating from one path, I could, with all my time and strength, enter on another, and with my methods, in my *Music of the Nineteenth Century*[10], in my choral method, in my *Beethoven*[11] and *Gluck*[12] – and whatever else I have tried to write – could further serve the art to which I have

[9] Like his earlier *Nahid und Omar*, this was a song-cycle, "three-times-three poems of Heine for voice and piano", published 1845.
[10] *Die Musik des Neunzehnten Jahrhunderts und Ihre Pflege*, Leipzig, 1855.
[11] *Ludwig van Beethoven. Leben und Schaffen*, Berlin, 1859.
[12] *Gluck und Die Oper*, Berlin, 1863.

consecrated myself. But how else would it have been possible for me to take on and to bear my lifelong work with undiminished freshness, if the golden images of my own creations had not beckoned me further and further? My greatest efforts in my career as an artist were not given for the time in which I lived. Willingly, and without pain I can listen, if someone punishingly answers me: you were not strong enough for your mission; you were too weak for what you took upon yourself! Well, then others may try themselves on this, or on higher things. I do not speak the word of the haughty Roman: You banish me? I banish you![13]— We men of our time feel and know that we are through and through one with our people. Our entire being and our efforts belong to that people without conditions; for it is rooted in the people, and has won its nourishment and power from its life. With our German people we have celebrated each moment of its exaltation, with the people solemnized the pride of its life in ideality and for ideality. Thus we will also patiently wait out the time in between, in which it rests in slumber, and gathers its strength to rise once more. And we, its musicians, will willingly retreat and let our work slumber, until the people has achieved a new existence in justice, freedom and elevated spiritual awareness. Then our art will become young once more with new power of ideas.

Should it be the case when this time has come that my works are granted continued life, or should another stand in for me: I will joyfully greet he who completes what I have wished, or something greater.

[13] Shakespeare, *Coriolanus*, Act 3, Scene 3.

CHAPTER 15

FREDERICK WILLIAM IV

Along with all that has been mentioned thus far, and an increasingly expanding literary activity – I had supplied detailed articles to the Halle Yearbooks, *Caecilia*, the *Lexicon of Music*, etc. — there was yet another special activity that occupied my time and my lively interest, even though its intended goal would remain unachieved.

Already, over the course of several years it had been the intent of the Ministry of Culture to found a Conservatorium of music in Berlin. More than once I had had occasion, or taken the initiative to express my expert opinion on this situation. King Frederick William IV[1] had striven, as soon as he had taken power, to surround himself with famed or beloved personalities from abroad. Thus, among others, the philosopher Schelling[2], the poet Friedrich Rückert[3], and the painter Cornelius[4] were invited here.

Schelling already had the heights of his career behind him. He had spent the last few years in Munich without any further literary activity. People talked considerably about his mystical seclusion: how those assigned to him were lead through a shadowy set of gardens into a salon, and there had to wait for him for a long time, until finally other doors would open and the already old man, with long and flowing attire solemnly entered like a wizard.

In Berlin he was supposed to be the replacement for Hegel at the University; the immediate predecessor of Hegel's would thus now be his successor. Hegel had not just died; but the absolute value of absolute philosophy had suffered a notable blow in higher regions, as it appeared. For, while earlier, it was not easy for a philosopher who was not an acquaintance of Hegel to hope for advancement, now there was a considerable yearning to see new paths opened

---

[1] Frederick William IV, born in 1795, acceded to the throne in 1840. His reign was characterised by a cautious liberalism, at least by comparison with his authoritarian father, and his flexible approach to political questions allowed his regime to ride out the turmoil of the 1848 revolutions. He died in 1861.

[2] Friedrich Wilhelm Joseph Schelling, 1775-1854, a contemporary of – and eventually rival to –Hegel.

[3] Friedrich Rückert, 1788-1866, best known for his works on Oriental themes, and translations from eastern languages.

[4] Peter von Cornelius, 1784 –1867, an artist best known for fresco work, including at the unfinished royal mausoleum in Berlin.

for speculative knowledge. People no longer trusted Hegel's teaching, or did not trust it enough.

Naturally I had already striven to become familiar with Schelling's thinking. Now I could have taken a spot among those listening to him speak. But I felt no yearning, and no express inclination for speculative philosophy generally; I, as former jurist and committed artist craved the reassuring ground of facts and experience. Schelling read his lectures in the largest lecture hall before an extremely numerous listenership. As had once been the case for Gans, here also one saw the first rows of seats monopolized by generals and privy councilors, along with a whole crowd of professors, including most of the students of Hegel. Schelling labeled what he had previously presented as negative philosophy; now he would expound positive philosophy, the philosophy of revelation (as it was understood, more or less). Directing himself to the Hegelians, he said: "You, gentlemen, have turned into a cul-de-sac with your philosophy! If you join with me, I will lead you out into the light. After a few hours the lecture hall had emptied to a shocking extent, and the lecture was not completed.

Rückert, to all appearances, had a happier situation. Rückert had first won broad recognition through his "Geharnischten Sonette", which were given a liberal and patriotic significance directed against Napoleon. His other poems, however, remained little-known in comparison, and were unable to put down roots in the people. His greatest significance probably lay in his applied art of versification, which he admirably brought up to date in his translations, the *maqamat* of Al-Hariri and others, and in which you might say that reflected the original, silver with silver. In fact, he wrote a tragedy, but without significant success. In order to also give him a public position, he was named a professor at the University, with permission to spend the summer six months of the year at his country estate near Coburg. This could have been advantageous for his poetical work, but his work at the University had to steal from the beginning of his printed editions, which demanded only uninterrupted activity. And so he soon left the circle of the University once again.

I interrupt myself here with the question: Did these recruitments deserve unconditional censure because of their minimal success? – and must, according to my views, answer "no!". Frederick William IV was receptive and active in many spiritual directions in the arts and sciences. Often, weekly I believe, he brought together important men of science, among them Bopp, in order for them to lecture; I have already related his sympathy for classical music (Vol. 1, p. 252 Proper page reference needed). Thus I had already seen a pencil sketch from his hand at the Mad. General Helwig's – if I am not mistaken, it was the representation of a confirmation, perhaps the first in Berlin after the Reformation – which in fact went far beyond the usual capabilities of a dilettante.

That such a lord such wish to have important men nearby is understandable; likewise, that the external form of the producing relationship was something less keenly perceived by him. One may say one what one wishes on the benefits of autocracy: it is simply impractical and unfeasible. No man, and thus no ruler, can know and understand everything; this was not granted even to the greatest rulers, to a Frederick II, to a Napoleon I, no matter how much their power of spirit stood above that of their contemporaries. And should there be a man who knew and understood everything, yet he could not be everywhere at the same time, where it was necessary to observe and act. The great Napoleon learned bitterly in his final campaigns that his spirit could not be reliably represented even through his most tested marshals, and that they were defeated where his eye and thought was lacking. No! no ruler, whether he call himself absolute or constitutional, can reign without the help of others. The question is only whence he will select his advisors and administrators, whether from the entire nation, or from a small, selected portion of the nation, the nobility, or the civil servants.

Frederick William IV followed the promptings of his soul toward spiritual surroundings and elevation. With regard to this impulse, and the more profitable placement of those recruited he lacked the intermediation which those recruits or confidants should have been able to offer. These men were joined by Peter Cornelius, the painter. He had been teacher at the Academy of Painting in Düsseldorf, which became a Prussian city. At that time King Ludwig of Bavaria, recognizing his high degree of talent with his artistically trained eye, had summoned him, still little-known to Munich. There in Munich he produced a whole string of great paintings – the frescos in the Glyptothek, the Last Judgment and other great wall paintings in the Aukirche and the great basilica, that put the name of Cornelius at the pinnacle of the new German school of painting.

Now he had been called to Berlin, in order to decorate the *campo santo,* the burial place of the Prussian rulers, with frescos. But this *campo santo* was not yet built, and even today has not yet been completed. Cornelius traveled to Italy, especially to Rome, in order work on and send back studies and drafts for the new works.

Along with those named above Felix Mendelssohn was also called.

Mendelssohn had earlier had, and indeed had constantly had a desire to move away from Berlin; Berlin was not sympathetic to him, no matter how many connections of relations and friendship might have been able to tether him there. After Zelter's death (1832) he was invited by the board of directors of the Singakademie to apply for the vacant post of director. He was unable to apply, no matter how much this would have been in line with the wishes of the family. My encouragement, my pointing to all the beneficial things that he could foster in that position, made the final difference. He applied – and was not selected, despite the assurance of a clear majority that he had received. Now he was first appointed as director in Düsseldorf, and then in Leipzig.

Mendelssohn, after his travels to England and then to Italy, did not return as the same person he had been at the time of our most intimate contact. When I first met him, he was entirely imbued with the power, depth and truth of Sebastian Bach; repeatedly and insistently he had striven to make clear to me, who had until that point been unreachable by the most important works of the master, the superiority of Bach over Handel. I am speaking here in his opinion, and perhaps also my opinion of that time; now I have been for a long time, and far enough removed from such measuring of masters one against the other. It was then also when Felix sought for truthfulness and fidelity in his own works. I can still see him, with flushed face, come into my apartment, stride through the room, and say to me: "Hey! I have a fabulous idea! – What do you think about this? I am going to write an overture to *Midsummer Night's Dream*." I spoke very warmly in favor of it. A few days later there he was once again, happy, free, and he had brought me the score, completed up to the second part. The dance of the elves with the introductory chords was just as we came to know it later. Then – yes, then followed an overture, cheerful, with charming motion, entirely enjoyable, entirely worthy of praise – I was only in disagreement with the "Dream". With loyalty, according to my duty as a friend, I said this to him directly. He was upset, irritated, indeed wounded, and ran off without saying farewell. I had to accept this and stayed away from his house for a few days, and indeed his mother and Fanny received me coldly, and were almost hostile at my final visit after that conversation.

After a few days the slender servant of the house came to me in the morning and handed me an envelope with the words: "A compliment from Mr. Felix!" When I opened it, great pieces of music-paper, ripped in half, fell to the ground, along with a piece of paper from Felix with the words: "You are right in everything! But now come and help." Perhaps it had been his very understanding and sensible father who had given the suggestions; perhaps, also, the young hothead had found his bearings by himself.

I did not make myself scarce, but hurried to him, and explained to him that such an overture, in my opinion, had to give the true and complete picture of the drama for which it served as prologue. With fire and unconditional devotion he set to work. The wandering of the loving couples, in the first motive (e, d#, d, c#), was salvaged from the first work, at least, but everything else was newly written. There was nothing for it! "It's too much! Too much!" he shrieked, when I wanted to see the rustics and even Bottom's ardent donkey-bray included in their places. It happened; the overture became that which we know today. Mother and sister were reconciled, since they saw the composer rushing about in the greatest excitement and joy. The father, however, explained to the many assembled for the first performance in his house that the overture was really more my work than Felix's. This was entirely unfounded, as is evident, simply the expression of his satisfaction with my behavior, perhaps a compensation for the earlier turning away by the women. The first idea and the execution belonged to Felix, only the advice was my duty and my portion.

At his departure before his trip to England[5] Felix had once spoken to me with great agitation: "You! If this and that comes to you and it does not seem right, don't be too quick to judge! I am coming back." I did not understand what he had said, but it would gradually become clear to me.

In England he had his C-minor symphony performed, but instead of the menuett had used the scherzo from the Octet; it did not fit with the character of the whole work, but now seemed to him to be more attractive. How often had he earlier scoffed and laughed about the French bad habit of mixing in movements from elsewhere, for example, grafting the scherzo of the A-major symphony by Beethoven into his D-major symphony!

At his return from Italy he brought a new composition with him, the *Walpurgisnacht*; Goethe himself had written a pair of verses for him at his request. I found the composition charming, but could not overlook the untruthfulness on which this charm rested, which certainly had its basis in the poem itself, but there remains unnoticed, while composition, more realistic, for which only has truth, not pretense, available, pulls the untruthfulness into the bright light of day. Goethe obviously attributes to the original residents gathering on the mountain peaks that which does not belong to them, but rather to Christianity – the urge to the eternal light as their belief, which they have to preserve against the "dull parson-Christians". For this reason they disguise themselves as witches and goblins. The description of this, "Come with teeth and forks, etc." was made into charming choruses for witches by Mendelssohn; his orchestra builds this up to the wildest noise of actual haunting. But now this itself is brought out; that the whole is only supposed to be pretense is not expressed by the music, since it is unable to; the poet can play lightly with his presentations; for the musician it must however become entirely serious, and thus has in this poem neither root nor place. And so the haunting cannot be a real haunting in its fearful power, but hovers between joking and truth.

[5] This was his first visit to England, in 1829. Mendelssohn visited the country nine further times until 1847.

Most musicians and friends of music will find such considerations too severe. But we had a very close example before our eyes, of what happens when a musician is more concerned with success than the most sincere truth. Near us lived Meyerbeer, called to be general director and music director of the opera by Frederick William IV. In my opinion he was far above all his contemporaries in talent. The most brilliant proof of this he had just set down in the opera which was soon to disappear in its original form: the *Feldlager in Schlesien*[6]. Here, especially in the soldier's songs, one is struck again and again by the most specific truth[7], which no composer of any time could have done better. This talent was assisted by a complete musical and humanistic education. But how far he fell from what he might, with such gifts, have been for music! Rather than staying true to his mission, he wanted to give everything to everyone, and so overloaded and disturbed one thing by the other. He was German, Italian and French at the same time; he spoke, now as one true spirit to another; now he was concerned to be obliging to this singer, or that instrumentalist, or to provide the most peculiar and variegated sights for the viewing pleasure of the crowd. And he also belonged to the false and frivolous period of the restoration, the aftereffects of which had not reached Mendelssohn.

Now, having arrived in Berlin, Mendelssohn, at the suggestion of the King, wrote the music for Sophocles' *Antigone*. Were this to happen, it could scarcely be better performed than here. Mendelssohn here followed, without antiquarian deviations, the style of Gluck. It must be noted once more, that the king's desire cannot be criticized; not he, but the musician, must consider whether the task is compatible with the essence of our modern music – and our stages and manner of life – or whether it compels inaccessibility and untruth. Mendelssohn had not been able to speak to the King regarding this.

Whatever one may decide about this, neither this individual activity, nor a few compositions for the Cathedral Choir, offered support for a continuing position for Mendelssohn in Berlin. He had been recruited, and only now was the question of what to do with him asked. Individual suggestions were made

---

[6] This opera of 1844, based on an episode in the life of Frederick the Great, was popular in Prussia, but never performed outside the kingdom and was not published. Meyerbeer re-used some of the material from the work for an *opéra-comique* of 1854, *L'Étoile du Nord*.
[7] Meyerbeer had invited me to the dress rehearsal and I wrote him, still quite pleased about the matter, in approximately the language given above. On the same day he came to see, and to express his joy about my letter. "But I will preserve it as a document!", he added, smiling significantly. The thoroughly good-natured man, who, however, was all too sensitive to praise and blame, certainly knew that I could not be entirely in agreement with his direction. He thought it advisable to simply take me at my word. For how serious I was with my utterances about the characteristic, how much I did not express that which had not taken lasting root in my convictions, this was not clear to him.

officially. He should perform church music; but where? With what purpose? — He should set up music festivals. — He should found a conservatory. When he told me about these and others, I tried to influence him toward the last suggestion, the only feasible one. But it was precisely this one that he would not hear of. "There is him…and him…and…; I cannot collaborate with them, our paths lie far apart, and I cannot dislodge them." In vain I tried to prove that one could use each in his place. In vain, I told him, half joking, half seriously: according to his view there was only a third possibility, that of waiting for those men to die off; until then, however, successors in the same sense would appear. Everything was fruitless, and Mendelssohn went back to Leipzig to his working circle there.

These things had flowed past. *Mose*, with the support of the King, was to be performed here.

Then, I received, unexpectedly, the request to …in the morning at ….report for an audience with the King[8]. Since the King had requested the performance, but, hindered by a departure for Palermo that had suddenly become necessary, was not able to be present, thus I assumed that he had the intention of saying a few kind words.

At the appointed time I entered the waiting room. The Wing-Adjutant on duty asked me to forgive him; at the moment, Count Stollberg was speaking, then there were a second and third waiting, and then he could announce me. Just then we heard the wagons of the King and the Queen departing; the adjutant told me that today the audiences had been going on since early in the morning, and their Majesties had decided to go to this exhibition and that, and finally to travel to dinner at Charlottenburg. With an entirely good intention, obviously with the naiveté of one rather inexperienced in these circles I asked, whether it might not be more appropriate to come back on another day. "I am entirely unable to answer that", came the reply. I remained. In the meantime, the door to the audience-chamber opened, and the last speaker exited. I walked cheerfully to the door so as not to waste a moment; the adjutant, however, held me back; we had to await the command first. Soon thereafter he himself went into the audience chamber.

It was not long until the voice of the king resound from inside with a loud "Mr. Marx!" I went in immediately and found myself close by the monarch, who was leaning on his long working table. I awaited a word in relation to *Mose*. Instead the King spoke: "I have heard of your ideas for the improvement of musical life. Present them to me!"

[8] TM: Exactly thus in the German.

Still guided by the assumption that the King only intended to show his grace toward me, and that the question had no more serious intent, particularly given the pressing time of his departure, I began a brief expression on the subject, but was immediately interrupted by the words of the King: "No! give me a thorough presentation." Now, I thought, that can happen. I began to develop my thoughts, tersely, but in detail. The King listened attentively and supportively, interrupted me several times with questions – and I cannot deny that I, entirely filled with the circumstance and elevated by the importance of the moment, also interrupted him; all of a sudden the formal audience had become a lively conversation.

The audience last, as I later learned, close to two hours. I had never found such deep and lightning-quick understanding, such animated involvement, with any minister or adviser. The King expressed his satisfaction and his decision to let the plan presented to him go into effect; the resources on hand for music would be used for this; he himself wanted to add from his funds annually the sum of three to four thousand thalers. "Go," were his final words, "to Geheimrat von Massow[9], to speak with him about the details; you will find him to be very affable and quite familiar with music." I left, extremely surprised, but even so, filled with thanks.

Early the next day a *Jäger* came to me with the message that Count Redern wished to ask when he could speak with me. I asked the *Jäger*: are you coming from his Excellence Massow? "No, from his Excellence Redern." I asked him to say that I would make my visit immediately.

Not long thereafter, a military gendarme brought me a large communication from General von Thile. The same, at the time Minister without portfolio, asked me for a brief communication of what I had presented to the King. I sent it to him and went to see Count Redern, with whom I had already become acquainted in the commission regarding the matter of the Königstadt Theater. He told me that the King had instructed him to discuss the musical matters I had presented with me in more detail. He had thus taken the place of Massow, with whom I no longer had any connection.

Thus the matter, having begun in such a lively fashion, seemed to be well under way; after the royal approval the discussions, so zealously begun, seemed to indicate this, at least to me.

"Now? And then what?" —

Nothing.

---

[9] Ludwig von Massow, 1794-1859, was the long-serving minister of the royal house and was indeed adept at carrying out the monarch's cultural wishes.

That was the end of the matter, as if it had all been a dream. Had there been opposition from some side? Had the King been drawn away by more important matters? I do not know. Not long thereafter the movements of the year 1848 began, and exclusively claimed the attentions of all.

But what had led to the King's invitation to present my ideas? It did not originate with me; I do not know whom it really came from. Possibly the late Archduke of Mecklenburg-Strelitz gave the suggestion. He had sent several of his seminar instructors to me to be instructed in composition; for the same purpose his chamberlain, the spirited Karl von Oertzen had stayed a longer time with me in Berlin. Then I had performed *Mose* in Strelitz, and written a piece of music for the festival of the *Volksschule*. During these occasions I had been asked about my intentions and plans and had presented my views, especially before and after a meal at the *Schweizerhäuschen*[10], to which the Archduke had invited only Oertzen and myself, and to which he himself had driven in his light hunting wagon through the magnificent beech forests. Whether something of this had made its way to the King, I know nothing, as I have said.

[10] A hunting lodge in the Carpin region, built in 1833, where the archduke later died.

Frederick William IV

CHAPTER 16

WEM GELINGT ES? TRÜBE FRAGE[1] .....

Goethe.

But what had I presented to the King?

I had made a connection with the Cathedral Choir, which the King had founded not long before. After my acknowledgement of that which anyone speaking about the accomplishments of this choir would appreciate, I had dared to mention the alternative: if church music does not belong in our Evangelical Church[2], it should likewise be inadmissible in the church visited by King and Court; if church music does, however, belong in the Evangelical Church – as the Lutheran Church always believed after its departure from the Mother Church, to win over and retain them, – then the last and poorest church in the kingdom has just as much right as the Court-church, or indeed much more need and duty, to provide itself with this.

This was the first thought that I presented, and it immediately awoke the attention of the King. Naturally I immediately added, that no state had the appropriate resources available to satisfy this requirement. Something that is a necessity of the entire people can only be effected directly by the people. With relatively little assistance on the part of the state, each congregation must from its own resources at the least provide the most important and indispensable element of church music: a choir; and certainly not a choir of paid or hired singers, but rather one created from the members of the congregation itself. Admittedly, the various choirs would, depending on the resources and level of education of the congregations have varying levels of performance abilities. But these varying levels correspond to the varying levels of all forms of church music generally, from the simplest responsories and chorales up to the great Passions and oratorios, which, as in the past, take their place in divine service at the high feasts of the church.

The means of creating these choirs would be a method that would descend to the sources of musical life, and from there would draw understanding and skill upward level by level to the highest and mostly highly developed endeavors. However, for this one would need capable and willing teachers and directors everywhere.

---

[1] "Who succeeds? A murky question,…." *Faust*, Part II
[2] The German collective title for the various forms of Reformed Protestant church in operation.

The method lay, founded according to its essence, in my composition method, already widely disseminated at that time; I followed this and to the general method (*Music of the Nineteenth Century*) with my choral method, though long after this period; I had however tested it practically several times already by this point.

Once the choirs and their directors were found, then folk music could also be enriched and elevated in all directions; natural singing and the monophonic song remain untouched, but one could according to desire and necessity overlook them.

This popular singing with the inclusion of choral singing seemed to me (and still seems to me) to be the true folk music, at least for us Germans.

For training of teachers and directors a conservatory would have to be founded. For the appointment and promotion of all musical functionaries, even for incentives for private teachers for improved education – there was planning for what was needed. Sections (but not as such) were later published in my essay on the organization of musical life[3]. The concept was my own individual work; the realization – did not depend on me[4].

---

[3] *Die Organisation des Musikwesens im Preussischen Staate: Eine Denkschrift*, Berlin, 1848.

[4] Although Marx's more ambitious notions for the reform of musical education were derailed by the events of 1848, he did become personally involved, along with Julius Stern, 1820-1883, and Theodor Kullak, 1818-1882, in the creation of the Berliner Musikschule in 1850. He withdrew from the project five years later. What came to be called the Stern Conservatoire continued to operate until the Second World War, after which it eventually became part of the Universität der Künste.

AFTERWORD IN PLACE OF A FOREWORD.

The previous pages were created at the end of the year 1864, and certainly at an unusual moment of my life.

With the idea of writing down my music history and musicology after more than thirty years of preparation, I was seized by a nervous morbidity, the result of an overload of work, and of a life full of inner storminess, and thus hindered in the completion of this work for the time being, or so I was assured unanimously by the doctors whom I consulted.

That which appeared in the form of severe unhappiness, would then be unveiled to me as a blessing. In this involuntary leisure time my opinions and thoughts were broadened and deepened so considerably that I, if this work were to appear to me now, as I had managed it up to my breakdown in spirit, I would have to turn away from it, entirely dissatisfied.

In my silent return to myself, the pictures of my past returned to me, so sharply etched and in living colors in my soul, that it was as if I experienced my life a second time. Thus, I wanted to know that it was depicted for my own recollection and that of my friends. Then, however, I was directed by this thought: it might be that what I experienced would also resonate in wider circles.

Full of longing, but entirely unconcerned, I look forward now to the day which will lead me back to that work, the highest task of my scholarly career. Unconcerned! – for in my life, as in that career, which has become clear to me, I have learned that no one dies until he has completed the duty assigned to him; I have already endeavored to show this for Beethoven and Gluck. If these works have meaning for the world, so I will live and write them. If I should die first, then their completion was not commanded[5].

It was my Therese, however, with the insightful and friendship-true advice of excellent doctors, who stepped forward to protect me against the frightening onset of the disease, which at the beginning made it seem that I was losing my sight. For my wife's love will stretch up to heaven and does not hesitate before the horrors of hell, if this means refreshing and rescuing her husband.

Berlin, March 4, 1865.

Adolf Bernhard Marx

[5] Although Marx had plans to write more deeply on musical history and theory, he produced little more of substance after this date, and died in May 1866; a work of idealist philosophy, *Das Ideal und die Gegenwart*, was published in 1867 under the auspices of his widow. It is not clear precisely what caused his death, which was ascribed by contemporaries to exhaustion.

TRANSLATOR'S NOTE ON INDEXING

As our society moves into its third decade of the Internet and World Wide Web, with every member of the American middle class, and almost every American more generally carrying a computing device with worldwide, instant access to net resources in their pockets (the smart phone), it seems that it is time to admit that some of our habits in scholarly communication, based as they are on the world of books printed on paper during a five-hundred year span, can reasonably be adapted to a world in which much knowledge originates and is disseminated electronically and instantly. Many of the footnotes beloved to scholars point to citations for material that was never and will never be printed. Many leading academic libraries provide solely electronic access to most of the periodic literature they select. In such a world, one may argue (and I am arguing) that the ease and facility of keyword searching for electronic texts mean that an extensive index created in addition to a scholarly text is a redundancy. Most, though not all, recently published books were born digital, and are transmitted digitally through much of their life. The electronic text for such a book can be interrogated as desired by the reader to locate precisely the information desired. The labor, effort, and cost involved in preparing and printing an index of names and subjects for the user who may only need a single particular piece of information (rather than the reader who will be reading the entire volume) is difficult to justify. We (publisher, translator, author) believe that this book makes a substantial contribution to the scholarly literature, and that it will do so without a pre-existing index, as we continue to move towards electronic publication.

- Stephen Thomson Moore